THE FORCE OF FAMILY

Repatriation, Kinship, and Memory on Haida Gwaii

Cara Krmpotich

The Force of Family is an ethnography of the Haida Nation's successful efforts to repatriate ancestral remains from museums around the world to Haida Gwaii, British Columbia. These remains were returned over the course of more than a decade and, in the summer of 2010, the Haida achieved what many thought was impossible: the return of ancestral remains from the Pitt Rivers Museum at the University of Oxford. After years of hard work, heartache, and celebrations, repatriation has become an indelible feature of contemporary Haida culture.

In her study, Cara Krmpotich focuses on the traditional objects made by Haidas to respect and honour their ancestors, as well as the large variety of contemporary objects that have been produced, sold, and circulated to cover the financial demands of repatriating some 460 human remains. She also examines the combination of new and old ceremonies intended to "set things right," the Haida ideal of *yahgudangang* ("to pay respect" and "to be fit for respect"), and the agency of ancestors in death. Since the 1990s Haidas have been making button blankets and bentwood boxes with clan crest designs, hosting feasts for hundreds of people, and composing and choreographing new songs and dances in the service of repatriation. The book shows how shared experiences of sewing, weaving, dancing, cooking, and feasting contribute to the Haida notion of "respect," the creation of kinship and collective memory, and the production of a cultural archive.

The first book-length ethnographic study of repatriation processes, *Force of Family* investigates, in depth and in cultural context, local motivations for repatriation. By taking an ethnographic approach, the work presents repatriation not only as a post-colonial act between museums and indigenous communities but as, first and foremost, an act of kinship among Haida families.

CARA KRMPOTICH is an assistant professor in the Museum Studies program, Faculty of Information, at the University of Toronto.

CARA KRMPOTICH

The Force of Family

Repatriation, Kinship, and Memory on Haida Gwaii

UNIVERSITY OF TORONTO PRESS
Toronto Buffalo London

© University of Toronto Press 2014
Toronto Buffalo London
www.utppublishing.com
Printed in Canada

ISBN 978-1-4426-4657-5 (cloth)
ISBN 978-1-4426-1450-5 (paper)

Printed on acid-free, 100% post-consumer recycled paper with vegetable-based inks.

Library and Archives Canada Cataloguing in Publication

Krmpotich, Cara, 1978–, author
The force of family : repatriation, kinship, and memory on Haida Gwaii/
Cara Krmpotich.

Includes bibliographical references and index.
ISBN 978-1-4426-4657-5 (bound). – ISBN 978-1-4426-1450-5 (pbk.)

1. Haida Indians – British Columbia – Haida Gwaii – Antiquities.   2. Haida Indians –
Material culture – British Columbia – Haida Gwaii.   3. Haida Indians – Kinship –
British Columbia – Haida Gwaii.   4. Haida Indians – British Columbia – Haida Gwaii –
Ethnic identity.   5. Human remains (Archaeology) – Repatriation – British Columbia –
Haida Gwaii.   6. Cultural property – Repatriation – British Columbia – Haida Gwaii.
7. Haida Gwaii (B.C.) – Antiquities.   8. Ethnology – British Columbia – Haida Gwaii.
I. Title.

E99.H2K76 2014   971.1004'9728   C2013-908549-1

This book has been published with the help of a grant from the Canadian Federation for
the Humanities and Social Sciences, through the Awards to Scholarly Publications Program, using funds provided by the Social Sciences and Humanities Research Council of
Canada.

University of Toronto Press acknowledges the financial assistance to its publishing
program of the Canada Council for the Arts and the Ontario Arts Council.

**Canada Council   Conseil des Arts
for the Arts   du Canada**

ONTARIO ARTS COUNCIL
CONSEIL DES ARTS DE L'ONTARIO
50 YEARS OF ONTARIO GOVERNMENT SUPPORT OF THE ARTS
50 ANS DE SOUTIEN DU GOUVERNEMENT DE L'ONTARIO AUX ARTS

University of Toronto Press acknowledges the financial support of the
Government of Canada through the Canada Book Fund for its publishing activities.

Contents

Illustrations

Photographs not otherwise credited were taken by the author.

Figures

Table

Acknowledgments

This book has come to have a geography about it. It has travelled with me across oceans, time zones, and countries. It went from Vancouver to Oxford, up to Haida Gwaii, down to Victoria, then to Nottingham, revisited Haida Gwaii, hopped over to Sault Ste. Marie, went east to Edinburgh, west to Old Massett, south to Skidegate, pit-stopped in Vancouver again, rode the train between England and Scotland regularly, and finally arrived in Toronto. At every stop, we have found a home. It is to the people who have made these places home that I owe my thanks.

I am indebted to Vince Collison, Lucy Bell, Ken Rea and Amelia Rea, Melinda Pick and family, and Irene Mills, who shared their homes with me at various times during this research. Committee members from both the Haida Heritage and Repatriation Society and Skidegate Repatriation and Cultural Committee generously shared their time and stories. There are many others in Massett and Skidegate whose friendship has endured, and who have influenced the beginnings and endings of this research, as well as the beginnings of new endeavours together. A special thank you is owed to Maureen Matthews and Laura Peers.

The Skidegate Repatriation and Cultural Committee and Haida Heritage and Repatriation Society shared images. The Council of the Haida Nation allowed me to adapt their maps for publications, and Mariange Beaudry expertly and swiftly produced the resulting map. This book has benefited from a most helpful editor, anonymous reviewers, and Haida reviewers: your careful reading and constructive comments have improved the book tremendously, though any omissions or errors remain my own. Chris, Will, and Juniper make every journey better – either by joining me or by welcoming me home: thank you.

Funding for this research came from the Social Sciences and Humanities Research Council of Canada, an Overseas Research Scholarship from the United Kingdom, and a Clarendon Bursary from the University of Oxford. An overview of the findings appeared in an earlier article, "Repatriation and Remembering: The Production of Kinship, Memory and Respect" (*Journal of Material Culture* 15, no. 2, 2010). Elements of this book pertaining to the creation of material culture for repatriation activities were previously published as "Repatriation and the Generation of Material Culture" (*Mortality* 16, no. 2, 2011). The argument for considering pre-colonial influences on people's decisions to repatriate forms the basis of a chapter entitled "Post-Colonial or Pre-Colonial: Indigenous Values and Repatriation" in *Anthropologists, Indigenous Scholars, and the Research Encounter: Seeking Bridges Towards Mutual Respect,* edited by Joy Hendry and Laara Fitznor (Routledge, 2012).

Note on Orthography

Currently, there is no standard orthography for the Haida language. It was not until the late 1800s that scholars, missionaries, and Haidas desired written alphabets to either record or communicate within the Haida language. Different systems exist as a result of the varied preferences of linguists (see, for example, Enrico 2005; Lawrence 1977) and of speakers of the dialects. I use those alphabets and phonetic systems currently being used within Haida language programs in Skidegate, Old Massett, and, where appropriate, Alaska.[1] Where Haida words appear within citations from other sources, the original phonetic system is retained; current spellings are provided in brackets when reading the word in question would require specialized linguistic knowledge on the part of Haida language speakers or students.

a   like the *u* in "but"; sometimes like the *e* in "net," "pen"
aa   long *a* sound as in "laugh"
ee   long *e* sound as in "to lay"; used only in the definite form of nouns
i   short *i* as in "skin"
ii   long *i* sound as in "machine"; before *hl* or *l* it sounds like "ey"
u   like the *u* in "put"
uu   long *u*, like *oo* as in "tool" or the *u* in "rule"
b   same as English; very rare
p   same as English; rare sound in Haida, mostly in borrowed words

---

1 Based on orthography from a *Xaad Kil* (Haida language) course designed by Marianne Boelscher and delivered through Simon Fraser University, and Sealaska Heritage Institute's *X̱aat Kil* online orthography (http://www.haidalanguage.org/ways-of-writing.html; accessed 5 June 2008).

m   same as English
w   same as English
d   same as English; only in borrowed words
n   same as English
dl   like the *dl* in "paddle"
tl   like the *tl* in "bottle"
t   same as English
l   same as English
j   like the *j* in "judge"
s   same as English
ts   like *ch* in "church"; like the *ts* in "pets" when at the end of a word
g   same as English
k   like the *k* in "kin"
k'   velar glottalized stop
ng   like the *ng* sound in "king"
y   same as English
h   similar to English *h* but voiced further down the throat, almost like $\underline{x}$
G̲   uvular stop; very rare in Massett Haida but common in Skidegate
g̲   "back *g*" (Massett dialect); pharyngeal stop
k̲   "back *k*"; an uvular aspirated stop
k̲'   an uvular glottalized stop
hl   lateral fricative
x   velar fricative
x̲   pharyngeal fricative
7   glottal stop
'   glottal stop

Abbreviations

DCMS   Department of Culture, Media and Sport
HGM   Haida Gwaii Museum
HHRS   Haida Heritage and Repatriation Society
HRC   Haida Repatriation Committee
INAC   Indian and Northern Affairs Canada (formerly Department of Indian Affairs)
NWC   Northwest Coast
OMVC   Old Massett Village Council
SRCC   Skidegate Repatriation and Cultural Committee
UBCIC   Union of British Columbia Indian Chiefs

THE FORCE OF FAMILY

Repatriation, Kinship, and Memory on Haida Gwaii

1 Introduction

My first encounter with Haida repatriation efforts was on a June day in 2005. The Skidegate Repatriation and Cultural Committee (SRCC) was hosting an End of Mourning ceremony – a kind of second funeral hosted by family that marks the end of their public mourning for the deceased. The day's events were a celebration of the successful repatriation of all Haida ancestral remains within North America to Haida Gwaii, and for the committee in Skidegate the end of public mourning for these repatriated ancestors.

A fire was lit on the beachfront. People gathered in the parking lot, on the grassy area above the beach, and eventually on the sand around the fire itself. I did not yet know the names of these people: the ones tending the fire and handing out tobacco, accepting the tobacco and sifting it through their fingers before sprinkling it into the fire, wearing button blankets appliquéd with shimmering buttons and family crest designs, woven cedar hats, or dress shirts with strings of trade beads hung around their collars.

As kids played on the beach and families and friends visited, the forty-two-foot red cedar canoe *Loo Taas*, its fibreglass twin, and their Coast Guard escort were spotted rounding the headland. Hereditary leaders stood in a line at the water's edge to meet the approaching canoes (figure 1.1). The paddlers petitioned Chief Skidegate, the late Dempsey Collinson, to land on the beach. A young man from Skidegate danced on the beach to show that they were welcome to land. The paddlers began to unload their cargo of painted cedar bentwood chests, passed from person to person, up the beach. Later, the repatriation committee presented the senior woman from each of the Skidegate clans with one of the chests as a gift in recognition of their families' support of the repatriation process.

Figure 1.1 Canoes approaching the beach during the End of Mourning ceremony, 2005. Photograph by Cynthia Frankenburg, courtesy of SRCC and the
National Museum of the American Indian, Smithsonian Institution.

At the fire, Haidas offered prayers before placing a cedar plank with
seafood and berries into the fire. The food and prayers were for people's repatriated ancestors, but also for the victims of a devastating
nineteenth-century smallpox epidemic – an epidemic that pummelled
Haida families, killing an estimated 90 per cent of the population and in
some cases exterminating entire Haida clans (Acheson 1998). New as I
was to Haida Gwaii and repatriation, I did not fully appreciate this act
of grieving, honouring, and remembrance. On that day, no one explained that this was the first time victims of smallpox were being com-
memorated publicly on Haida Gwaii, and that for the first time people
felt safe enough to collectively confront this massive loss of life affecting all Haida families. Haidas spoke of their fears that the survivors of
smallpox might not have been able to provide funerals or an End of
Mourning feast for the family members they lost. It is quite likely that
among the repatriated ancestors were victims of smallpox.

As the day proceeded, thousands of sandwiches and hundreds of cans
of juice and bottles of water were distributed to those in attendance.

Afterwards, a procession set out from the beach to the cemetery, a few hundred metres down the road. There were around a hundred people gathered near the back of the cemetery where a row of mounds had been marked with large cedar plaques carved with the number of repatriated ancestors buried there, the names of the institutions from which they were returned, and the date of their return. Women poured water from porcelain jugs into bowls and washed the cedar plaques standing as headstones. During the washing of the plaques, the handle of one jug broke, snapping audibly and causing everyone to start. Haidas likened the sound to the crackling and popping sounds made when offerings are put into a fire – signs that the *kuniisii*, their ancestors, have received the offerings and are grateful.

From the cemetery, people made their way over to the George Brown Recreation Centre, a gymnasium that doubles as a hall for large gatherings. The centre was set up with long decorated tables and special seats for honoured guests and chiefs. The middle of the room was left clear for dancing, general traffic, and as a place to set up the enormous pots of stews to be served. Over six hundred guests came for the feast, filling the tables and settling in along the bleachers against the walls. After dinner, members of the repatriation committees donned white spirit masks and danced to the spirit song. The first notes of the song transformed the room of chatting people, clanging crockery, and rambunctious children into a still, haunting space filled with a drumbeat, the notes of the song, and memories. When spirit dancers emerged into the open space at the centre of the hall, they scattered and were undirected in their movements. The spirit dancers were followed by repatriation committee dancers who moved about the floor, gathering the spirit dancers, calming and unifying them, placing them as if in a canoe and then transporting the spirits away, dancing as though they were paddling the canoe. There were dances and songs for pure entertainment as well. The men's competition dance showcasing stamina and strength and the women's dance focusing on elegance and form gave delight to and were encouraged by all present. Dancers from Skidegate, Old Massett, and Alaska worked the crowd in friendly competition. *Gaagiid* danced – the tall, hairy being with sea urchin spines around his mouth and an unpredictable wildness scared and entranced young kids. Kaigani Haida from Alaska performed a new song they had written specifically in response to the repatriation efforts.

To ensure the day's events and significance would be remembered, and hence be efficacious, all those present were gifted with headbands embroidered with the SRCC butterfly logo, mugs with the same logo, and "Haida roses" fashioned from cedar bark. People's acceptance of these items demonstrated their support for the work of the repatriation committee and the statements made, in words and actions, during the feast. Now, as I remember the day's events and write these words, I sip water from the mug presented to me at the end of the feast.

A few months later, I returned to Haida Gwaii expecting to learn about the interconnectedness of Haida repatriation efforts and Haida political movements for recognition of their sovereignty. The very public displays such as the End of Mourning hosted by the SRCC would have been, I imagined, an extension of Haida political identities and claims. Not exactly: during a second, nine-month stay on Haida Gwaii I learned that understanding the repatriation process, the people and objects that are part of it, and Haida political identities requires viewing these through the lens of kinship. Kinship is a powerful force on Haida Gwaii: it is the basis of personal and collective identities, social obligations, and relationships. It undergirds value systems. I believe it even shapes how Haidas remember, know history, and reckon time. It is structural and constructive.

What became resoundingly clear in talking to members of the Haida Repatriation Committee, attending community events, and visiting with people in their homes and their territory is that time does not minimize Haidas' sense of family. This conclusion is in tension with repatriation literature, in which some archaelogists display marked tendencies to assign a temporal limitation to affect (discussed in Zimmerman 1987, 1989). For example, Clement Meighan, a vocal critic of repatriation legislation in the United States, asks, "How could I [an archaeologist] harm any person who had already been dead for thousands of years? How could anything that I did with the bones of these ancient people harm any living person?" (1992, 706). In 2011 Soren Holm similarly responded to repatriation debates in Europe by refusing to recognize that people could – and do – imagine kinship relationships across centuries or even millennia. Human remains distanced by more than three or four generations are imagined to be "too past" to evoke grief or mourning in the living (see also Pullar 1994). They are thought to be too removed to resonate emotionally, or within family histories. Russell Thornton (2002), by contrast, points out that when museums persist in holding aboriginal human remains, this makes historic actions all the more pressing; the keeping of ancestral remains continues to wound the living and prevents any semblance of closure for past trauma. As

I came to know the story of Haida repatriation efforts and the values inherent in Haida kinship better, the questions I heard being voiced by Haidas and the questions I came to ask were not only about ancestors in the past, but also about relatives in the present. If the remains of your family members are locked away in a museum's storage unit, what does that say about your family? What kind of story can you tell about yourself? Alternatively, if you find your ancestors' remains, honour them, return them to their homes, remember them, and visit them in the graveyards, how do those stories change? How do those people – family members living and deceased – change? And of equal importance, what aspects of self, family, community, and cultural practices continue?

A Time for Repatriation

During the nineteenth and early twentieth centuries, Western scholars were building their own stories of race and biological and cultural evolution. To build robust scientific theories, they frequently sought specimens of the world's "others" – non-Europeans and marginalized groups within Europe. Crania from aboriginal populations were collected as comparative phrenology specimens, while more complete skeletons facilitated physical anthropology studies (see Harrison 2012 for a nuanced cross-cultural history of these practices). We do not have a clear sense of the scale of these activities, except that it was vast. No one has undertaken a survey of human remains held within Canadian institutions, and arriving at even an approximate number is an elusive task. We do know that the physical remains of over three hundred thousand aboriginal people were deposited in American institutions such as natural history and ethnology museums, archaeology laboratories, and universities (Stuart 1999; see also Beider 2000; Hinsley 2000; Mihesuah 2000; Stocking 1968). Cubillo (2010, 20) records 7,200 indigenous Australian remains in museums, some 5,500 of which lack the provenance to identify them more specifically (for parallel processes in New Zealand and Tasmania see Fforde 2002, 2004.)[1] Remains from at least 1,000 indigenous North Americans were sent to the United Kingdom, and contribute to the 61,000 human remains in British collections (DCMS 2004, 11–12).

Increasingly since the 1980s, indigenous communities have endeavoured to repatriate their ancestors' remains by appealing for empathy, applying political pressure, and lobbying for legislation (Atkinson 2010; Riding In 2000; Thornton 2002; Trope and Echo-Hawk 2000; Turnbull

2010; Yellowman 1996). Rather than pursue legislation, in Canada the Assembly of First Nations and Canadian Museums Association developed a set of principles advocating ethical working relationships in all facets of museum work, including conservation, exhibitions, interpretation, education, training, and employment equity (Nicks and Hill 1992). The policy encourages museums to contact people biologically and/or culturally related to human remains in their collections. It also stresses that museums welcome aboriginal participation in determining how any remains retained within the museum's care are handled and kept, including setting parameters for scientific study. The policy's position on the repatriation of human remains is best summed up in the following two guidelines:

> v) Museums that acquire human remains through any means must involve the appropriate First Nation in the treatment and disposition of the remains.
>
> vi) The retention of Aboriginal human remains for prolonged periods against the expressed wishes of First Peoples is not acceptable. (Nicks and Hill 1992, 9)

Not withstanding these clear guidelines, it is difficult to determine how often or thoroughly museums or aboriginal nations have abided by the policy; a systematic review of the report is lacking.[2] Ruth Phillips' recent *Museum Pieces* (2011) suggests that Canadian museums have internalized aspects of the task force, and more specifically of aboriginal decision-making practices and philosophies, to such an extent that they are undergoing a process of "indigenization" – an indication that museums have taken the policy seriously.

Members of the Haida Repatriation Committee are well versed in the task force report and the principles (and to a lesser degree, the legal mechanisms) of the United States' Native American Graves Protection and Repatriation Act.[3] Yet the socio-political climate expounding collaboration and reparation for aboriginal peoples was far less influential in their repatriation process than was Haidas' own cultural impetus to act as kin. From an outsider's perspective, it is easy to perceive colonial collecting as having created the need for repatriation and post-colonial attitudes as having made repatriation possible. But from a Haida perspective, although colonialism corrupted their ability to care properly for their ancestors, they frequently explain the timing of their repatriation activities as the result of their own ancestors' agency: it is their ancestors who prompted Haidas to begin repatriating. The ancestors wanted this to be done and sent signals accordingly, such that people would come together and know repatriation was both possible and necessary. Christian White, who has been active in the Haida Heritage and Repatriation Society (HHRS) in the village of Old Massett, explained:

> In a way, you know, it was meant to happen. That's what we always used to hear when we were younger: it'll happen if it's meant to happen. So I believe that it was meant to happen. Sooner or later, really. They were calling us to bring them home. And some of us listened, I guess. If not, we'd go to those museums now and we'd still hear them calling us to bring them home. I think if the people had learned about them, then there would have been an effort. (19 November 2005)[4]

Similarly, Irene Mills of the SRCC explained:

> It's like everything has a germination time. So the seeds that were planted, however subconscious at the start of it – whether it was written in the paper or whatever – the ancestors have a way of working their magic to say "Okay, I think they're ready now. Let's send a few little signals their way." And that's how it started. (11 May 2006)

Since the mid-1990s, the repatriation of Haida ancestral remains has been a joint initiative between the Haida villages of Old Massett and Skidegate. The villages are represented by the HHRS and the SRCC, who work together as the Haida Repatriation Committee (HRC). The HRC receives strong moral support, but acts independently from, the Council of the Haida Nation, the village band councils, and hereditary leaders. Both committees seek the advice and participation of their village's elders. Their priority has been the return of their ancestors' remains, but they have also advocated for the return of their material heritage.

The exact number of ancestral remains taken off Haida Gwaii is difficult to know. Haidas have repatriated over 460 individuals from North American collections alone – an achievement described in more detail in chapter 3. They are currently pursuing the repatriation of significant Haida artefacts as well as the return of their ancestors' remains held in European institutions. In July 2010, Haidas welcomed home their first ancestor from overseas, repatriated from the Pitt Rivers Museum, University of Oxford, England. The feast to welcome this *kuniisii* was a jumble of emotions – joy, grief, relief, pride, anxiety; bringing *kuniisii* home instils pride in Haidas but also reminds them that the need to repatriate persists. The HRC continues to negotiate with the British Museum for the return of a cranium to Haida Gwaii. They are conscious that their family members continue to lie in boxes and shelves in museum storerooms, and as curios in people's living rooms and cupboards.

Anthropological Understandings of Repatriation

In this book I make an argument for understanding Haida repatriation efforts first and foremost through the lens of kinship. But I also argue for a more ethnographic and more context-specific approach to the study and understanding of repatriation. In attending to repatriation ethnographically, scholars can avoid essentializing "source communities" as undifferentiated indigenous peoples (Curtis 2006). On Haida Gwaii, repatriation has not occurred in isolation. The organized location and repatriation of ancestral remains has been ongoing for more than fifteen years, occupying thousands of person-hours spent in public meetings and committee meetings and involving fund-raising, travelling to museums, hosting feasts, and creating bentwood boxes, cedar mats, and button blankets. Throughout this time, people have navigated and refined their ideas about the reasons for repatriating their ancestors' remains, what it means to their nation, what is still to come, and how this new practice aligns with longer-standing Haida values. The continuing and evolving practices of repatriation can provide a focus for understanding Haida culture and people more broadly.

As both an ethnography of repatriation and an ethnography of the Haida, this book joins a slim body of literature and documentaries[5] that situate repatriation within local cultural and historical contexts rather than juxtaposing a number of case studies in order to illustrate broader historico-political movements or museum–community relations (Barkan and Bush 2002; Greenfield 2007; Killion 2008; Mihesuah 2000; Simpson 1996). In much of the repatriation literature, repatriated bodies become objectified and politicized and the repatriation of human remains is frequently presented as a political act, a means of correcting colonial wrongdoings, achieving self-determination, or reinforcing burgeoning identities (Crawford 2000; Fforde et al. 2002; Scheper-Hughes 2001; Verdery 1999). I am not suggesting these cases have been misinterpreted, but rather that these models are not the best fit for understanding

Haida repatriation efforts and their effects on people's lives. I approach Haidas' relationships to their ancestors' bodies and to the process of repatriation through their creation of, uses of, and ideas about memory and material culture – not the bodies themselves. There is much to learn from the things made for the *kuniisii*, the personal and family possessions Haidas integrate into the repatriation process, the things made and sold to cover the financial costs of repatriation activities, and the ways Haidas incorporate repatriation-linked objects into their everyday lives.

On Haida Gwaii, the way kin relationships are performed through the use of material culture and remembrance within the process of repatriation reflects a longer legacy of object, memory, and kinship performances occurring across a broad range of Haida cultural practices. Using an ethnographical approach, we can better appreciate why particular actions resonate within Haida repatriation efforts, and who those actions are aimed at. We more clearly understand that when Haidas speak of national efforts and community efforts, they are imagining their nation and their villages as comprised of interdependent families.

Objects and remembering are at the core of my understanding of Haida repatriation efforts for interrelated reasons. The HRC was at a time of rest and recuperation when I was on Haida Gwaii for nine months in 2005 and 2006. The End of Mourning ceremony that opens this book symbolized more than a decade of continuous searching for and repatriating Haida ancestors – tasks that required extensive fund-raising and travel preparations, but also carried tremendous emotional weight. Leaders and members of the HRC needed time to focus on the well-being of themselves and their immediate families. No ancestors were brought home during my main fieldwork. It was not until the summer of 2010 that I witnessed a reburial, and this was not as a researcher, but as someone affiliated with the returning institution – an event I return to in chapter 8. As a result, we largely talked about the past. I learned from people's memories. But I also attend to memory because the act of remembering emerged during my fieldwork as a crucial component of repatriation. Forgetting, in contrast, connoted negative values of loss, apathy, and crucially, unfamilial behaviour among Haidas. Nevertheless, the repatriation process has allowed for a degree of forgetting – namely, a forgetting of negligence, powerlessness, despair, or unfamilial behaviour.

In the course of my field research, Haidas' stories of repatriation presented a constant movement between personal memory and collective memory, triggered by contact with the things made for repatriation.[6]

Juxtaposing memory and material culture presents interesting opportunities for understanding these concepts individually and relationally. While memory is often considered as essentially ephemeral and material culture is by definition tangible, both memory and material objects have the potential to be "lost," "regained," or "manipulated." The uses of memory and material culture can be habitual or conscious, and are almost always inevitably both. There is an interdependence between the mnemonic potential of objects and the memory required to use or create objects in socially effective ways. Memories and objects can be both public and private, and often gain their social purchase through their use in performances. The memory work encouraged by Haida repatriation efforts, including forgetting and painful reminiscences, has joined a broader network – or more aptly a complex, multinodal meshwork (Ingold 2007) – and structure of memory practices on Haida Gwaii. As one repatriation committee member put it, repatriation has altered the way people remember the past so substantially that it has changed and even made history.

Haida repatriation efforts have left a number of material traces: grave plaques and headstones in cemeteries; casual clothing embroidered with the committees' butterfly logos; bentwood boxes carried from carving sheds to community centres to graveyards; tote bags with the butterfly logo that transport groceries or get collected by museums; the *Migration Home* pole that was commissioned to symbolize Haida repatriation, travelled to Germany, and now stands in front of an elementary school. These objects transcend the graveyard (and museum) as a place associated with death, mourning, or repatriation and materialize repatriation within public and private spheres throughout Haida Gwaii and beyond (Hallam and Hockey 2001). These objects foster repeat, often unanticipated, embodied interactions that recall the repatriated and the repatriators and provide broader opportunities for remembering (see also Saunders 2004). The material evidence of repatriation shapes Haidas' landscape.

Collective memory is being made on Haida Gwaii as a result of repatriation efforts. People's memories of repatriation are finding an enduring place in their biographies and in family, community, and national histories. Following decades of research in the Sudan and with displaced Sudanese refugees, Wendy James (2007) imagines a "cultural archive" external to the minds of individuals but grounded in encounters with everyday sounds, concepts, rhythms, tastes, movements, people, and places. Although textual records or photographs can comprise a part of this archive, it is not the things themselves but what people do with them, and how they remember through them, that constitutes the archive. James and Judith Ashton created the multimedia website *Voices from the Blue Nile*[7] to serve as a companion to James' (2007) book *War and Survival in Sudan's Frontierlands: Voices from the Blue Nile.* The website highlights the ways memory is a key component of James' investigation, including the recuperation of memories of lapsed performances. The ability to re-experience elements of the cultural archive supports relatedness and continuity through time and space. James' attention to lapsed practices is an important component of memory studies in postcolonial settings, and is especially pertinent to studies of memory within aboriginal communities in North America. On Haida Gwaii, the recuperation of memories and practices through repatriation is being used to support a sense of continuity, a concept defined ambiguously by Haidas, at times linear and uninterrupted, at other times cyclical or intermittent though not necessarily concerned by interruptions (see also Kramer 2006).

The relationship between cultural archives and collective memory requires clarification and exploration. Investigating the cultural archive in the context of the Haida repatriation process reveals it to be less dependent on commemoration and memorialization and more a product of embodied, emplaced, sensory, and verbal remembering and communication. A cultural archive seems to work in tandem with the structured remembering proposed by Bloch (1996) and Halbwachs (1992); in the emerging cultural archive of repatriation, the structure, obligations, expectations, and objects of Haida kinship loom large. There is a relationship between memory, kinship, and material culture.

The objects of material culture made and used in repatriation settings express Haidas' family identities and their intentions and states of being. They also act as mnemonic devices and function as sites for collective remembrance. Thus, the objects made for repatriation contribute to anthropological understandings of the interplay between memory and material culture, but more specifically they extend anthropological understandings of how kinship and memory are co-produced (Carsten 2000, 2007). By adding material culture into the equation, we can reconceive memory as a shared substance of kinship.

Given the force of repatriation in people's lives and histories, it is not surprising that the thought of another anthropologist writing about "the Haida" provoked anxiety among some HRC members; academic modes for describing and explaining aboriginal peoples or cultures do not always resonate with those for whom it is life lived. And yet, it was during our conversations about my choices of theory that Haidas felt increasingly secure that I understood what I was hearing and seeing, and what they were feeling. In the earlier months, for example, we explored ideas about inalienability (Weiner 1985, 1992) and the potential for Haida to co-opt the media as, essentially, potlatch witnesses. While people could readily understand their ancestors as inalienable from them, I found the exchange framework that comes with inalienability to be misplaced in much the same way that Renato Rosaldo came to accept grief rather than equalization as the impetus for Ilongot actions (1984). Conversations with Lucy Bell and Andy Wilson, two leaders of the Haida Repatriation Committee, probed the tensions between process and product, and what this tension had to say about repatriation on Haida Gwaii. Conversations with others tackled ideas about "authenticity," tradition, and change over time. During a later phase of my research, I returned to Haida Gwaii to discuss Janet Carsten's theory of the co-production of kinship and memory stemming from her work with Scottish adoptees and its fit with what I had observed and recorded on Haida Gwaii. Her ideas resonated with repatriation committee members as an explanatory and translating tool, and people were intrigued by and curious about the parallels with adoption – a relatively common Haida practice that both expands families and expresses esteem and honour.

Anxieties about my ability to translate Haida experiences of repatriation accurately were tempered by Haidas' sense that increasing academics' and museum professionals' awareness of their accomplishments and their reasons for repatriation could foster further dialogue. In particular, Haidas were keenly aware that I was coming to them as a doctoral student at the University of Oxford, under the supervision of Laura Peers, curator at the Pitt Rivers Museum and a leading figure in museum and source community relations. Haidas had "unfinished business," as they put it, with Pitt Rivers Museum: the museum held one of their ancestor's remains. They described efforts in 1998[8] to discuss the return of their *kuniisii* with museum staff as leaving them feeling deflated but determined. Through time, I came to understand that whereas I imagined myself as an individual researcher, Haidas saw in me an opportunity: I was evidence of a new willingness on the part of the museum to engage in a dialogue about repatriation. And so repatriation committee members took a chance on me and my ability to translate their experiences of repatriating their ancestors' remains.

Translations

Haidas make clear that anyone seeking to understand "Haida culture" must come to Haida Gwaii. In this, they share anthropology's tenet that you cannot understand a place from a distance. Chapters 2 and 3 bring us closer to Haida Gwaii – its families, history, ecology, landscape, and repatriation activities. Chapter 2 highlights the history of the cultural encounters between Haida and non-Haida that led to the removal of ancestral remains and material culture from the islands and that posed substantial challenges to Haida families. In chapter 3, I discuss the history of repatriation in North America and repatriation as a facet of life on Haida Gwaii. I compare various possible contexts for the return of Haida ancestral remains – ownership, the global indigenous rights movement, decolonization and reparations, and twentieth-century debates regarding the value of human bodies – but show how the Haida repatriation process is rooted primarily within the moral values, expectations, and obligations of Haida kinship.

Chapter 4 expands upon the values associated with Haida kinship. A significant aspect of the chapter is the connection between kinship and Haida notions of "respect," or *yahgudang*. *Yahgudang* is also the word Haidas use to characterize the work of the HRC. Ethnographic examples from the past and present show how kinship is continuously made and remade through objects, activities, and shared experiences. This lays the groundwork for exploring repatriation as part of a Haida cultural archive, as similar objects, activities, and experiences recur throughout Haida repatriation activities. This prepares us to look more closely at material culture in chapter 5. In order to understand how *yahgudang* is manifest within the process of repatriation, we need to know the ways in which *yahgudang* is expressed through the use of material objects and intangible property, especially during times of death and mourning.

Chapter 6 pays special attention to memory and the social functions of remembering, including how a sense of belonging can be communicated through interactions with material objects. This opens up the theoretical basis for combining kinship, material culture, and collective memory. I look at different spaces created by the repatriation process that support collective remembering and question the kinds of narratives and memories fostered in those spaces. The role of kinship in structuring people's encounters with objects, how they remember these encounters, and the creation of a cultural archive come to the fore.

Chapter 7 looks more specifically at how individual and collective remembering (or, conversely, forgetting) are strategies for overcoming traumatic events such as the loss of ancestral remains. Repatriation narratives expose contemporary Haida attitudes towards loss, continuity, and adaptability that are essential to understanding the force and the future of family on Haida Gwaii. The narratives also further our understanding of how a cultural archive comes to inform people's sense of self and their history.

The final chapter returns to the most recent repatriation events on Haida Gwaii and revisits reasons why kinship and, ultimately, repatriation are powerful forces in Haidas' lives.

To understand how cultural patterns shape social action, Clifford Geertz (1968, 111) offered two distinct measurements: "force" and "scope." Force describes the thoroughness, the "centrality or marginality," of a cultural pattern in one's life, whereas scope expresses how widespread a cultural pattern is across a population. Ideally, for my Haida colleagues, there will come a time when repatriation activities no longer need to be part of daily Haida life. For now, *The Force of Family* attests to the centrality of repatriation activities within Haidas' lives at the turn of the twenty-first century, and the enduring centrality of kinship for generations of Haidas.

2 Departures and Arrivals

The culture's just as much about going out clam digging, for a huge part of our population that's what they do for a big chunk of the season – they clam dig. And that's Haida culture. Going out salmon fishing, halibut fishing, or any of that stuff, that's what we've been doing forever. That's all part of Haida culture, that's who we are. The "fancy part" of it – the singing and dancing and the art of it – everyone's proud of that because we're good at it, but that's only a reflection of what we do in the ocean and the beaches. And that's really more of what we are. That art wouldn't exist without all that, without the land.

Jaalen Edenshaw, 18 January 2006

Government people come and go, you have other people come and go, but this is our homeland. People who live away call this their old country. Because, you know, this is where we have started from, from our stories.

Irene Mills, 11 May 2006

Haida Gwaii has been and continues to be people's home, islands of opportunity, and more recently in its history a field site for archaeologists, ethnologists, collectors, ethnobotanists, biologists, environmental scientists, and linguists. For the Haida, the waters and lands of Haida Gwaii are the homes of their supernatural ancestors, and where their human ancestors were created and have lived ever since. In the Haida language, Haida Gwaii means "land of the people." Haida history attributes the creation of this archipelago to the supernatural being Raven. Prior to Raven's meddling, there existed only a reef where other supernatural beings gathered. Raven, unable to find a place to land and rest on the reef, travelled to a village in the sky where he received various gifts and instructions on how to use them. Among these gifts are stones that Raven used to create Haida Gwaii and mainland British Columbia. The supernatural beings – including the supernatural ancestresses of Haida lineages – spread out from the reef across the islands (Enrico 1995; MacDonald 1983.) During a symposium in honour of Haida artist Bill Reid, Gwaaganad[1] (Diane Brown) shared a story she learned from Nang Ḵiing.aay 7uwans (James Young) describing the start of the k'waalaa (moiety) system:

> In the beginning of time, the sgaana gid iids – the supernatural killer whales – were the first beings to come to Haida Gwaii. There were few humans around then. The killer whales landed on Rose Spit around the Tow Hill area. They were the first supernatural beings, and they brought their wives with them, their killer whale wives. These supernatural killer whales had special markings. At will, they could come out of their killer whale skins and become human beings. The killer-whale beings wanted to have children. They could not have children with their wives. (Gwaganad 2004, 64)

Gwaaganad later explained to me that in order to have children, the killer whales went to Masset Inlet and found wives from the Old Massett area. These wives had different markings; thus this story tells of the origins of the k'waalaa system. "If you're a Haida, you are either an Eagle or a Raven, and this is how far back in the beginning of time that we got our crests: from the Beginning-of-Time people" (Gwaganad 2004, 64).

The places in which the supernaturals settled continue to be visible on the landscape today, rooting Haida families and history within the land (figure 2.1). For Haidas, the beauty of this place rests in its history, as the site of Haida origins, their capabilities, achievements, and their families. It is a place of identity, homecoming, nostalgia, and longing. However fraught conceptions of history, family, and identity may be, this complexity only increases the centrality of Haida Gwaii as a place for living, leaving, returning, remembering, forgetting, preserving, and developing.

In Haida history, Haida Gwaii was the epicentre of creation and geography; visiting the continental land mass required travel "seaward," away from the centre (Acheson 1998; MacDonald 1983). North America and the archipelago of Haida Gwaii are separated by Ḵandaliigwii, called Hecate Strait in English, a deep passage of the Pacific Ocean running along the northern coast of British Columbia, Canada. The islands fall

Figure 2.1 Agate beach with Tow Hill, home of the *Sgaana* (killer whale super-naturals), in the background. Northeast coast of Haida Gwaii, 2005.

within the provincial boundary of British Columbia although the archipelago is approximately forty kilometres offshore at its northern end and one hundred kilometres offshore at its southern end. The mountainous Alaskan panhandle can be seen on a clear day from the northern beaches of Haida Gwaii, while ocean views from the east, west, and south coasts extend uninterrupted. Today, the kilometres of unpaved logging roads far outnumber the kilometres of paved roads on the islands, and the southern half of the islands is only accessible by float plane or boat. Hundreds of islands sit in the bays and along the rocky and sandy shores of the two major islands, Graham and Moresby. The majority of islanders live in one of seven small towns or villages found along the paved roadway, which extends 110 kilometres along the eastern half of the islands (figure 2.2). A vehicle ferry to and from the mainland transports people, groceries, building supplies, mail, and other goods daily or weekly depending on the time of year and the weather, supplemented by daily commercial flights.

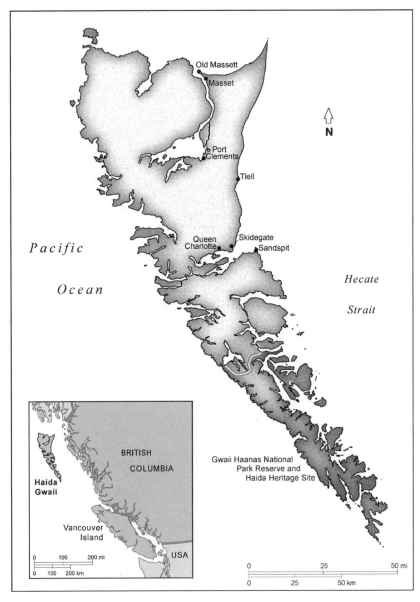

Figure 2.2 Map of Haida Gwaii showing current settlements. GIS and Cartography Office, Department of Geography and Planning, University of Toronto, modelled on a series of maps provided by the Council of the Haida Nation.

Of the 5,000 people living on Haida Gwaii today, just under half are Haida (Council of the Haida Nation 2008). A definitive figure for the Haida population is difficult to obtain. There are approximately 1,400 members of the Skidegate band, with about half living in Skidegate village (Indian and Northern Affairs Canada [INAC] 2008). The Old Massett band has always been slightly larger, with a population of about 2,650 people, 700 of whom live in the village of Old Massett (INAC 2008).[2] Taking into account band membership numbers and Council of the Haida Nation estimates, we arrive at a total population of 4,500. However, individuals suggested to me that a population of 6,000 is more accurate. Haida not living in Skidegate or Old Massett might live in one of the predominantly white settlements on the island – New Masset, Port Clements, Tlell, Queen Charlotte City, or Sandspit – or in more urban centres off-island such as Prince Rupert, Vancouver, or Victoria.[3] There are also Haida living in Alaska, the descendents of Haidas who emigrated from northern villages on Haida Gwaii in the second half of the 1800s.

The distance from the mainland and the turbulence of the waters surrounding Haida Gwaii meant that for much of their history – estimated to be at least 10,500 years (Fedje and Mathewes 2005) – Haida were almost the only people departing from or returning to these shores. Only over the last three centuries did trading vessels, steamships, and later airplanes shift this dynamic, bringing traders, homesteaders, missionaries, government officials, tourists, entreprenuers, scientists, and labourers to Haida Gwaii. Each group wanted varying degrees of control over the lands, waters, resources, and people. As Canada and British Columbia expanded and enveloped Haida Gwaii, both levels of government sought to control the resources and the people. Title to land on Haida Gwaii was distributed to early settlers, providing them with a place to call home while recategorizing Haida villages as reserves[4] on Crown land. Visualizing the islands as a place of untapped natural resources, government officials and entrepreneurs set their sights on its timbers, minerals, fish stocks, and tourist appeal. Questions of title, sovereignty, and control persist among the Haida, corporations, and government.

New arrivals are at first astounded at the number of deer on the roadside, ceasing their photography of the animals only after they have clicked their fiftieth frame in as many kilometres. During deer season, Haida hunters take many of the animals with little impact on their population. Deer meat appears on dinner tables, but more significantly in the enormous stockpots used to make venison or fish stews for feasts and potlatches. Hunting and gathering, or, more accurately, fishing, hunting, and gathering continue to make important contributions to local diets. Salmon is a key dietary element among many Northwest Coast aboriginal populations (Adams 1981), and while it is a common dish in Haida homes and at feasts, a significant portion of the Haida diet consists of the massive halibut caught in the waters around the islands (see also Acheson 1998). Other seafoods, such as scallops, clams, crab, black cod, ling cod, octopus, and _k'aaw_ (herring roe on kelp), are enjoyed alongside huckleberries, salmon berries, wild strawberries, and blackberries.[5] "Grease," a condiment made on the mainland from the oil extracted from putrified eulachon fish and treasured throughout the Northwest Coast (Jonaitis 2006), is obtained through trade or as give-away items at feasts. These foods are supplemented with rice, potatoes, macaroni salad, Asian noodle salads, convenience foods from grocery stores, soy sauce, and (a Haida favourite) sushi made with their own freshly caught seafood. Haida women enjoy a talent for baking bread, pies, and sweets, and Haida recipes in general contain enough servings for an extended family.

Old cedar roofing shingles can become thick with moss in this place, much like the tree limbs drip with thick layers of soft moss. It is possible – though not always desired – to build one's home from flotsam and jetsam collected on the beach. The spaces between houses contain wild strawberry patches and huckleberry and salmonberry bushes, scenting the air in summer. Eagles sit on the beach to eat their fish. Pebbles softly clatter against each other as they roll in and out with the ocean waves. A week of gale force winds astounds you with their power and perseverance. Drivers interrupt their errands to watch migratory whales emerge and submerge offshore, rolling and splashing and shimmering in the sun. Island residents need to know the islands' cycles and weather – the tides, harvesting times, spawning seasons, winds – for survival and for quality of life.

The northeastern corner of Graham Island consists of Naikoon Provincial Park, encompassing a handful of protected ecological reserves. Its northwestern corner is protected by the Council of the Haida Nation as Duu Guusd Protected Area (Forest n.d.).[6] The southern third of the islands comprises the Gwaii Haanas National Park Reserve and Haida Heritage Site – recently named the best national park in North America for its "natural beauty and the authenticity of the local Haida culture" (Ward 2005; see also Lukovich 2005; Tourtellot 2005[7]). During tours of the Park Reserve, the remnants of Haida villages – toppled house poles and mortuary poles, sunken floors of longhouses, massive stand-alone house posts, cave sites, and Christian-influenced cemeteries – confound one's sense of time. For city slickers, the abundance of wildlife can have the same impact. Humpback and killer whales, sea lions, puffins, porpoises, sea urchins, a subspecies of black bear found only on the islands (*Ursus americanus carlottae*), deer, eagles, ravens, and ancient murrelets all benefit from the islands' unique ecology.

This unique ecology also attracts the attention of conservationists and naturalists. It has been billed as a northern Galapagos. Haida Gwaii is a mixture of ecological zones, with alpine and intertidal regions, dense old-growth forest and expansive reforested areas, marshlands, prairie, and rock and sand beaches (see Turner 2004). There is a grandness to the flora and fauna, to the energy of the wind and waves, and to the expansive vistas. This grandness is equally evident in the artistic displays of Haida culture. There is a formidable presence to Haida singing, dancing, and carving that commands attention. Unsurprisingly, then, Haida Gwaii has also been sought out by anthropologists and art historians wanting to document, understand, preserve, "salvage," and acquire the products of Haida culture.

Knowledge of the history of cross-cultural encounters on Haida Gwaii is critical for understanding the circumstances under which repatriation happened, but also because these historic encounters continue to influence people's lives and the choices they make in the present. The loss of ancestral remains and artefacts and the disruption of family were linked historically, while the return of ancestral remains, reengaging with heritage objects, and the strengthening of Haida kinship continue to be intimately connected.

A History of Encounters on Haida Gwaii

The relationships between Haida and those who have joined them on Haida Gwaii are complex owing to the variety of circumstances under which off-islanders have arrived. They came, and continue to come, as aboriginal trading partners or spouses, labourers, missionaries, environmentalists, loggers, sports hunters, homesteaders, scientists, businessmen, politicians, tourists, cottagers, friends, family, health professionals, and artists. Each incoming group or individual, myself included, brings expectations of and demands on the resources and people of Haida Gwaii. In this section, I focus on those interactions between Haidas and non-Haidas that led to the removal of ancestral remains from Haida Gwaii, and those that challenged Haida values of kinship, entitlement, and, ultimately, identity.

The first recorded encounter[8] between Haida and Europeans was in 1774 with the arrival of Juan Perez to Haida territory, followed by a series of explorers-cum-traders. One of the first characteristics ascribed to Haida people was that of skilled and discerning traders. Diaries and reports of traders bartering with Haidas depict a rich, strong, impressive population. Their villages made positive first impressions: large, multifamily, permanent houses all facing towards the sea, dwarfed – despite their size – by spectacularly carved poles. The natural resources of the Haida, especially sea otter pelts, and Haida material culture were objects of desire, collected as items of commerce, curios, and symbols of trading partnerships. In return, the *yaats xaadee* (literally translated as "iron people" but more generally translated as "white people") provided objects admired and desired locally, such as iron objects, beads, wool broadcloth, guns, officers' uniforms, and, later, alcohol. In one case, a Haida chief from Kiusta was pleased to exchange names with his favoured British trader; the chief proudly continued to use the name "Douglas" for many years (Acheson 1998, 101; Wright 2001).

Early traders reaching Haida Gwaii remarked on the autonomy Haida individuals exercised in trading their furs for European goods. Captain George Dixon recorded:

> Though every tribe we met with at these islands is governed by its respective Chief, yet they are divided into families, each of which appear to have regulation and a kind of subordinate government of its own: the Chief usually trades for the whole tribe; but I have sometimes observed that when his method of barter has been disapproved of, each separate family was [sic] claimed right to dispose of their own furs, and the Chief always complied with this request. (quoted in Acheson 1998, 65)

During this initial period of visiting Haida Gwaii, *yaats xaadee* traders travelled throughout the bays, inlets, and narrows, stopping in at one of the many villages perennially inhabited by Haida lineages.[9] Scores of seasonal camps for harvesting and processing various natural resources were also in use. With the steady stream of trading ships came new sources of wealth for Haidas and a steady source of iron ideal for the production of new tools. New tools in turn supported an efflorescence in the production of traditional material wealth such as houses, canoes, poles, or coppers, used for supporting or claiming immaterial wealth such as names, songs, or titles. The combination of increased traditional wealth with newly introduced forms of wealth underpinned the material richness of this period, depicted by many as the zenith of Haida culture (Davidson 2006; Gunther 1966; Stewart 1993).

Potlatching – the social institution used to demarcate successions of chiefly titles, claim or share rights to property, give a name to a newly constructed house, compensate for social blunders, or mark transformations of social identities (as a result of, for example, marriage, adoption, death, or menstruation) – grew in grandness as potlatch hosts sought to provide their guests with more food and more gifts (many of European origin) (Blackman 1990; Boelscher 1988; Murdock 1936). Over time, the artistry and craftsmanship of the regalia and monuments that marked these changes or claims became ever more impressive, as did the paraphernalia of dancers and entertainers.

Throughout this time, Haida lineages continued to intermarry and trade with mainland native populations, exchanging well-made canoes, sea otter pelts, slaves, finely crafted objects, songs, and names for prized materials and foods such as eulachon grease. As Fort Victoria on Vancouver Island became a trading hub within the Pacific Northwest, increasing numbers of Haida canoed south to sell their own wares and acquire novel forms of wealth for personal use or to give away at their potlatches. In the 1860s, however, Haida traders were falling ill en route back to Haida Gwaii. Stories recall times when ten canoes departed from Victoria but only one or two reached their destination.[10] Smallpox spread rapidly throughout Haida villages, decimating the population and extinguishing lineages. This was the second deadly epidemic of smallpox on Haida Gwaii; the first came in the 1790s. Estimates for the pre-contact Haida population range from six thousand people to ten thousand and even as many as thirty thousand (Acheson 1998, 61; N. Collison 2006, 58; Duff 1964). What is easier to determine is the population after the epidemics. An 1881 Canadian census recorded only 829 Haida; by 1915, a count recorded only 588 Haida (Duff 1964).

The arrival of Christianity on Haida Gwaii followed closely on the heels of the 1860s epidemic. The first mission to be established on Haida Gwaii was in Old Massett in 1876, by the Reverend W.H. Collison. Collison's (1981) memoirs of this period record how it was his ability to heal medical ailments that won him favour in the village, and ultimately redirected Haida allegiances from their shaman to Collison. A Methodist missionary established himself in Skidegate in 1883 (Enrico

1995, 1), and later a rival Salvation Army brigade was established in the village. Early missionary accounts do not capture the sense of grief that . contemporary Haidas empathically imagine must have been felt in the wake of the smallpox epidemic. For them, the decimation of one's family is beyond words, beyond knowing.

Within three decades, Christianity became the outward form of Haida religious practices. Christian Haidas have retained certain social and spiritual values from pre-Christian days and may continue, for example, to adhere to Haida creation stories, as other Christians may read Genesis alongside Darwinian evolution. Although the Church advocated for belief in Christianity to the exclusion of Haida beliefs, in practice Haidas do not seem to see the two as mutually exclusive. Respect for food sources and for animals' giving themselves up for nourishment, for example, has continued, though the performance of these beliefs was not always publicly enacted. The Return of the Salmon Ceremony continued to be practiced quietly within families, and in recent years has been re-enacted publicly. The effects of the Church's work in removing Haida cultural practices from the public sphere and removing Haida children from their homes is a topic I return to below.

After the 1860s smallpox epidemic, the surviving Haida families began clustering around two sites: Skidegate in the south and Old Massett in the north (figures 2.3, 2.4). Previously, social divisions were based on a combination of geography and lineage. Today, within Old Massett and Skidegate, Haida lineage members retain the memory of their natal villages and the movements of their lineages across the Haida Gwaii landscape. Haida language speakers – almost all of whom are in their seventies or older – retain separate village identities in their dialects.[11] The post-epidemic resettlement added new social categories of "north" and "south," or "Massett" and "Skidegate." This division became an administrative one, as the resettlement coincided with the arrival of missionaries and the installation of magistrates and, later, government Indian agents. Indian agents recognized the Haida as consisting of two bands, Old Massett and Skidegate, a division still maintained by the Department of Indian Affairs and Northern Development. The division between the two villages has come to carry a good deal of weight with Haidas as well. Each compares itself with the other regarding fund-raising success, entrepreneurship, athletic prowess, community spirit, how meetings are conducted, and speech mannerisms, among other things. The comparisons are alternately competitive, joking, hostile, and familial – there is, after all, a lot of shared family between the two villages.

Figure 2.3 Village of Skidegate, *HlGaagilda*, 2006.

Figure 2.4 Village of Old Massett, looking out towards Masset Inlet, 2005.

At the same time that the Haida population was dropping dramatically, the number of *yaats xaadee* arriving on the west coast of North America skyrocketed. Competing traders, settlers, and entrepreneurs were lured to the west coast of North America by pelts, land, gold, other minerals, timber, and fish stocks (Fisher 1992).[12] In the last decades of the 1800s, increasing numbers of white traders and settlers landed with the intention of remaining permanently on Haida Gwaii. Trading, scientific, geological, ethnographic, and capitalist expeditions eventually turned into a continual presence on the islands. Dogfish oil and gold mining had minimal success, while the logging and fishing industries were, and continue to be, highly lucrative. Today, in the midst of indigenous land claims and environmental degradation, they are also highly contentious. Concerns about commercial logging practices on the islands prompted the establishment of the Council of the Haida Nation in 1974, the political body that advocates for and protects Haidas' collective aboriginal rights and title.

Douglas Cole captures the rapid pace of colonial settlement in the Pacific Northwest in the latter half of the nineteenth century:

> Spectacular growth began in the 1880s, the decade opening with a gold rush to Juneau and the beginning of western construction of Canada's Pacific railway, completed in 1885 ... Immigrants and capital, attracted by the burgeoning timber trade, by the development of the salmon canning industry, by rich agricultural land ... and by commercial opportunities of growth poured into Washington, British Columbia and Alaska. Forestry, fishing, and mining caused intensive intrusions into previously remote locations ... Seattle boomed from 3,533 people in 1880 to 42, 837 in 1890, and Vancouver was called into existence as the terminal city of the Canadian Pacific. (Cole 1995, 89–90)

With this huge influx of people to the Pacific coast came greater demands for access to and ownership of land and resources. While newcomers imagined the west coast as uninhabited, unowned, and ripe for the taking, aboriginal peoples had been exercising their rights to particular lands and resources for thousands of years.

Although contact between Europeans, Euro-Canadians, and Haida had been ongoing for a century, by this point Haida Gwaii is best described as a "contact zone," a "space of colonial encounters ... in which peoples geographically and historically separated come into contact with each other and establish ongoing relations, usually involving conditions of coercion, radical inequality, and intractable conflict" (Pratt 1992, 7).

Such a "'contact' perspective emphasizes how subjects are constituted in and by their relations to each other [stressing] co-presence, interaction, interlocking understandings and practices, often within radically asymmetrical relations of power" (Pratt 1992, 7; see also Clifford's 1997 application of the idea to museums and Boast's 2011 critique of museums' neoliberal rendering of the term). One of the most striking depictions of co-presence and asymmetry of power in this contact zone was the implementation of the reserve system by Euro-Canadians.

Indian reserve commissioner Peter O'Reilly arrived on Haida Gwaii in 1882, demarcated some twenty small, unconnected plots of land as reserves for Haida people, and opened the rest of the islands to outside purchasers and speculators. Historic geographer Cole Harris observes that, prior to the creation of Indian reserves, "the Haida had been in sole possession of the island, [in the words of Haida chief Alfred Adams] 'with our houses scattered at the mouths of every river and stream'"; afterwards they "had five acres of land per person" (Harris 2002, 213). Alfred Adams and fellow Haidas Amos Russ and James Sterling were among the aboriginal representatives who argued their case to the 1913 Royal Commission, pressing for their ongoing rights to their territories. Sterling, reflecting on the hammering of stakes, and the dividing and selling of land by Euro-Canadians, told the Royal Commission, "We tried to make ourselves believe we were in our own country, but we are more and more reminded that what we supposed was ours, is said on many cases to belong to men who never saw these islands" (Harris 2002, 214).

While the natural resources of the Haida were being targeted by capitalist interests, and while Haida souls were being targeted by Christian missionaries, the highly decorated and well-crafted material culture of the Haida was being targeted by a different set of newcomers to the islands: ethnographic collectors. The "scramble" for Northwest Coast materials was hastened by the presumption that aboriginal peoples living along the coast would be lost in a matter of generations, as a result of either disease or assimilation (Cole 1995; Rosenblum 1996). The Berlin Museum, the newly founded Smithsonian Institution, Chicago's Field Museum, the American Museum of Natural History, the Bremen Geographical Society, and to a lesser degree the Canadian Geological Survey, British museums, and the British Columbia Provincial Museum sent curators and collectors to the Pacific Northwest, contracted local buyers, and solicited already formed collections for their growing anthropological collections (Cole 1995). Collecting was highly competitive. Local collectors worked for multiple museums (and themselves) at any one time, raced to new areas of Christian conversion to snatch up ceremonial items for sale, collected from people in times of duress, jealously guarded knowledge of unprotected burial sites ripe for looting, compared prices, both purchased and stole items, and sought insider knowledge from native colleagues.

Franz Boas spent considerable time on Vancouver Island and the Northwest Coast more generally, collecting for the Chicago World's Fair and the Jesup North Pacific Expedition. For the latter, Boas and his staff – including John R. Swanton – amassed an impressive ethnographic collection for the American Museum of Natural History in New York City, including textual records of songs, histories, stories, and mythologies of the Haida as well as general ethnographic observations and artefacts (Cole 1995; Swanton 1905a, 1905b, 1908). Swanton stayed on Haida Gwaii in 1900–1, and produced seminal ethnographic works on Haida culture. He often asked people to speak about historic (and thus, to him, his colleagues, and readers, "more authentic") practices. Much of what Haidas shared with him they shared in their own language, and Swanton frequently included both Haida and English transcriptions in his publications. For both of these reasons, Swanton's work and especially his *Contributions to the Ethnology of the Haida* are highly valued resources among Haidas. *Contributions* was reprinted by the Council of the Haida Nation in 2004 with a new introduction, with proceeds from sales supporting the council.

Victoria-based medical doctor C.F. Newcombe assisted Swanton in his endeavours, but also sent many Haida collections to Boas' competitor George Dorsey at Chicago's Field Museum, the National Museum of Man in Ottawa, British Columbia Provincial Museum in Victoria, University Museum in Philadelphia, the British Museum in London, and to Edward Burnett Tylor at the University of Oxford (Cole 1995). During his lengthy career with Ottawa's National Museum of Man, ethnologist Marius Barbeau researched, documented, and collected specimens of Haida argillite carving and Northwest Coast pole carving (Barbeau 1953, 1957, 1990).

Often, collectors obtained the assistance and made use of the influence of local missionaries. Missionaries were variously driven in their collecting by intellectual curiosity, a desire to purge "excess" and "idolatry" from traditional ways, or a desire to prevent newly converted Christians from slipping back to their traditional ways. The Reverend Charles Harrison in Old Massett sent collections of Haida materials to Tylor at the University of Oxford. These materials, some 140 objects, are now part of the collections of the Pitt Rivers Museum (Harrison 1925).[13]

The Reverend Crosby also collected Haida materials, as well as materials from the northern river systems in British Columbia (Cole 1995; Hare and Barman 2006; Neylan 2003).

Native guides and friends, on the other hand, were useful for navigating local inheritance and ownership patterns, providing detailed provenance for objects, and obtaining access to objects before they reached the public market. Johnny Kit Elswa of Skidegate, for example, provided assistance to collector James G. Swan, who was under contract to the Smithsonian (Cole 1995).[14] But collectors also pursued their ends without Native guides or local colleagues, particularly when grave goods and human remains were their target.

Collectors solicited the location of burial caves, sometimes bribing locals for assistance, at other times returning later in secret to disinter the remains (Thom 2000). A telling episode from this time was Boas' refusal to have John Swanton collect Haida human remains. Boas knew that if Swanton collected human remains it would violate Swanton's working partnerships and jeopardize his magnificent success at recording Haida myths and cultural traditions (Cole 1995, 185), and so he enlisted Newcombe for this task instead.

While removing remains under Haida surveillance was difficult, the massive loss of life from disease on Haida Gwaii meant that remains could be found strewn along the long coastline of Haida Gwaii, which was largely uninhabited after the epidemics. When survivors of the epidemics began to congregate in the towns of Massett and Skidegate, a physical distance anywhere from two to two-hundred kilometres was created between Haidas and their ancestors' graves. Lucy Bell recalled her *naanii* (grandmother) mentioning that when she was a young girl Haidas were nervous about entering the old villages with remains lying everywhere. Professional and amateur collectors alike collected physical remains with minimal difficulty and without being seen. Despite Haida efforts to protect their ancestors' remains, over 460 were removed from Haida Gwaii and deposited in North American museums, universities, and private collections (Haida Gwaii Museum 2013; SRCC 2006). The number of remains sent directly to European museums, or traded there by North American museums, is as yet undetermined.

Collecting property – whether objects and bodies or land and resources – was encouraged by newcomers to the coast. From 1875 to 1925, the intensive, competitive collecting of material culture by North American and German museums in particular is credited with "denuding" the Northwest Coast of physical objects (Cole 1995; King 1999; Meuli 2001).[15] Indeed, Cole (1995, 286) surmises that by the time the frenzied collecting ended "the city of Washington contained more Northwest Coast material than the state of Washington and New York City probably housed more British Columbia material than British Columbia herself." Appropriations of lands, resources, and material culture thus coincided throughout the Northwest Coast as intersecting processes.

Haidas responded to these changes in various ways. Carver Charles Edenshaw and weaver Isabella Edenshaw, for example, supported their family by creating argillite models, silver bracelets, woven baskets, and woven hats for sale to collectors and tourists (Blackman 2011). The missionaries posted on Haida Gwaii had been impressed with the work ethic and abilities of Haida men and women. Haida women and children could find ample work in the canneries. By the 1930s, Haida men had gained a widespread reputation as superb builders of fishing boats, which is not surprising given their reknown as expert canoe builders. The village of Old Massett had as many as thirteen seine boats owned by Haida men, with Haida crews. The building and operating costs for the boats had been financed through the bank; following a few lean seasons, in the 1950s and 1960s the boats were repossessed. With the loss of their livelihood and of the means to provide food for their famililies, and with diminished access to waters and lands, the male population experienced a severe blow to their morale. Alcoholism became one coping strategy, and families became dependent on social assistance from the government. In a few short years, the economic centre of the islands moved from Old Massett to New Masset, as both the grocery store and the cannery shifted location from the former to the latter. Today, New Masset is the site of the post office, restaurants, hardware stores, garage, harbour, and most services. More recently, the economic centre of the islands shifted again, to Queen Charlotte City, located approximately seven kilometres west of Skidegate and comprising mostly non-Haida residents. Still, a number of the most recent economic developments are located in Skidegate, suggesting another shift may be happening. Old Massett has a handful of small businesses run from homes – convenience stores, gifts, Haida regalia, fishing charters, and bed and breakfasts – plus a café and Haida art store. Skidegate has a grocery store, gas station, clothing store, gift shop, take-out eatery, fishing charter, and home-run businesses similar to those of Old Massett. There are also resource-based businesses, education-related operations including a satellite for Northwest Community College, and tourism- and heritage-based operations including the Haida Heritage Centre and Haida Gwaii Museum, as well as Parks Canada and Haida operations tied to Gwaii Haanas National Park Reserve and Haida Heritage Site. While the vast majority of Haida men have worked on a commercial fishing or crabbing boat during their lifetime, today few such boats are owned by Haidas (figure 2.5).[16]

Christian White, a repatriation committee member, carver, grandfather, singer, and dancer in Old Massett, reflected:

> A hundred and some odd years ago, some of my family members were documented and they were chiefs, their mothers were chiefs' daughters, and they were chiefs' sons. And they were wealthy, they were wealthy people. Very highly intelligent, and became educated also. They were very trustworthy. I think, in a way, over the past hundred years, we've kind of stepped *back*, because if our ancestors a hundred years ago could become that highly educated to actually translate the Bible, to translate a thousand pages of English into Haida, it shows how intelligent they were. And nowadays, we're having a hard time doing that sort of thing. I think we were a bit, like I said, we went through this wave of bitterness after we lost our livelihoods. And then also we realized that we, when we saw all our other losses, we saw the loss of our culture too. You know, when we were doing good in the fishing industry, we kind of – it cushioned the effects of the loss of our culture. But then when we realized we had lost our livelihoods and we had also lost our culture, then you could see how the bitterness crept in there. So from there, we've been trying to recover what's left of our culture. (19 November 2005)

Cultural attrition has been attributed to a multitude of factors working in concert. Potlatching was made illegal by the Canadian government in 1884 in an attempt to prevent non-capitalist attitudes towards wealth and to encourage assimilation of the aboriginal population (Cole and Chaikin 1990). For two decades, lineages continued potlatching in secret, assisted by winter travelling conditions that dissuaded most Indian agents from visiting the remote islands during the season. Eventually, the creation of regalia for dancing, large-scale carving of poles, and carving of bentwood boxes and mountain goat horn spoons ceased as the law was increasingly enforced (Thom 2000) and missionaries increasingly discouraged its practice. Missionaries disapproved of the materials – the masks, rattles, and blankets – and activities that connected participants with supernaturals and other spirits. They encouraged the sale or donation of the materials to collectors, and discouraged dancing and the singing of old songs (Jensen and Sargent 1986). Despite

Figure 2.5 The harbour at the start of fishing season in New Masset, May 2006.

their disapproval, missionaries were among the guests who attended potlatches, and they directed the payments they received for offering prayers, singing hymns, or witnessing the events to the church's coffers. Blackman (1973, 51) clarifies that these potlatches were much transformed in appearance, having "undergone a considerable amount of external and superficial change while remaining structurally and functionally unaltered" (see also Codere 1966; Jonaitis 1991; Seguin 1985).

The potlatch itself did not cease: it became disguised, and incorporated within Christian and Western traditions such as Christmas, funerals, and birthdays. Grand public potlatches transformed into smaller affairs. The new style of single-family home was built with combined living and dining rooms, providing a large open space where teas and meals could be served in place of large dinner feasts. Church hymns and a prize-winning brass band became new musical foci within the villages. Names, titles, rights, and privileges remained in old people's memories more often than they were transferred.

Across Canada, further attempts to "civilize" aboriginal people were focused on children. Church and state together removed thousands of children from their homes and placed them in boarding schools aimed at alienating the students from their languages and traditions and the "negative" (i.e., cultural) influences of their families (Milloy 1999). Recently, the federal government began to financially compensate individuals who were sent to residential schools. On Haida Gwaii, such individuals are now between the ages of fifty and one hundred years. Whether or not this compensation will be sufficient for Haidas to reconcile the legacy of residential schools, which includes cultural loss, language loss, alcoholism, drug addiction, sexual and physical abuse, and the weakening of the family, remains to be seen.

Another hurdle for Haida communities (indeed, aboriginal communities throughout Canada) has been the federal government's removal of "status" in certain circumstances. "Status" Indians are entitled to particular concessions or services from the federal government as set out in the Indian Act. Growing out of the Royal Proclamation of 1763, the Indian Act served as a means of compensating First Nations for loss of lands and as a way of integrating them within the burgeoning nation. (A less flattering reading of the Proclamation sees it as a means for enabling colonialist expansion and assimilation; see Harris 2002.) Indian status could be retracted from people who obtained university degrees or from women who married non-Native men; paradoxically, when male status Indians married white women those women *gained* Indian status. The loss of status through marriage was challenged by aboriginal people across Canada and defeated with the passing of Bill C-31 in 1985 (Fiske and George 2006), although a series of loopholes still jeopardizes the ability of future generations to claim status. The bill has been hailed as a triumph for the rights of aboriginal women, was viewed with apprehension by many, and caused highly charged interactions within communities. Women from Skidegate and Old Massett spoke of the conflict Bill C-31 had caused in their own communities. Status Indians were afraid that they would have to share the precious few resources coming from the government with even more people, while Bill C-31 women and their families who moved back to the Indian reserves of their youth sometimes felt snubbed by people or alienated from a way of life that was no longer familiar. It was Haida women mostly who shared these stories, and often did so quietly, noting the subtlety with which such interactions took place among their neighbours. For those willing to vocalize the problem, there seemed to be a level of shame stemming from the ill treatment that passed between Haidas, within villages and families, over the matter. Although it has been twenty-five years since the passing of the bill, families, friends, and band councils are still working through the intended and unexpected consequences of the bill.

As politics and attitudes have changed, so has Haida practice. Knowledge of Western law, negotiation, bureaucracy, ethnography, archaeology, and history have formed a new tool set as people seek to communicate their sense of territory, property, and rights to outsiders. As commercial fishermen, food fishermen, logging operators, and fallers, Haidas are keenly aware of the tensions, persistent throughout the twentieth century, among commercial regulations, industrial harvesting methods, and traditional harvesting methods. Haidas have staged protests and blockades throughout the islands and waters of the archipelago to protect the islands from clear-cutting, halt sports fishing and trophy hunting, and demonstrate their ownership of the land, water, and resources. This apparent move to national action and national responsibility is a theme I return to at various points throughout this book. The question of how such national efforts compare and compete with familial responsibility – presenting alternative frameworks for remembering history and locating identity – is of increasing relevance to First Nations communities (see also Kramer 2006) as well as to this investigation of how Haidas structure history, remembering, and social encounters. National identity on Haida Gwaii is premised upon a relatedness and interdependence of clans, and political action is most efficacious and national or international in scope when families agree.

There have also been changes in Haidas' relationships with material culture. In 1969, the first pole raising in Old Massett in eighty years was hosted by carver Robert Davidson (gii-dahl-guud-sliiaay 1995; Stearns 1990, 265). The impetus for carving the pole, according to Davidson, "was so that people could celebrate one more time before they die, especially the elders" (Jensen and Sargent 1986, 21). Yet as Davidson himself points out, "We're still celebrating" (ibid.). Rather than being an isolated event, poles continued to be carved and raised, along with the renewed creation of button blankets, masks, and bowls to complement the small carvings and prints people had in their homes and the jewellery they wore.

Stearns describes how the process of creating material goods led to a parallel interest in traditional knowledge and the practices allowing for the display and use of such wealth:

> For a time more than 30 artists were at work in Masset alone. Looking back to the traditional culture for inspiration intensified their interest in other aspects of old Haida culture – the food, the beliefs, the medicines. The making of red-bordered dance blankets [button blankets], with crest out-lines in pearl buttons, became a cottage industry. Dance groups appeared, and soon every public event featured native dancing, drumming, and singing. (Stearns 1990, 265)

Today, button blankets, vests and tunics, raven's tail robes and head-bands and woven cedar hats in traditional, top hat, and fedora styles may be worn for special occasions such as graduations, weddings, feasts, repatriations, and potlatches. Since the 1980s, potlatches have increased in frequency, continuing to honour the passing of chiefs, to transfer rights and property, and to mark life events (Steltzer 1984; Virtual Museum Canada 1998; Webster 1991).

The historic fame and value of Haida canoes, objects admired by in-digenous and European seafarers alike, was reinvigorated when Bill Reid made a fifty-foot canoe for Expo '86 in Vancouver. The canoe was paddled back to Haida Gwaii from Vancouver the following year (a distance of nine hundred kilometres), retracing old trade routes and being celebrated with feasts along the way. In 1989, the canoe was brought to France and paddled along the Seine to mark the opening of an exhibition of Haida art at the Musée de l'Homme (Virtual Museum Canada 1998). It has also been paddled to Alaska and today resides in Skidegate, where it is used for different community events, including the Skidegate Repatriation and Cultural Committee's End of Mourning ceremony in June 2005. The Haida Gwaii Museum published *Gina 'Waadluxan Tluu The Everything Canoe* (Ramsay and Jones 2010), and Haida canoe culture has become a part of the local school curriculum.

Lucy Bell and Vince Collison (2006) of the Haida Heritage and Repatriation Society in Old Massett have characterized the cultural production associated with the repatriation process as a resurgence in *cultural pride* as opposed to a revitalization of "culture." According to the eldest Haida generations, pride and self-respect should be insepa-rable. As ideals of behaviour, they are linked conceptually. As practices, they are expressed through adherence to cultural protocol involving actions and objects, property and ownership, lineages and moieties (*k'waalaa*). Moreover, the Haida concept of *yahgudang*, "to be fit for respect," is central to understanding how repatriation committee members explain repatriation and the procedures surrounding the return of their ancestors' remains.

Challenges, Change, Continuity, and Adaptability

Assimilationist and racist policies and laws, Christianity, new economic opportunities, an influx of non-Haida people and interests to their islands, and increasingly varied influences from off-island have had a complex influence on Haida people and their cultural practices. Haida responses reflect processes of adaptation, coercion, acceptance, and rejection, all coexisting in different measures throughout this time.

As we shall see in subsequent chapters, the continuous presence of Haida families on Haida Gwaii is an important means of creating shared experiences between generations of Haida, including those who lived in the past and those who are to come in the future. The removal of Haida ancestral remains from Haida Gwaii, and from Haida family social interactions, needs to be understood within this context. The historic removal of remains only partially explains the need for repatriation; we also need to understand Haida sensibilities of family and respect.

In the next chapter, I look more closely at the history, process, and outcomes of repatriation on Haida Gwaii. There are a number of different contexts in which repatriation may be read, but it is the values and ideals of Haida kinship, including *yahgudang*, that are central to understanding the Haida repatriation process.

3 Family, Morality, and Haida Repatriation

They used to say they never settle. Their spirits can't settle unless they are in their own home ground. They used to say that, eh, because they're so far. Quite a distance between here and there. I know the first one we went to, the caretakers there, when we went to check them out, there was Gertie, Rayno Russ, and Lucille and them, and the caretaker was telling us before he took us in to see where the remains are, showing us, pulling out the drawers. And then we went out, and sat around and talked with us, and he told us sometimes there's kids running down the hallway. Sometimes he'd hear laughter. That's what the elders used to talk about. They're not settled unless they're on the reserve where they belong. So I told them what the elders used to say, "As long as they're not buried in their own home grounds, their spirits won't rest." And he was really amazed when I told him all this. He asked me where I heard these stories. I told him when my dad owned the mill – he brought it over from Howkaan Alaska, this was in the twenties. Anyways, when all the elders stopped in for tea or coffee, they used to talk about these remains that were taken off the island. No one couldn't say anything because they couldn't speak English, they couldn't stop them. So I told him, some of the elders used to cry when they talked about it. It was really sad for some of them, knowing that some of their relatives were taken off the island like that. I told him about that, and once we took the remains down to the cemetery, everything will change. A lot of elders used to say, once we bury our remains here, things will start getting better in the village. As long as the spirits are wandering around, things wouldn't be the same. This is what they used to say. I often think about it because it really bothered me. The first trip we went on, you know, Gertie White and I being elders, we felt like, you know, it just happened. We were both really sad and she said to me in Haida, the second day we were there in Victoria – we were the first ones to go with the group as elders – we got up really early, we were sitting in the sitting area – I can't remember if I put hockey on – and she said in Haida, "Gee Mary, I'm feeling really badly. I feel like it just happened." I said, "I know, Gertie, I feel the same way. I'm really sad today too. But we have to think about the better, we have to think about that too. Because it's going to be better for us when we get home, when they bury them, and then they have the feast for them." I said "Think about that, and it wouldn't be so bad." So we went to the museum that afternoon, the second day, third day, they wrapped the bones up and put them in totes and we had the burning of the food and oh, there was so many people. We had a chief [from southern British Columbia], I can't remember his name, he and his wife were supporting us right and left. They were so kind.

Mary Swanson, 13 January 2006

During my fieldwork, repatriation committee members generally spoke of repatriation in ways that evoked past, present, and future relationships, especially relations of kinship. Irene Mills spoke to me of a hope that repatriated ancestors will, once rested, reincarnate and bring with them old skills and knowledge. In our conversations on the topic, Lucy Bell and Mary Swanson situated the ancestors within ongoing family lines, speaking in the present tense: "That is someone's grandmother," or "It could be your uncle, one of your family members from years back." In the quotation from Mary Swanson that opens this chapter, she recalls the words of her elders that returning her ancestors' bodies to Haida Gwaii would help the villages stabilize and proceed in positive directions.

Now that Haida repatriation efforts have been going on for more than ten years, the repatriation process is developing its own history and its own role within the Haida nation that, largely, is seen as positively influencing the future of the Haida nation. To my question of how things would be different if they had not repatriated, Christian White responded, "I think it pretty well changed a lot of our history. It made history. So, in a way, a lot of our history would be different right now if it didn't happen." This is an idea I return to throughout this book as I explore how the process of repatriation has helped to shift the perspective from which Haidas remember their history and incorporate it within their contemporary identities. In order to do this, we require a more thorough understanding of the motivations for repatriation and the form these efforts took. We also need to appreciate the interconnectedness of the Haida concepts of family and respect, and the ways in which these concepts are realized through objects and interpersonal exchanges.

Literature examining the lengthy history of repatriation on a global scale shows two main agendas for repatriation: its use to achieve political goals and to fulfil moral obligations. For the Haida, repatriation is not grounded solely in a need to address colonial encounters and historic wrongs, but in a far longer and more deeply rooted tradition of familial relations and responsibility. Although there was no direct precedent for repatriation en masse within Haida history, committee members acted on the advice of elders and their cultural protocol that dictates appropriate ways to conduct family relations, care for the deceased, and bring respect to oneself and others.

"Repatriation" and "Community": A Few Definitions

It is important to clarify the word "repatriation," as its denotations and connotations have varied across times. According to the Oxford English Dictionary (2002), "repatriation" originally referred to persons returning to their country. The OED defines the current usage of "repatriate" in somewhat more ambiguous terms – to "send (someone) back to their country." These definitions only hint at the political processes surrounding repatriation. As Glass (2004, 188) clarifies, current usage of the term involves determinations about self-prescribed and imposed national and state identities and forced displacements. Although indigenous people's requests for the return of ancestral remains occurred as remains were being collected in the late nineteenth century and throughout the twentieth, the use of the term "repatriation" to describe this process did not become common until the 1970s when indigenous peoples organized politically on a global level, advocating for indigenous rights that included the return of human remains from museums and other research institutions (Fforde 2004; Fine-Dare 2002). Sledge (2005, 143) explains the difference a word can make: "'Return,'" he writes, "has more of the connotation of getting back that which was lent, while 'repatriate' conveys the meaning that the desired object is subject to another's control and must be 'freed' in order to be returned."

Today, "repatriation" is used to refer to the transfer of human remains (Bray and Killion 1994; Fforde et al. 2002; Mihesuah 2000), as well as being used alongside "restitution," and "reparation" to refer to the return of physical objects from museums to individuals, source communities, or nations (Greenfield 2007; Leggett 1999; Merrill et al. 1993; Merryman 2006; Tapsell 2000). Increasingly, visual repatriation, knowledge repatriation, virtual repatriation, and figurative repatriation are additional possibilities alongside artefact or human repatriation. These terms describe the processes of returning records, information, archival material, photographs, or images more generally (Binney and Chaplin 2003; Brown et al. 2006; Fienup-Riordan 1998; May et al. 2005), field notes from ethnographic work (Jaarsma 2002), intellectual property, digital surrogates, or representations of objects, images and records (Brown and Nicholas 2012; Hennessey et al. 2012), control over space and thus the interpretation, representation, and construction of knowledge (Kramer 2004, 2006; see also Isaac 2007). These processes have been deemed concessions in lieu of returning artefacts or remains, but they have also at times been a primary goal of source communities.

Kramer's (2004) use of "figurative repatriation" diverges most obviously with the classical definition of repatriation in that it entails returning control over how space is used in order to return control over how one (as a member of a group) is represented. In the examples Kramer provides of figurative repatriation between the Museum of Anthropology in Vancouver, Canada, and Kwakwaka'wakw artists, it is not simply a reassertion of indigenous presence on indigenous lands. This does happen, but in an indirect way, since the museum is situated on the traditional territory of the Musqueam First Nation (a Coast Salish, not Kwakwaka'wakw, group). Kramer argues convincingly that the Kwakwaka'wakw artists "capture Kwakwaka'wakw cultural objects within their own system of culture, thus turning 'foreign terrain' into familiar, comfortable space" (2004, 179). The objects are not travelling to their "home territory"; their home territory is travelling to the objects through the intervention of the artist. Figurative repatriation, then, can present feasible opportunities for "restoration" or the reinstatement of prior ways of being tied to broader projects of cultural revitalization.

Requests for repatriation frequently come from "source communities," defined as "the communities from which museum collections originate" (Peers and Brown 2003, 1). Frequently, source communities are imagined as indigenous populations, though nation states and diaspora communities may also be conceived in this way. In using the term "community," I support the notion – though I do not take it for granted – that people can be joined across time by shared space, beliefs, kinship, laws, language, interests, and/or cultural identification and that this continuity creates a community. The shared experiences that Haidas privilege in the building of their sense of continuity and collective identity include being born or adopted into a *gyaaying.aay / gwaay gaang*

(matrilineage) and spending time on Haida Gwaii. Haidas have organized regular "Homecomings," for example, for Haida children who
have been adopted or live off-island. The Homecoming welcomes these
children to Haida Gwaii with songs, a feast, and opportunities to develop experiences in and memories of Haida villages and territory.
Thus, however fraught the term "community" has become within academic discourse, I use it here because it continues to mean something
to Haida people.

What ties a person to or distances them from the Haida community
is exceptionally difficult to isolate. "Belonging," emotional integration,
social acceptance and, conversely, alienation occur in degrees. When it
comes to artefacts and ancestral remains held in museums, however,
there was little discrepancy among Haidas I spoke with, who felt strongly that the people alive today are very much part of the same community from which Haida objects and remains were bought, collected,
traded, or stolen. As Vince Collison expressed the matter:

[Museum staff] don't realize the Haida are still alive, are still thriving, are
still culturally strong in a lot of different ways. In a lot of ways in places
like Chicago where they tried to take ownership over a couple of totem
poles they had to be reminded that the poles came from these islands, they
didn't belong in Chicago. It was interesting to see how much ownership
these places do take over our collections. For us, it's about a lot of our ancestors worked on these pieces and these pieces were meant to be used,
and they're not meant to be stored away. (22 December 2005)

For the Haida I worked with, a "Haida community" is not so much a
point for debate as it is something that exists continuously, maintained
primarily through the occupation of Haida Gwaii and the reproduction
of lineage members belonging to both Raven and Eagle k'waalaa (moieties). As Irene Mills explained to me:

The [repatriation] work that we've done and how we've included the
community – everybody knows what we do and why we do it and they
support us because we all still have not only strong ties to our community,
but we have strong ties to our ancestors because we all still know where
we come from. They're buried in our graveyards and so how can you discount, or you know, I don't even think it's a real issue – because we can
take our kids to the graveyard and we can say, "Here's our lineage," and
that's an amazing thing to be able to do. And I think that's why some

people [Kaigani Haida in Alaska] say this is their old country because they, there's no other place where they can do that. And we are so strong in our clan system still. (11 May 2006)

This sense of identity, of genealogical and territorial continuity, is markedly different from the racialized identities physical anthropologists were attempting to decipher (or create, depending on the perspective), and the evolutionary identities cultural anthropologists were trying to exhibit through crania, anthropometry, objects, and cultural traits in the late nineteenth and early-to-mid-twentieth centuries.

Situating Haida Repatriation Efforts

I had expected to find an amalgamation of the political and the sacred underlying the repatriation of Haida human remains from museums. Repatriation, I supposed, would provide an opportunity to assert political and cultural self-determination, mirroring other Haida efforts in land and resource negotiations. In 2010, Haidas celebrated the twenty-fifth anniversary of Lyell Island – an occupation and protest against unsustainable logging practices on Haida Gwaii and a call for the recognition of aboriginal rights and title that garnered national attention beginning in 1985 (see *Haida Laas* 2010 and Pynn 2010 for overviews of the events and their legacy). An outgrowth of the protest was the first aboriginal/Parks Canada co-management plan that provides for stewardship of Gwaii Haanas National Park Reserve and Haida Heritage Site. Haidas have continued to protest unsustainable fishing and logging practices in other areas of their territory, and their government, the Council of the Haida Nation, successfully advocated for *Sgaan Kinghlas*, the Bowie Seamount, to be designated a Marine Protected Area in Canada.[1] Repatriation may have even been an extension of the expressions of political and cultural sovereignty expressed in treaty and land claim negotiations. I suspected Haida repatriation efforts could be situated within the context of British Columbia's "New Relationships"[2] between the province and indigenous peoples, created out of greater sensitivity for the cultural, economic, and social well-being of indigenous people within nation states.

More broadly still, I surmised that Haida repatriation efforts could be framed within the growing fields of cultural, intellectual, and property rights. After all, repatriation as a global and modern process has been located within the context of a heightened and shared awareness among international groups (such as the United Nations or the International Working Group for Indigenous Affairs) of the rights of indigenous peoples to be free of political and cultural oppression. These models imagine repatriation as a political act, a result of post-colonialism, of shifting government relations, a symbolic end to persecution, or a trend of political correctness.

It is possible to insert Haida repatriation into this discourse. Indeed, the Haida Heritage and Repatriation Committee, with support from the Skidegate Repatriation and Cultural Committee, have organized international conferences for other indigenous groups, museum professionals, and archaeologists concerned with repatriation. They have provided advice and support to other First Nations engaged in repatriation. They encourage reporters writing stories on repatriation to consider some of the other pressing matters of their nation: title to their land, sovereignty, sustainable economic development, and government accountability.

But political spheres are not the parameters or contexts Haidas invoke when talking about repatriation. The Haida Heritage and Repatriation Society in Old Massett and Skidegate Repatriation and Cultural Committee in Skidegate try to keep the political sphere at bay. Although they are authorized to undertake repatriation efforts on behalf of their nation, they maintain their autonomy as bodies independent of the communities' respective band councils, hereditary chiefs, and Council of the Haida Nation. Repatriation committee members made a conscious decision to distance repatriation efforts from Haida politics and political agendas.[3] The Haida do not see the return of their ancestors as a matter of negotiation, nor did they want to endure the lengthy treaty process before being able to repatriate their ancestors' remains.[4]

More specifically, I found the language of politics failed to provide people with the necessary vocabulary. When positioned within a framework of aboriginal rights and title, my discussions with repatriation committee members were stunted and unproductive. By contrast, employing the vocabulary of kinship with Haidas produced long, lucid, evocative, and provocative conversations about repatriation. Repatriation became a node in a "meshwork" of people, obligations, expectations, and values (Ingold 2007). In response to this pattern, I pursued an understanding of Haida repatriation efforts that began locally in an ideal, rather than externally in a process. Rather than frame Haida repatriation as a post-colonial response, I understand it as people's desire to treat their ancestors with respect and fulfil their familial obligation to protect their ancestors' well-being. The approach I take is not entirely separable from political processes, but it does require the consideration of alternative sets of motivations, an alternative understanding of time, and an alternative understanding of agency. Put plainly, it requires an awareness of and appreciation for the enduring moral relationships that exist between and create kin among the Haida.

Why Repatriate?

The most striking element of the Haida repatriation process that forced me to consider the role of kinship, and not just politics, came in Haida explanations of *why* and *how* repatriation became known to them as a possible course of action. In both Old Massett and Skidegate people intimated that it was time for repatriation. It was the ancestors themselves who encouraged it, followed by the pledging of support from families and friends.

During interviews, repatriation committee members frequently explained that their prime motivation for repatriating Haida ancestral remains is to ease the anxiety and sorrow of their displaced ancestors. The disturbance of resting places (be they caves, trees, mortuary poles, or grave interments) distresses the spirits associated with those remains. As these remains were surreptitiously taken from Haida Gwaii and then shipped to museums around the world anywhere from thirty to one hundred years ago, Haidas lament that these ancestors have been held in strange, foreign places where no one has talked to, fed, or prayed for them. In their remote locations they are prevented from being fully active in Haida life, while their descendants have been prevented from being fully active in attending to the well-being of their ancestors. The goal of the repatriation committees is to make them well again, to allow them to re-engage with their home and their world. Irene Mills, who has been active with the SRCC since its early days, elaborated upon this idea:

CARA: With repatriation is it important that the ancestors – like, do they need to be back home in order to be back in the cycle of reincarnation? Do you know what I mean?

IRENE: That's a difficult one, because of course, we don't know who the ancestors are who are gone. So if someone comes home and they're finally at rest and their spirit's at rest then they are able to do other things. So that then, those kinds of things become possibilities, but how do we know if we haven't heard the names? So right now, we have people who are reincarnated into grandparents, or aunties or uncles or brothers or sisters – it's because we know their name and we might not have the ability any more to recognize – if we're dreaming of people, because that's how people kind of get that. And if we dream of elders, how do we give them a name? Because we're a little bit further away from all those gifts that they had. I mean, how do we pinpoint those kinds of things? I believe that when our ancestors come home they're just so happy, that's what gives us the calm within our people, our community. It gives everyone a sense of relief. I think at some point, when those people are able to be reincarnated, we're going to have more of the old knowledge come back. Because right now our elders say it was so long ago, they don't remember some things. But I think then we're going to have children being born with memories. And that's such an amazing thing. I know my brother used to walk around and talk about who he was before he even knew what he was talking about. We have instances of that. And again, it's being brought up with that knowledge of this is how our people come back ... What we believe – I mean, I was told since I was little we're all reincarnated into somebody and sometimes it comes through strong and we know. Like my daughter, both my kids actually, are natural weavers – they're amazing. They picked it up and April [Churchill] just loved my kids weaving because they just caught on. Then my daughter doesn't touch it for a decade, comes home, weaves with me, weaves a basket, then she's gone again. So it's that stuff that we inherit from those reincarnations, that we're so lucky for too. So I think when those spirits have rested enough and want to come back that our nation is going to have some amazing knowledge come forward.

CARA: So what do you think things would be like here if you hadn't repatriated?

IRENE: I think there'd still be lots of unrest. I think the elders – I think people really feel good about what's happened. I think our school system would be not as rich because the kids are so involved and because we've been doing it for so long – I mean we've been doing it for eight years now down at this end. Well, longer than that if you count the repatriation that the museum started [...] And now we have kids in our schools for eight years who have been making button blankets, who have been painting on boxes and have been getting in touch with their community and non-Haida kids too, getting that understanding that these are our people and this is important. (11 May 2006)

I return to Irene's suggestion that Haidas can be born with memory in chapter 4. Presently, we see in Irene's responses the idea that her repatriated ancestors will feel relief at being back on Haida Gwaii, but relief also comes to the living in a variety of ways: from having healthy ancestors, through the return of old knowledge and capacities, from an increased sense of belonging and purpose. The agency of ancestors – from within an afterlife and through rebirth into lineages – is central in her understanding of the effects of repatriation.

Repatriation is a pursuit that respects and uses Haida values and it also rights a historic wrong: what Haidas perceive as the dubious and underhanded removal of their ancestors' bodies by outsiders. As Natalie Fournier, a member of the SRCC, sees it, because families have always been the source of power and authority among Haidas, families need to be at the root of re-establishing balance and well-being among Haidas. Historically, wars, alliances, and politicking, she reflected, were

> about how you as a family, or as a clan, or as a people, can hold yourself up in reflection of how you're taking care of your ancestors, or taking care of business, or taking care of your reputation. And winding my way back to repatriation, Haidas – we were aggressive, we were dominant. We still can be in a lot of situations. This is about us taking care of business. At the end of the day, it's about how we look at ourselves and how we see ourselves. We felt so disempowered, and I think part of the rage that happens along with knowing these bastards stole our bones – *they stole our bones* – is the lack of power we had in this era. (4 May 2006)

Marcia Crosby (2004, 110) offers an astute observation on the matter of self-identity: "I couldn't help thinking about the way we tell stories about ourselves and how these can sometimes intersect with, and are informed by, the enormous body of academically constructed work about aboriginal peoples." Natalie's comments integrate colonial politics into the local setting and local experiences. Her analysis of her experience living within a community actively repatriating their ancestors echoes her post-secondary education in the field of First Nations Studies, but only to a degree. Her characterization of repatriation not so much as a post-colonial action but as part of a larger political dynamic between Haida families points to other ways of structuring knowledge and experience.

Natalie suggested that one of the "first and most important things it [repatriation] does is remind us what happened." For her, the history that needs to be remembered begins with the horrendous loss of entire families and villages. This is not a simple narrative of victimhood, however. Natalie tried to imagine how the survivors of smallpox would have responded, and how surviving lineages would have struggled first to survive and then to establish themselves in new positions of power and leadership according to their cultural values and practices. She tried to imagine the intertwining role of the federal government, offering help with large and strong strings attached (such as the negation of status), and the interlineage competitiveness that is part of Haida life. Although the story is not one of victimization, Natalie still believes the resultant fractures in her community need to be healed, and she suspects that success at repatriation can be seen as a metaphor for bringing back other alienated Haidas:

> Bringing them back, doing what we need to do culturally with the End of Mourning, is a step down the road to start pulling in the fractured pieces of this village and other Haida communities and saying, "We take you back and what happened was wrong and we bring you back and we honour you." It's a long drawn story, but I don't see it as disconnected. I see how it affected our community, when you lost that many people. (4 May 2006)

Natalie uses the End of Mourning here as a starting point, but the repatriation process itself started much earlier.

Ready for Repatriation ·

The presence of Haida artefacts in museums around the world was common knowledge among Haidas. In the 1950s, Haida artist Bill Reid worked with museum directors in Vancouver and Victoria to salvage poles from historic Haida village sites and relocate them to museums in the cities (Duffek 2004, 78–80; Townsend-Gault 1994). But the presence of hundreds of their ancestors' remains in museums around the world remained outside the public consciousness on Haida Gwaii. Before the formation of the Haida Heritage and Repatriation Society (HHRS) in Old Massett and the Skidegate Repatriation and Cultural Committee (SRCC) in Skidegate, isolated incidents of repatriation had occurred. In 1976, poles that had been cut down and removed from four Haida villages were repatriated from the Royal British Columbia Museum to the Queen Charlotte Islands Museum (QCI Museum, now called the Haida Gwaii Museum) (SRCC 2006). The first repatriation of human remains occurred when QCI Museum staff sought to recover archaeological artefacts found to be missing during an inventory.

In 1989, Nathalie MacFarlane was hired as director/curator at the QCI Museum, located on the edge of Skidegate at the site of Second Beach, or _Kaay Llnagaay_, Sea Lion Town. MacFarlane continued as the museum's director until 2013, and recently oversaw a major expansion of the museum alongside a new cultural centre built on the site. Prompted by the suspicions of the board of governors and the greater Haida community, MacFarlane ordered an inventory to determine if archaeological materials excavated at the Haida village of Kiusta were missing from the museum. The excavation of the Kiusta site was led by archaeologist Nick Gessler who, along with his wife, served as co-director/curator of the QCI Museum. Gessler had received permission from the Old Massett Village Council (OMVC) and a permit from the Provincial Archaeology Branch to excavate the site, which he did with the help of Haida crews between 1973 and 1987 (MacFarlane 1993). He had obtained permission from the OMVC to do particular analyses on the remains; however, the OMVC was not informed that such analyses would need to take place in California. When Gessler left Haida Gwaii in 1985 to complete his doctoral work in California, he took some of the archaeological material with him. Subsequently, he was granted permission from the Heritage Conservation Branch to export additional materials from Kiusta with the stipulation that they be returned to British Columbia within five years. However, the material Gessler took with him included uncatalogued and incompletely catalogued artefacts and human remains from other sites, and uncatalogued donations of artefacts from Haida to the museum. His catalogue of Kiusta artefacts and remains was equally incomplete (MacFarlane 1993).

In 1991, materials began to be shipped back periodically to the museum from California, but it was not until the museum retained the services of the Royal Canadian Mounted Police to impose the Canadian Cultural Property Export and Import Act that it received the human remains and an abundance of other archaeological material, filling a total of eighty-five boxes (MacFarlane 1993). When museum employees began to unpack the boxes arriving at the museum they found artefacts and remains scrambled together with little documentation. A physical anthropologist from the Provincial Archaeology Branch came to identify the remains (see Oliver 1993 for the analysis of the remains). Four of the human remains excavated from Kiusta, including one of a high-ranking woman still remembered by elders living in Old Massett at the time of the excavation, were taken to Old Massett for burial.

Other remains and artefacts were kept within the museum for a number of years. Over time, more and more employees became unsettled by experiences in the museum: strong feelings of sadness, hearing voices when no one was in the building, catching glimpses of light or movement. In response to people's sense of apprehension and sadness when working in the museum, the remains were put in an on-site mortuary house[5] that resembles a longhouse, at a fraction of the size; the house continues to act as a repository until ancestral remains can be interred. It once stood fairly separate from the museum, but today is surrounded by the new Ḵaay Llnagaay Heritage Centre, nestled between the Heritage Centre's new longhouses.

The return of these remains was not, however, the catalyst for further repatriation in either community. As Vince Collison explained to me, it never occurred to him that Gessler's actions mimicked those of so many others; that so many more of their ancestors would be kept in museums and laboratories. There are few people alive today who can bridge the generations between those who were present when bones were leaving the islands and those who are now bringing them back. Mary Swanson, now in her eighties and a member of the HHRS, recalled her parents' and grandparents' generation talking about and crying over the removal of their ancestors' remains. A sense of helplessness arose from their being unfamiliar with the institutions and language of those who took the bones, and the uncertainty of their destination. The knowledge that so many remains were removed from Haida Gwaii was not passed on in any formal or communal sense. I suspect that this was part of the information "lost" – or incompletely transmitted – during the decades when Haida families resettled after smallpox epidemics, children were taken off-island to attend residential schools, and people accustomed themselves to the new language, conversion to Christianity, and the new economy that initially brought prosperity via boat building, fishing, and canneries.

In Old Massett, the repatriation committee was formed in 1996, prompted by an experience of its co-chair, Lucy Bell. Lucy was interning at the Royal British Columbia Museum in Victoria, BC, in the early 1990s after finishing her degree in anthropology. While working late one night, she heard children playing although only she and the security guards were in the museum. Later, she learned that Haida remains, including the remains of children, were being kept in the RBCM and in museums throughout the world. She connected her experience of hearing the children with this information. Lucy was grieved by the disrespect shown to her ancestors and the ancestors of other Haidas, how they were removed from their graves and homes and transformed into specimens. She was determined to do something about it, but the task of repatriating the remains was extremely daunting.[6] During one of our conversations, Lucy remembered having the unsettling idea of packing all the remains in her suitcase so she would not have to leave them behind in Victoria when she returned to Haida Gwaii.

Once home, Lucy approached the Old Massett Village Council and received their endorsement to search for Haida remains in museums around the world. She began writing letters to different institutions inquiring into their Haida collections – a task summer students at the Haida Gwaii Museum also undertook. Initially, the support of the band council was a necessity; museums would not work with Lucy as an independent person without the support of the band's elected government or council.[7] Lucy hosted a meeting in Old Massett to inform people that their ancestors were being stored in museums around the world. She sought guidance from the assembly on how best to proceed with the information. Lucy was joined by Vince Collison, and the two continued to serve together as co-chairs of the committee until 2012. Vince (who continues to chair the committee) had worked with two other men from OMVC and with museum staff to inventory the materials returned by Gessler. Through Lucy, he became aware of the Haida remains dispersed around the world. Volunteers began to come forward, both as a result of the meeting and through family and friend networks. One of these volunteers was Mary Swanson, who raised the culturally specific idea of *yahgudangang* (plural, "to be fit for respect" and "to pay respect") as a means of explaining and encouraging repatriation efforts.

In 1994, the Haida Gwaii Museum, represented by staff member Terri-Lynn Williams, met with leaders to open conversations about a repatriation initiative in Skidegate. The term *yahgudangang* was similarly applied by Niis Wes, the late hereditary leader Ernie Wilson, and was adopted by other leaders in Skidegate. In 1996, Nathalie MacFarlane had approached Gwaaganad (Diane Brown), a recognized elder who is often called on to offer prayers at gatherings and worked for the Skidegate Haida Immersion Programme: she advised Nathalie that things would happen when people were ready and able. The Council of the Haida Nation and the Haida Gwaii Museum had already been grappling with the practicalities of how to deal with human remains, as they are unearthed with regularity on Haida Gwaii. Although islanders were advised to leave remains where found, they continued to bring recovered remains to the museum. It was two years before the people of Skidegate began to seek out their ancestors in museums and work to bring them home.

In 1998, Nathalie MacFarlane approached Nika Collison and Andy Wilson, who began to work together on the return of ancestral remains from off-island. They were joined by a number of other men and women, and Andy and Nika coordinated and co-chaired the Skidegate Repatriation and Cultural Committee (figure 3.1). The idea of respect has become a maxim for both repatriation committees. As *yahgudang* is a fundamental concept in understanding Haida repatriation as well as Haida social interactions, it should not come as a surprise that repatriation committee members' memories of their experiences frequently include the unassailable appeals of their elders for committee members to embody *yahgudang*: to treat their ancestors, museum employees, co-committee members, and themselves with respect. People's memories of childhood are also filled with admonitions to act with respect, and it forms the core of what is considered appropriate behaviour. The ideal of respect occurs throughout Haida historical narratives and is embedded in everyday and ceremonial situations on Haida Gwaii, including those found in the repatriation process.

The Duties of Repatriation

To date, the Haida have succeeded in repatriating remains from the Canadian Museum of Civilization (Gatineau, Quebec), Royal British Columbia Museum (Victoria), Lab of Archaeology at the University of British Columbia (Vancouver), the archaeology department at Simon Fraser University (Burnaby, British Columbia), American Museum of Natural History (New York City), Field Museum (Chicago, Illinois), the Oakland Museum of California (Oakland, California), the Pitt Rivers Museum, University of Oxford (Oxford, UK), the University of Oregon's Natural History Museum (Eugene, Oregon), and several private collections (Table 3.1). Increasingly, the committees are focusing their work on museums in Europe. They are beginning to build alliances with staff and researchers associated with museums in the UK and in Germany, and looking to overcome issues of access (geographic space, language barriers, and receptiveness to non-academic researchers in collections space) to get a better sense of where ancestral remains and Haida collections are located. In 2009, as part of a Leverhulme-funded International Research Network, I helped the Pitt Rivers Museum, British Museum, and Haida Repatriation Committee

Figure 3.1. Women from the Skidegate Repatriation and Cultural Committee and guest Dr Laura Peers, Pitt Rivers Museum, 2005. *Back row, left to right*: Natalie Fournier, Ruth Gladstone-Davies, Melinda Pick, Darlene Squires, Irene Mills. Front row, left to right: Jenny Cross, Sue Gladstone, Nika Collison with daughter Gid K̲uuyas, Laura Peers.

facilitate a three-week collections-focused visit for twenty-one Haida delegates to the UK (Krmpotich and Peers 2011, 2013; and see www .prm.ox.ac.uk/haida.html for the documentary film *Everything Was Carved* about the need for and outcomes of the visit). Integrated into the itinerary was a one-day conference in Oxford where curators from fifteen UK museums were invited to provide an overview of their holdings to Haida delegates and to come equipped with paper and digital copies of inventories, catalogue records, and images for Haidas to take back to their communities.

Although the HHRS and SRCC desire the return of artefacts as well as their ancestors' remains, both have prioritized the return of their ancestors. To the best of their knowledge, the Haida repatriation committees

Table 3.1 Locations of Ancestral Remains Repatriated to Haida Gwaii

Source of Repatriation	Number Returned	Year
Royal British Columbia Museum	43*	1993, 1998, 2000, 2001
University of British Columbia Laboratory of Archaeology	6	1999
Canadian Museum of Civilization	148	2000
Oakland Museum of California	1	2002
American Museum of Natural History	48	2002
Field Museum	160	2003
University of Oregon, Museum of Natural History	2	2005
Simon Fraser University, Department of Archaeology	4	2005
Private Collections	53**	1991–2006
University of Oxford, Pitt Rivers Museum	1	2010
Total	466	

Source: Haida Gwaii Museum 2013

* Includes twenty-three sets of remains that had not been returned following an archaeo-logical excavation.
** Includes forty-nine sets of remains taken off-island by Gessler and returned with the assistance of the Royal Canadian Mounted Police.

had returned all known Haida remains from museums and other pub-lic institutions in North America, though recent news from repatria-tion partners indicates this is not the case: the American Museum of Natural History found additional skeletal remains in their holdings from ancestors repatriated in 2002, and the remains of at least one per-son from the village of Skedans have been turned in to the University of British Columbia Laboratory of Archaeology. That some of these re-mains were returned by individuals acts as a bitter reminder for Lucy Bell that Haida ancestors likely still remain as specimens or curios held off-island, while these updates from partner institutions further high-light the ways repatriation remains an ongoing concern for Haidas. Lucy also fears that tourists and seasonal workers continue to remove ancestral remains from Haida Gwaii. The committees' choice to bury their ancestors in the graveyards of Skidegate and Old Massett rather than in their original villages reflects the perceived need for surveillance in order to prevent the remains from being disinterred and once again taken away, for many of the older villages are accessible only by boat, making them difficult to monitor on a regular basis.

The size of the committees is always in flux. New volunteers come forward, and HRC members will approach people for help because of a particular skill they possess, such as speaking Haida or singing. People also periodically leave the committee to pursue other projects or to recoup emotionally and mentally from the experience. A number of elders active on the committee have also passed away. While there was a general sense of support for the work, there was also uncertainty and unease. Mothers did not want their (grown) children handling the remains out of concern over the emotional impact and the "unnaturalness" of handling the long-dead bodies. Fears of "witchcraft" or malevolent powers still lay under the surface on Haida Gwaii, though "superstition" is what people are likely to call it today. For Haidas, dead bodies are particularly susceptible to malevolent beings, and various measures should be taken to protect them, such as drawing the curtains, covering mirrors, and paying members of the opposite *k'waalaa* to stay awake and sit with the body during the night. When large numbers of repatriated remains were brought back to Haida Gwaii, the SRCC temporarily kept those to be buried in Skidegate in the George Brown Community Centre and people stayed with them throughout the night, just as family members ensure the body of a recently deceased relative is safeguarded through the night.

The concern for personal well-being has been taken seriously by those engaged in repatriation. Younger HHRS committee members credited the *naaniis* (grandmothers, older women) who have served on the committee with providing the emotional grounding for the group. The elders who have joined the HHRS possess a stability that comes with age, parenthood, grandparenthood, and great-grandparenthood. They embody perseverance. Elders on the HHRS advise on protocol, inspire the committee with their enthusiasm and work ethic, lead prayers and direct ceremonies, and are able to speak to the ancestors in their own language. In an interview, Lucy Bell, Vince Collison, and Candace Weir reflected upon the contributions of the elders:

LUCY: The *naaniis* always talk about just being respectful to the ancestors
 – pay them the highest respect that we could. To be kind to each other,

cessary for Haidas to travel to the museums to retrieve the
mains; the remains were not to be sent back via the post or
Andy Wilson, former co-chair of the SRCC, explained to
sion to send people to the museums to retrieve their ances-
action to the haphazard manner in which Gessler returned
s and remains from Kiusta. The hereditary leaders and el-
bered the shock, sadness, and offence they felt when their
emains were returned home with so little respect, and in-
aidas be the ones to prepare their ancestors' remains for the
ensure this would always be done in a respectful manner.
ases, the number of remains held at an individual institu-
a delegation of repatriation committee members from both
nd Old Massett were needed to prepare the ancestors for
ack to Haida Gwaii. This is partially because of the sheer
work that is required, partially because of the variety of
eed to be done (different people pray and make offerings,
to the remains, provide emotional support, and prepare and
mains for travel), and partially because the emotional strain
quires the presence of friends and family and of taking turns
ce the formal handover of human remains has been made,
uest privacy when they prepare their ancestors for travel
da Gwaii. There are no photos, no intrusions.
was shown by wrapping each set of remains in a button
a woven cedar mat and then placing them in cedar bent-
s to be buried. The use of such objects in daily life and cere-
is recorded in Haida oral histories from the time before
habited Haida Gwaii, and have become, again, important
family identity and status. (The production of both blankets
ood boxes was a rarity in Haida villages during the early to
entieth century; see also chapter 2 and Stearns 1990.)
n White in Old Massett and Andy Wilson in Skidegate led the
bentwood boxes for repatriation, and were assisted by vol-
vers, elementary and high school students, and community
in general. Bentwood boxes are made by kerfing a single
ood so that, when steamed, it will bend to form all four sides
, including ninety-degree corners, without splitting. A base
e fitted to allow the square box (or rectangular chest) to nest
m. Historically, Haida used bentwood boxes to store dried
h as fish, seaweed, ḵ'aaw (herring roe on kelp), and berries,
e cedar bark and spruce roots for weaving. As they are

in the process, because in the end of the day we still have to get along
and work with each other … [It's] so much more bearable at the end of
the trip, or when there's just a couple of us sweeping the floor at the hall
after we've just put our ancestors in the ground, it's like "Oh my God!
Why do we keep doing this?" We're exhausted! And then we remember
the *naaniis* coming to everything.

VINCE: I think it was a Nuu-chah-nulth lady that gave us the advice of
bringing elders with us on our next trip, the RBCM one. About talking
to the ancestors, and I think that was something – that these people were
human beings once and you've got to talk to them and obviously these
people never knew English. Bringing along the elders was part of that.
I think the smartest thing we did was bringing the elders along because
there's a lot of strength – we couldn't have done it in a lot of ways without them. They kept a lot of us on an even keel with some of the emotional stuff. And getting ready – we all knew it was going to be difficult.
The first one, I found it difficult too. We were going into unknown territory – we didn't know what the protocols were. We didn't know what
we were supposed to be doing. We were kind of making a lot of things
up as we were going along. It turned out everything we were doing was
leading to the right way, but getting there was full of a lot of confusion,
but it didn't look like it.

CANDACE: I remember we were sitting at Co-op [grocery store], flogging our
merchandise [repatriation committee merchandise, sold to raise funds for
repatriation work] one day, and I'm at the table and Naanii Ethel is walking by and she's like "I'm coming! I'm coming!" She's shopping away,
and Vince and I are at this table and it wasn't even a hardship or anything. Things like that make the whole process easier with their support
… And then at another fund-raiser, Naanii Mary was at the table and it
was a big seller and a big item one year to get ladies' butterfly thongs,
and men's briefs and bikini bottoms and Naanii Mary's really pitching
our underwear line! Selling our thong underwear! (22 December 2005)

Both committees are self-sustaining: they fund-raise locally, and apply to various businesses and granting agencies for services and funds.
Local fund-raisers include sushi sales, "loonie" and "toonie" (colloquial terms for one- and two-dollar Canadian coins) auctions (figure 3.2),
sales of merchandise such as t-shirts, jackets, hats, aprons, canvas bags,
and even underwear printed with the repatriation logos, and a fashion
show featuring Haida blankets and garments. Local businesses and individuals donate goods and services for auctions and raffles, such as

Figure 3.2 Items including clothing, children's toys, fleece blankets, and DVDs are displayed as part of a loonie and toonie auction fund-raiser for the Haida Heritage and Repatriation Society, 2005.

plane tickets to Vancouver, homemade bread or pies, crocheted garments, or artwork. In Skidegate, seafood dinners featuring local seafood, Haida dancing, and a slide show to explain repatriation are geared towards summer tourists.

The monetary cost of repatriation is considerable. The repatriation work began with committee members and staff from the Haida Gwaii Museum compiling an inventory of Haida artefacts and remains in international museum collections. In time, hundreds of letters were sent to institutions around the world to ascertain the location and types of Haida materials held in museums. In many cases, no response was received, while in many American museums the Haida request for an inventory was put in the queue with other American Indian tribes who had asked for inventories under the Native American Graves Protection and Repatriation Act (NAGPRA). Students were employed through grant monies during summer months and sent to museums to sift

through archives and catalogue the provenance of Haida remains There are also administrative costs calls, faxes, mail, and stationery. In provides training and staff for rese supporting about half of the coordi travel, accommodation, and food journey to museums across North museums are substantial. But there paring the ancestors for transportat port itself. There is the constructi woven cedar mats, button blankets like cedar shavings, all of which a travel and burial. Each burial was a requires the feeding of hundreds o contemporary form of a long-stand lineage hosts a meal. Today, lineages lowing the funeral service, open to f

It is the disturbance of interments and spiritually damaging. For most final resting place and to remove the for the purpose of gathering inform Such acts simply fall outside the bou ble. The disturbance of the deceased ceived in institutions were described "inhuman." People felt this indignity treatment of their family members. Th cultural protocol, thus making their g ingful to their ancestors and to thems als surrounding death are the prerc members. Close family members may of mourning, decide whether to bury it on to another family member, or de and imagery that will appear on a h however, happens at all levels, k'waalaa vidual. Since there was no precedent a triation en masse, elders advised on hov repatriation.

The committees determined that the Gwaii deserved and were in need o

deemed it
ancestral re
couriers. A
me, the dec
tors was a
the materia
ders remem
ancestors'
sisted that
trip home

In many
tion meant
Skidegate
their trip
amount of
tasks that
sing, spea
crate the r
involved r
at tasks. C
Haidas re
back to H.

Respec
blanket ar
wood box
monial lif
humans i
markers o
and bent
middle tw

Christi
making o
unteer ca
members
plank of
of the bo
and lid a
inside th
foods su
or to st

watertight, they were also used to store eulachon grease and seal oil, and to boil soups and stews. Elaborately carved bentwood boxes served as containers for important property such as regalia, spoons, rattles, and bowls. When finely carved, the boxes were themselves valued property. High-ranking people were interred in decorated boxes and placed within mortuary poles (Swanton 1905a).

Christian White began working with his carving apprentices and brother-in-law on the boxes in 1998 or 1999. He had no experience making boxes before this time, though a family member gave him two sides of an old box found inside the wall of a house being torn down. The group of carvers used these pieces to help them while they experimented with how thick to plane the boards, and to determine the exact dimensions for each side so that the ends join properly. Christian recollected:

> I really felt that we should make bentwood boxes for that. I think in a way, by initiating that – making the bentwood boxes – I don't know if I was asked – I used a lot of my own materials I had on hand the first couple of years. It was like I was prepared already. I had material cut even though I didn't know, even a couple of years prior – four or five years before – I didn't have any idea our ancestors were in museums. I didn't realize that until my friends were working on the ancestors' remains that were returned from California – the ones Gessler collected. I did hear a bit about it over the years following that, when I joined the cultural committee. Sitting on that board, I started to think that this would be the proper way of honouring the ancestors. We also heard the word *yahgudangang*, to pay respect. It was the right thing to do. (19 November 2005)

In Skidegate, the making of bent boxes for repatriated remains began with the return of remains from the Laboratory of Archaeology at UBC, but then expanded to include the remains returned by Gessler. Making bent boxes is material and labour intensive; when the decision was made in Skidegate, they were only looking to make four boxes for the UBC remains, which seemed a reasonable task for the assembled team. But with the repatriation movement now underway in Skidegate, the community and committee decided to make an additional forty boxes for the remains returned by Gessler but not yet buried. Nika Collison explained that the committee saw people's involvement in the repatriation from UBC as a sign that villagers were now ready to work through the challenges and responsibilities of repatriation. To make the boxes for repatriation, Andy Wilson (figure 3.3) pieced together different parts

Figure 3.3 Andy Wilson bending a cedar plank to make a bentwood box. Photograph by Jack Litrell, courtesy of SRCC.

of the process by talking to people in Skidegate and studying the construction of the boxes at the Haida Gwaii Museum. Steaming and shaping each plank three times (the fourth corner is created by sewing, nailing, or gluing the two ends together) is the most time-consuming element in the production of bent boxes (figure 3.4) To speed up production of the additional boxes, Andy and his team began experimenting with plastic tubing and heating water-filled kegs to enable all four corners to be steamed at one time. To date, the two communities have produced well over four hundred boxes in which to bury and honour their ancestors.

Historically, Haida bentwood boxes and chests were painted with the lineage crest of the person who owned and used it and was possibly even interred inside it. In the case of the remains held in museums, the village name was usually the only piece of provenience recorded; lineage, let alone individual, names rarely appear in museum records. In response to this dilemma, the elders in Skidegate advised their committee to work with the boxes as a group and to place all the southern in the process, because in the end of the day we still have to get along and work with each other ... [It's] so much more bearable at the end of the trip, or when there's just a couple of us sweeping the floor at the hall after we've just put our ancestors in the ground, it's like "Oh my God! Why do we keep doing this?" We're exhausted! And then we remember the *naaniis* coming to everything.

VINCE: I think it was a Nuu-chah-nulth lady that gave us the advice of bringing elders with us on our next trip, the RBCM one. About talking to the ancestors, and I think that was something – that these people were human beings once and you've got to talk to them and obviously these people never knew English. Bringing along the elders was part of that. I think the smartest thing we did was bringing the elders along because there's a lot of strength – we couldn't have done it in a lot of ways without them. They kept a lot of us on an even keel with some of the emotional stuff. And getting ready – we all knew it was going to be difficult. The first one, I found it difficult too. We were going into unknown territory – we didn't know what the protocols were. We didn't know what we were supposed to be doing. We were kind of making a lot of things up as we were going along. It turned out everything we were doing was leading to the right way, but getting there was full of a lot of confusion, but it didn't look like it.

CANDACE: I remember we were sitting at Co-op [grocery store], flogging our merchandise [repatriation committee merchandise, sold to raise funds for repatriation work] one day, and I'm at the table and Naanii Ethel is walking by and she's like "I'm coming! I'm coming!" She's shopping away, and Vince and I are at this table and it wasn't even a hardship or anything. Things like that make the whole process easier with their support ... And then at another fund-raiser, Naanii Mary was at the table and it was a big seller and a big item one year to get ladies' butterfly thongs, and men's briefs and bikini bottoms and Naanii Mary's really pitching our underwear line! Selling our thong underwear! (22 December 2005)

Both committees are self-sustaining: they fund-raise locally, and apply to various businesses and granting agencies for services and funds. Local fund-raisers include sushi sales, "loonie" and "toonie" (colloquial terms for one- and two-dollar Canadian coins) auctions (figure 3.2), sales of merchandise such as t-shirts, jackets, hats, aprons, canvas bags, and even underwear printed with the repatriation logos, and a fashion show featuring Haida blankets and garments. Local businesses and individuals donate goods and services for auctions and raffles, such as

Figure 3.2 Items including clothing, children's toys, fleece blankets, and DVDs are displayed as part of a loonie and toonie auction fund-raiser for the Haida Heritage and Repatriation Society, 2005.

plane tickets to Vancouver, homemade bread or pies, crocheted garments, or artwork. In Skidegate, seafood dinners featuring local seafood, Haida dancing, and a slide show to explain repatriation are geared towards summer tourists.

The monetary cost of repatriation is considerable. The repatriation work began with committee members and staff from the Haida Gwaii Museum compiling an inventory of Haida artefacts and remains in international museum collections. In time, hundreds of letters were sent to institutions around the world to ascertain the location and types of Haida materials held in museums. In many cases, no response was received, while in many American museums the Haida request for an inventory was put in the queue with other American Indian tribes who had asked for inventories under the Native American Graves Protection and Repatriation Act (NAGPRA). Students were employed through grant monies during summer months and sent to museums to sift through archives and catalogue records to determine more precisely the provenance of Haida remains and Haida artefacts in the collections. There are also administrative costs associated with long-distance phone calls, faxes, mail, and stationery. In Skidegate, the Haida Gwaii Museum provides training and staff for research and administration, as well as supporting about half of the coordination activities of the SRCC. The air travel, accommodation, and food costs for as many as thirty Haida to journey to museums across North America to retrieve remains from museums are substantial. But there are also costs associated with preparing the ancestors for transportation, as well as the cost of the transport itself. There is the construction of individual bentwood boxes, woven cedar mats, button blankets, and other "packaging" materials like cedar shavings, all of which are all important for the ancestors' travel and burial. Each burial was also accompanied by a feast, which requires the feeding of hundreds of guests – repatriation feasts are a contemporary form of a long-standing practice where the deceased's lineage hosts a meal. Today, lineages often provide an afternoon tea following the funeral service, open to friends, family, and acquaintances.

It is the disturbance of interments that Haidas find most troublesome and spiritually damaging. For most Haidas, to intentionally disturb a final resting place and to remove the remains of another human being for the purpose of gathering information is beyond comprehension. Such acts simply fall outside the boundaries of what should be possible. The disturbance of the deceased and the neglect the deceased received in institutions were described to me as "cruel," "wicked," and "inhuman." People felt this indignity deeply and wanted to rectify the treatment of their family members. The committees sought to abide by cultural protocol, thus making their gestures recognizable and meaningful to their ancestors and to themselves. Normally, events and rituals surrounding death are the prerogative of close lineage family members. Close family members may choose to crop their hair as a sign of mourning, decide whether to bury someone with regalia or pass it on to another family member, or determine the form, inscriptions, and imagery that will appear on a headstone. Honouring the dead, however, happens at all levels, k'waalaa (moiety), community, and individual. Since there was no precedent among Haida protocol for repatriation en masse, elders advised on how best to go about the process of repatriation.

The committees determined that the remains removed from Haida Gwaii deserved and were in need of respectful treatment. Elders deemed it necessary for Haidas to travel to the museums to retrieve the ancestral remains; the remains were not to be sent back via the post or couriers. As Andy Wilson, former co-chair of the SRCC, explained to me, the decision to send people to the museums to retrieve their ancestors was a reaction to the haphazard manner in which Gessler returned the materials and remains from Kiusta. The hereditary leaders and elders remembered the shock, sadness, and offence they felt when their ancestors' remains were returned home with so little respect, and insisted that Haidas be the ones to prepare their ancestors' remains for the trip home to ensure this would always be done in a respectful manner.

In many cases, the number of remains held at an individual institution meant a delegation of repatriation committee members from both Skidegate and Old Massett were needed to prepare the ancestors for their trip back to Haida Gwaii. This is partially because of the sheer amount of work that is required, partially because of the variety of tasks that need to be done (different people pray and make offerings, sing, speak to the remains, provide emotional support, and prepare and crate the remains for travel), and partially because the emotional strain involved requires the presence of friends and family and of taking turns at tasks. Once the formal handover of human remains has been made, Haidas request privacy when they prepare their ancestors for travel back to Haida Gwaii. There are no photos, no intrusions.

Respect was shown by wrapping each set of remains in a button blanket and a woven cedar mat and then placing them in cedar bentwood boxes to be buried. The use of such objects in daily life and ceremonial life is recorded in Haida oral histories from the time before humans inhabited Haida Gwaii, and have become, again, important markers of family identity and status. (The production of both blankets and bentwood boxes was a rarity in Haida villages during the early to middle twentieth century; see also chapter 2 and Stearns 1990.)

Christian White in Old Massett and Andy Wilson in Skidegate led the making of bentwood boxes for repatriation, and were assisted by volunteer carvers, elementary and high school students, and community members in general. Bentwood boxes are made by kerfing a single plank of wood so that, when steamed, it will bend to form all four sides of the box, including ninety-degree corners, without splitting. A base and lid are fitted to allow the square box (or rectangular chest) to nest inside them. Historically, Haida used bentwood boxes to store dried foods such as fish, seaweed, k̲'aaw (herring roe on kelp), and berries, or to store cedar bark and spruce roots for weaving. As they are

Figure 3.4 Steaming cedar, a part of the bentwood box-making process. Photograph by Nika Collison, courtesy of SRCC.

lineage's crests on the group of boxes. In this suggestion, as at other times during the repatriation process, we see a blurring between family and village, or family and nation, in terms of responsibility and identity. Yet this collective strategy relies on individual team members' contributing their knowledge of their own family's lineage crests. The significance of family – or more specifically, lineage – is not effaced by a broader collective identity. Rather, the interdependence of Haida families is reaffirmed in the elders' advice. The Haida Repatriation Committee conceives of itself as a body that represents Haida lineages. This sense of collectivity and interdependence of lineages is critical when speaking of "community" on Haida Gwaii. It represents a traditional ideal that is part of a growing and explicit discourse on Haida Gwaii emphasizing the importance of lineages within Haida history, sociality, and identity.

In Skidegate, a teacher in the Haida Studies program at the high school became aware of the bentwood box–making project and of the need for assistance in completing the boxes. She suggested her high school students become involved. That fall, their classroom turned into a makeshift painting studio where the pupils learned about lineages and crest designs, painted boxes, and even began designing unique crest forms (figure 3.5).[8] While I was visiting a Haida Studies class with Andy Wilson in January 2008, that teacher told us about being on

Figure 3.5 Students painting crest designs on bentwood boxes. Photograph by Nika Collison, courtesy of SRCC.

Vancouver Island a few weeks earlier and meeting a student who had worked on the boxes years earlier. The student recalled the time spent painting the boxes as the highlight of the class, a joyful time yielding happy memories. Together, the two reminisced about how two male students in particular became very good at drawing formline and began experimenting with new designs for lineage crests. This reminiscing, and the development of drawing and design skills among Haida youth, demonstrate some of the ways in which the process of repatriation has become a source for collective memory and shared experience on Haida Gwaii, a topic I return to in chapters 6 and 7.

Upon learning of the high school's participation, the elementary school Haida Studies teacher asked the SRCC how their school could contribute. Elementary school children were given the task of sewing button blankets, a sample of which is on display at the Haida Gwaii Museum. Like the boxes, the blankets have designs appliquéd and outlined with buttons that signify the interrelatedness of the two Haida *k'waalaa*, Eagle and Raven. The design is of a double-bird, raven with eagle, similar to the designs used by the Old Massett Village Council, the Skidegate Band Council, and the Council of the Haida Nation.

Bestowing the blankets on the repatriated ancestors emphasizes those ancestors' inclusion within ongoing *k'waalaa* relations.

In Old Massett, Christian was able to work in the high school with students and his carving apprentices, building the boxes and using crest templates made by artists to paint on designs. Leona Claw and Mary Swanson from the HHRS had worked in the local schools for many years, and used their time in the classroom to teach the elementary school students about the importance of repatriation. Leona and Mary, along with other teachers and committee members, worked alongside the students to produce small button blankets to wrap the remains in, and made crepe paper flowers to put on the graves in the cemetery. The children also created paper decorations for the burial feasts and the repatriation conference hosted by the HHRS in 2004.

The burials were accompanied by church services and feasts, to which the island community (Haida and non-Haida) was invited. The repatriation committees bear most of the physical and economic brunt of organizing, setting up, and carrying out burial ceremonies, in addition to the fund-raising events beforehand and the cleaning up afterwards. The majority of this is unpaid volunteer labour. The amount of work undertaken by the committees since their creation is formidable, and yet when Nika Collison was preparing the SRCC's *Haawa* (Thank You), a notice to appear in the island newspaper recognizing the people and businesses who contributed to the repatriation effort over the previous eight years, her list extended across four pages.

Another task that falls to chairs of the HRC is talking to local, national, and international media. The repatriation committees have used media coverage (i.e., Bohn 2005a, 2005b) to introduce non-Haidas, Haidas living off-island, and other indigenous peoples to their goals for repatriation. Knowing items such as bentwood boxes and button blankets appeal to the public, committee spokespersons often used such objects to catch the attention of non-Haidas in order to further educate them about the importance of Haida social relations, cultural traditions, land claims, and political aims. Repatriation committee members reasoned that their positive portrayal in the media assisted repatriation efforts by provoking donations of goods and services from companies who had learned of their efforts. They believed that crossing the Canadian/American border with human remains was made easier by their positive presence in the media. Lucy Bell, Vince Collison, and Candace Weir of the Haida Heritage and Repatriation Society explained their relationship with the press as follows:

LUCY: We thought it [positive press] would help. It would help get us across the border, get people on our side. It would help if we got good press from going to the Museum of Anthropology [in Vancouver] – that will help us to be more accepted when we go to the CMC [Canadian Museum of Civilization] or when we go to the States. It's all part of planning, to get as good coverage as we could and just get people more involved and –

VINCE: Especially in Canada, because there were some Haidas living in Vancouver and Victoria and it was a way to get the word out before the Internet, before email got so big, so in some way it was getting a hold of people.

CANDACE: Moccasin Messenger. (22 December 2005)

Vince described dealing with the press as a "necessary evil." He was remembering back to a time when he had to teach himself how to write press releases, searching the Internet for examples to learn from. Media also became a means of reaching other First Nations trying to repatriate their ancestors. Lucy explained that articles in newspapers helped create a network among indigenous peoples:

After a while we realized that there weren't that many people doing it [repatriating their ancestors] and that they were looking for guidance. So if we could say something about it in the newspaper – about how we did it – that might help. And I think it has. I don't know how many people we've helped but we've certainly got a lot of thanks along the way from other Nations trying to get their ancestors back: "Thanks for opening the door."

To which Candace added, "And then they've helped us in return. When we've been on other peoples' territory, they've given their assistance, their guidance. Shared some of their medicines, some of their wisdom and advice too. That helped us."

While at museums to repatriate their ancestors, committee members take fullest advantage of their situation to explore the Haida materials on display and in storage, to network with museum staff and discuss exhibition techniques or content, and to share Haida songs and dances with museum visitors. As well as being used in ceremonies and to mark significant events, singing and dancing is one way Haidas have fun, express their competitive side and their pride in being Haida. They also see it as a counterpoint to the inanimate displays of their material culture, for both visitors and museum staff. Being able to dance with old masks or headpieces, play an old flute, or examine the construction and materials of an artefact up close are often monumental and deeply moving moments for Haida. There is honour for Haidas in reinstating an object's earlier function. Objects people have only heard of in stories materialize for them in museum storage rooms. The opportunity to see collections of artefacts that no longer exist in peoples' homes and are not part of today's feasts and potlatches – mountain goat horn spoons and grease dishes, for example – is relished, and often emotionally charged. When the Haida delegation visited the Pitt Rivers Museum and British Museum in 2009, they sketched the designs carved on goat horn spoon handles, and requested callipers as well as using their own hands to measure the thicknesses of paddles and coppers. One woman brushed her cheek with the soft fur affixed to a mask. People talked rapidly together, piecing together how the articulated eye mechanisms on one particular mask might have worked, what the mask would have looked like in firelight, and which of the stories they knew might pertain to the mask. They photographed themselves while posing as though supping from spoons or playfully clubbing a sibling with a halibut club. These photos were posted to Facebook within hours, as people sought to share what they had seen with family and friends at home. Sometimes people just sat quietly, gently laying a hand on an apron's fringe. Language teachers and learners worked collectively to try to remember and record vocabulary for objects. They came prepared with a Haida language dictionary on their own laptops, and provided a digital copy to museum collections staff as well.

It is important to note that the visit to the UK was focused on object-based research with the vast majority of time and resources dedicated to this function. When delegations visit museums with the express purpose of repatriating their ancestors, they usually see their objects in museum storage spaces – pulling out drawers and peering into shelves. The Haida Repatriation Committee has also coordinated access to other museum collections on occasions where return of ancestral remains was not part of the purpose. For example, I spent one day in January 2006 making sushi with a number of volunteers from the HHRS and women from Lucy's family, the proceeds from the sale of which helped to fund a trip to the National Museum of the American Indian in Washington, DC, to mark the opening of the exhibit "Listening to Our Ancestors." Lucy, Nika, and their colleague Jolene Edenshaw curated the Haida component of the exhibit, and members of the Massett and Skidegate committees danced at the opening.

   Criticism of the repatriation committees from within Haida communities is often directed at the travel involved in the process. Short comments such as "It's a club – they just want to travel" or "They just want
to go away with their friends" were offered, but requests to elaborate
on these ideas were consistently declined. Public criticism on Haida
Gwaii is often carefully constructed, extremely subtle, and extremely
political (Boelscher 1988). People are reluctant to explicitly criticize
someone on the record (the public record, or the anthropologist's record). Casual griping, on the other hand, is frequent if not endemic and
is more a feature of conversation than something meant to harm. Acting
like a clique or a club is a common charge levied against different Haida
initiatives. As a result, it is difficult for me to gauge the depth of this
particular criticism of the repatriation committees. The overwhelming
turnouts for fund-raising activities, reburials, and End of Mourning
ceremonies, the quantity of "repatriation wear" sporting the committees' butterfly logos that is worn by Haidas, and the length of time this
support has been given (for more than twelve years in Old Massett and
ten in Skidegate) suggest that the majority of people view the committees and their activities with favour.
   Those who disagreed with the need for repatriation did elaborate upon
their perspective. A few people told me that they did not believe the spirits of the ancestors were tied to the bones. They thought the spirits would
be able to return to Haida Gwaii on their own because geographic distances were inconsequential on a spiritual and supernatural level and not
a hindrance to spiritual beings. Despite their belief that returning the
physical remains was metaphysically unnecessary, many of these people
still appreciated the efforts and intentions of the repatriation committee
and supported them by attending fund-raisers and feasts, and by not
vocalizing their opinions too strongly in public forums. Interestingly, one
of the persons who in 2005 expressed uncertainty about the spiritual
need for repatriation was later involved with a repatriation and spoke of
how unprepared he was for the immense impact of being with his ancestor's remains. He described his previous reflections on repatriation as
intellectual – something he had given significant metaphysical and ratio-
nal thought to, but not something he had experienced. Once he had the
experience of being with the bones of an ancestor, he saw with new eyes
and developed a new understanding of – and support for – the efforts of
the repatriation committee members.
   Elder members on both committees maintain that it is necessary to
bring back the physical remains. At eighty-plus years of age, Mary

Swanson is currently one of the most senior members of either committee whose advice is sought by the more junior members (figure 3.6). In turn, she relied on what she has learned from elders during her lifetime.

CARA: For yourself, what has been the most positive outcome of being involved in that work?

MARY: [Some] people don't believe in bringing back the bones, because they were saying they hear all kinds of different things [they are worried about unsettled spirits]. I don't think so. I think that was one of the best things that Lucille started. Some elders used to say as long as their spirits are wandering, nothing goes right in the village. That's their belief.

CARA: What do you think has been the most positive outcome for Old Massett?

MARY: When they buried all the remains – that was one of the best things that ever happened for the Haida people. A lot of elders were happy that was happening, because they used to wonder about their families who got taken away, off-island.

CARA: What's been the most difficult thing about repatriation, for you?

MARY: When they start taking the remains out, to wrap them up. The first time, we heard little footsteps down the hallway when we were waiting for the remains to be put out. After they were put in boxes, everything seemed to be settled. Us elders used to talk to them before they put them into the totes. We used to tell them they were going home to where they belong and all the ancestors will be happy they are back in their own home ground and that we're going to have a big celebration with them after they are buried, and they have a big feast for them after. (7 November 2005)

Mary's sentiments, especially when paired with Irene's explanation of the possibilities for ancestors to be reborn with old knowledge, described above, suggest how repatriation acts as one means of healing and improving the well-being of multiple generations of Haidas, past, present, and future.

Repatriation and Healing

Haidas' location of repatriation within a discourse of healing coincides with a general movement initiated by Haidas to improve the health and well-being of people in their families and communities. Grief, alienation, dispossession, and shame have occurred on a national level, both

Figure 3.6. Mary Swanson, member of the Haida Heritage and Repatriation Society, 2006.

among First Nations throughout Canada and among the Haida nation itself. Yet the latter half of the twentieth century has been witness to Haida events, predominantly political actions, based ·on nationally felt indignation, pride, conviction, and responsibility. On a day-to-day basis, humour and generosity are pervasive in Haida social interactions and coping strategies. Solutions to personal and community hardships are being sought in economic development, opportunities for youth, education, law suits, drug and alcohol rehabilitation; in convincing the federal government to be accountable in their dealings with bands; and in providing spiritual guidance through traditional teachings and a return to Haida cultural values.

There is no clear path between the major crises faced by individuals, families, and villages and the desire for repatriation. Neither has repatriation been the sole answer to these problems. It has, however, had the effect of strengthening the individuals who have worked on the committees. Many committee members reported that the experience of working on repatriation made them realize cooperation was not only possible but productive; they could work together as Haidas, and succeed at a task that was originally unimaginable. Candace Weir noted her growth as a singer as a result of working on the committee. Whereas at one time she would never sing alone, Candace now has a large repertoire of Haida songs she sings with confidence. As a singer and dancer, she is called upon to perform at headstone movings, potlatches, and even exhibition openings in museums around the continent.

For other committee members, helping to ease the pain of the displaced ancestors and knowing they could effect changes that would turn wrong things right has fostered their emotional and spiritual well-being. Andy Wilson referred to healing as an unexpected outcome of repatriation. He remembered going to the University of British Columbia in Vancouver for the repatriation of Haida remains in 1999. As many as one hundred Haidas attended the ceremony, and he remembered them singing, drumming, dancing, and crying. He began to understand how repatriation could bring relief to people, that it could work in unimagined ways. From then on, the committee made a concerted effort to involve as many Haidas as possible in the process, including those who were living in the cities where the museums were located. Andy also framed the decision to include non-Haidas in the repatriation process within a discourse of healing. Whether non-Haidas should be allowed to help in repatriation was discussed at length over the SRCC's first years; in the end the committee thought it likely that non-Haidas also needed a way to come to terms with the actions of their own ancestors. Non-Haida islanders, Andy explained to me, live and build on Haida territory, and visitors come to enjoy and experience the land and Haida culture. Yet it may have been these people's grandparents or great-grandparents who stole or sold Haida ancestral remains. The cultural and historical legacy of non-Haidas includes the collecting of remains, the taking of land, and the sending of children to residential schools. The SRCC suspected that many Euro-Canadians today want to come to terms with this legacy, change their relationships with Haidas or First Nations more generally, and be able to feel healed from the past. By initiating an invitation to participate in repatriation, Nika Collison thought, the SRCC would be more able to ensure Haida intellectual and property rights were being respected, and to create situations that fostered empathy, openness, cooperation, and mutual respect – key goals for the committee.

During my fieldwork in 2005, I asked Lucy Bell if my attention to the *process* of repatriation was misguided. I feared that current academic interests in process (cf. Goldstein-Gidoni 1999; Morphy 1994; Stoler 2008; Thomas 1992) were potentially in conflict with the interests of Haida people. I wondered whether the physical return of the ancestors was the most important aspect of repatriation, and if I should therefore be focusing on Haida spirituality. Lucy responded that, at the outset, the well-being of the ancestors was the sole motivation for repatriation, but over time committee members began to recognize the positive impact their experiences were having on each other and on the volunteers more generally. The acquisition of new skills, the growth in committee members' self-esteem, an increasing sense of being in control of one's life, finding inspiration for new works of art (songs, dances, carvings), gaining opportunities for travel, and establishing partnerships with major cultural institutions became a further incentive to continue with the work of repatriation.

Less altruistic emotions are entwined within the cultural and spiritual growth. Lucy revealed her sadness – and anger – that her daughter, throughout her whole life, has had to travel from museum to museum to repatriate her ancestors' remains, fund-raise continuously, and endure committee meetings in her living room for the purposes of repatriation. When the repatriation process began, Lucy was not yet a mother. Her goal was to bring every Haida ancestor home so that her own children would never have to do such work. And yet, my first morning on Haida Gwaii, I sat with Lucy's daughter, then only four years old, watching children's programs on television as she explained how they wrapped the bones in cedar mats and why they were bringing the bones home. Lucy is grateful for the love the repatriation *naaniis* have shown to her daughter and is proud of her daughter's entrepreneurship in service to her ancestors (as young as four, she set up her own sales area in her parents' café selling raffle tickets to raise funds in support of repatriation efforts), but it is not the life Lucy would have chosen for her daughter. Spending time in cosmopolitan cities with museum collections does not erase the sorrow of having to retrieve one's ancestors.

Although repatriation committee members were leery of characterizing repatriation as a "cultural saviour," those I spoke with tended to focus on the positive outcomes of their work for themselves as artists, singers, family members, Haida language students, contributing community members, and human beings more generally. I return to the cathartic qualities of repatriation and the place of remembering as an active, and often collective, element of healing in chapter 7. First, though, it is necessary to understand how family, respect, and remembrance are connected within Haida society through a closer examination of Haida kinship, the concept of *yahgudang,* and the extent to which repatriation reflects, reproduces, and develops these cultural ideals.

4 The Structural Qualities and Cultural Values of Haida Kinship

Matrilineages, *K'waalaa*, and Social Identity

Fundamentally, Haida are part of a complex social system that marks them in relation to consanguines, affines, and non-relatives. Haida society is composed of two *k'waalaa*, or moieties, Raven and Eagle. Each *k'waalaa* consists of a number of matrilineages. In the Haida dialects, matrilineages are called *gwaay gaang* (Massett), *gyaaging.aay* (Skidegate), and *gwáayk'aang* (Kaigani). At birth, a child's social identity is derived from his or her mother's *gwaay gaang/gyaaging.aay* and the *k'waalaa* to which her lineage belongs. Today, Haida colloquially refer to both lineages and *k'waalaa* as "clans." As "clan" can be ambiguous, I retain the anthropological terms "matrilineage" (or simply "lineage") and "moiety," and make use of the Haida language terms *gwaay gaang/gyaaging. aay* and *k'waalaa*.

The division into two *k'waalaa* has its origins in the pre-human days of Haida history, when there were only supernatural beings. Raven *k'waalaa* have their own origin stories involving the ocean, ultimately tracing their ancestry to the supernatural being Foam-Woman, who was sitting atop a place named Xā'gi when the flood waters receded. From Foam-Woman came three branches of Raven lineages on Haida Gwaii: the Xā'gi branch, Ata'na branch, and Rose Spit branch (Swanton 1905a, 76–7; see also Wright 2001). Eagle *k'waalaa* have their origins in the supernatural being Djila'qons. Whereas Foam-Woman appears in only one Haida story – that which tells of the creation of the Raven lineages – Djila'qons appears frequently in Haida stories. The creation of Eagle lineages occurs in different places and at different times. Djila'qons begot three daughters, Greatest-Mountain, Property-making-a-Noise, and Labret Woman, from whom the Eagle lineages trace their descent (Swanton 1905a, 92–3).

The construction of a sense of kinship among Haidas continues to be affected by the location of their relatives and ancestors on and in the land. When driving along the beach for scallops, people pass the Hiellen River and are in the shadow of Tow Hill: places where lineages were formed and established villages and, a century ago, where canneries provided wage earnings for relatives. The continuous chattering and mid-flight acrobatics of ravens recall Raven, the main figure in Haida oral history, while a murder of ravens along a power line is humorously referred to as a "clan meeting." People remember "the Prairie" as a place of family picnics and, later, teenage escapades. Photographs of the Yakoun River prompt memories of deceased relatives who used to fish there. Among the Haidas I spoke with were people who relished working in Gwaii Haanas National Park Reserve and Haida Heritage Site, living without electricity or plumbing but in close proximity to remnants of historical villages and sites of Creation, including the place where Foam Woman sat upon the reef. As Carol Zane Jolles writes of Yupik relationships to their home, St. Lawrence Island, Alaska:

> I believe the landscape itself, expressed through ... the daily experience of traversing the land, with its multitude of names, in order to hunt or to visit family or to seek comfort and assurance through prayer, also summarizes and affirms histories. Surely this deep familiarity affects how people feel about their homeland and how they think. (Jolles and Mikaghaq Oozeva 2002, 3)

As a homeland, Haida Gwaii is both familiar and familial, known to Haidas through the continued presence of their families on the islands. It is the familial that guides the familiar, as kinship forms the basis for organizing histories, memories, a sense of ownership, daily activities, and identity. The study of kinship systems has a long history in anthropology, but I take my lead from Leila Abu-Lughod (1999) who finds the relationships – or the ideology[1] – of kinship to be a critical factor in Bedouin identity and in turn the kinds of everyday social relations Bedouins engage in and navigate. Kinship becomes the idiom through which people express and understand feelings and actions. My interest in Haida kinship lies in its ability to express and frame cultural values (cf. Schneider 1980).

One particular quality of Haida kinship I pay attention to is the agency of deceased ancestors. To understand repatriation from a Haida perspective, it is necessary to address the ongoing social relations between the living and the deceased, the cycle of reincarnation, and the relationships that are possible as a result. With this as background, the concept of "ancestor" from a Haida perspective becomes clearer, as does the relationship between an individual and their lineage. The relationship between personhood, identity, and kinship is integral to understanding the force of kinship in decision making on Haida Gwaii.

Still, measuring the force of individual kinship acts is exceedingly difficult, if not impossible. Kinship is a cumulative process, a succession of what Janet Carsten (2000) calls "unmarked" and "marked exchanges," where unremarkable everyday exchanges act as signifiers of time and care invested in a relationship and become critical components in the construction of meaning, memory, and kinship during more ritual or formal occasions. In her study of Scottish adoptees looking to reunite with their birth parents, Carsten provides thought-provoking comparative material to understand how the production of kinship and the production of memories can occur simultaneously and be mutually constitutive: the troubles adoptees have in overcoming years of separation as they try to create meaningful familial relationships with biological parents or siblings shed light on the reasons why Haidas put such great effort into both mundane and ceremonial interactions with their ancestors' remains, objects, values, language, and other cultural practices.

The Interdependence of Ravens and Eagles

Ethnographies often describe Haida society as being based exclusively upon Raven and Eagle interactions (see, for example, Murdock 1936). Ravens, *yahl* or *Ḵaay xil*, and Eagles, *guud*, *Gidins*, *Gitans*, or *Ḵuustaayak*, rely upon the existence of the other, most noticeably through exogamous marriage practices. In the past, "marriages were ... contracted between two members of different lineages or opposing moieties, that is, between two people with rights to different tangible and intangible property" (Boelscher 1988, 117). Arranged marriages were common until the beginning of the twentieth century, and multiple marriages between two specific lineages were used strategically to keep power and wealth within higher-class lineages.[2] Today, love matches are sought, though still largely between Ravens and Eagles.

There are mechanisms to "correct" or "create" an intended spouse's lineage. Pearle Pearson related a story about her grandmother's strategic adoption by a lineage of the opposite moiety so that she would be an appropriate partner for a respected and high-ranking chief:

> My grandmother came down from Alaska. She married a young chief in Massett [but] she was Raven and he was a Raven. So he gave a huge potlatch to change her to Eagle. She was adopted into the Eagle clan. So that's how we became Eagles. We can still use the Raven crest too, but we don't. I don't think any of us use it. I don't. (1 May 2006)

People also use adoption to integrate a non-Haida spouse into a lineage and into the larger community. This is particularly important if the non-Haida spouse is female, as any children from the marriage will be part of her lineage.

Adoption is used in non-marriage circumstances too. For instance, if someone loses a sister, another woman may adopt the person who lost the sister and become a sister to them. Adoption can be used to show respect or bestow honour. Canadian prime minister Pierre Elliott Trudeau was adopted into the Yaghu'laanaas lineage when he visited Haida Gwaii in 1976. Remembering his death in 2000, *Yaghu jaanaas* (women of the Yaghu'laanaas lineage) lamented that no one from their lineage attended his funeral in Ottawa, despite being family. Adoptive relationships are formalized in front of witnesses, with a feast and give-away, often taking place as part of a larger potlatch. Adoptive relationships are not symbolic; they come with feelings of obligation, responsibility, and often affection. They are used to normalize, formalize, and reaffirm Haida kinship as the dominant social institution on the islands.

As work and social responsibilities are largely determined by *k'waalaa*, it is infinitely easier to navigate social gatherings, as well as social conflicts, if one is aware of his or her position within a lineage and therefore within a *k'waalaa*. Aside from marriage, Ravens and Eagles rely on each other for a wide variety of physical and social work, such as preparing and serving potlatch meals or funeral teas, carving memorial poles, or sitting with a recently deceased body until it is interred. The hosting lineage will hire workers from the opposite lineage to fill these roles. Meanwhile, the individual host of a potlatch, the commissioner of a pole, or a close relative of the deceased may call on his or her own matrilineage to provide support through monetary donations, fish or game for the meal, items to be given to the witnesses of potlatch transactions, or other objects useful for paying those of the opposite lineage.

The clarity regarding social responsibilities and divisions of labour for funerals, weddings, potlatches, and feasts is not always as easy to distinguish within day-to-day interactions. On a daily basis, the values of kinship are revealed in more subtle ways. Everyday family interactions are likely to include parents, siblings, grandparents, aunts, uncles, and cousins, all of whom spend considerable time together, working, playing, eating, providing child care or elder care, celebrating, and sharing news, gossip, and opinions. Glimpses of social values are seen in the conviction that although children may divide their affections and time equally between lineage and non-lineage grandparents, it is one's lineage grandparents who are imagined to be particularly responsible for fostering well-being and providing care. Similarly, aunts and uncles are deemed necessary for child-rearing because parents will be "too soft" on their children, being so deeply fond of them; aunts and uncles provide the necessary discipline. Mothers and children seem to have particularly strong bonds, as do siblings and lineage cousins (who are reckoned as siblings within the Haida language).

A Haida's "extended family" – comprising genealogically close lineage mates and affines from opposing lineages – is the major source of his or her education. Irene Mills from the Skidegate Repatriation and Cultural Committee put it this way: "the extended family is so important here, in all aspects of life, and that's where you learn." Watching is spoken of as a prime means of learning: explanations are not given so much as an example is set – an example that ideally is seen year after year, season after season, event after event. For example, Irene, speaking with me about learning to "put up," or can, fish, explained how important it was for her to ensure that her children and grandchildren who live off-island see her doing this: "If you don't have a visual – then how do you take the first step towards doing it?" For her, having visual referents in common was a critical part of knowledge sharing. She transitioned from preparing fish to repatriation activities, saying, "I think that goes back to the kids learning how to make blankets for us and getting it back in the schools and making it something that's talked about everyday."

For Herzfeld (1995), "watching" is very often a multisensory act and a form of apprenticing (see also Downey 2010; Henze 1992; Marchand 2001, 2009, 2010; Sutton 2001). I witnessed the same synesthetic approach on Haida Gwaii. Haida men I spoke with frequently learned how to work on fishing boats from their uncles (both maternal and paternal), out on the water. Women often learned how to make button blankets by watching their mothers, aunts, and grandmothers. An older man explained his process of learning to carve, describing seniors sitting, watching, and critiquing the forms and shapes he was producing; while his audience did not always have the vocabulary to coach him on *how* to carve, they drew upon memories of how a pole, a set of eyes, or a wing should look and had him amend his work until it resonated with their visual memories. Family outings might centre on crabbing, clamming, scallop harvesting, and berry picking – activities in which even small children are included. In fact, children are rarely left out of activities. Babies and toddlers are carried by dancers during formal performances, as well as during dances open to the audience. Young girls learn how to bend and dip one shoulder to show off their button blankets and poise during the women's dance by mimicking the women around them. Collectively, members of a family know how to complete the individual tasks it takes to can fish. Children may be given the simpler task of putting lids on jars of fish, graduating through various stages of the canning process until, as adults, they are entrusted with filleting the fish. Children of all ages are brought to weddings, funerals, headstone movings, and potlatches. There is, then, a significant amount of intergenerational interaction within Haida families, which is in turn a quality of kinship that Haidas value highly.

In contrast to models of Haida kinship that focus on the oppositional qualities of Ravens and Eagles, Swanton (1905a, 68) assessed the lineage as the "fundamental unit of Haida society." In 1900–1901, he recorded elders as remembering a time when there were twenty-two Raven lineages and twenty-three Eagle lineages; however, by the time he conducted his interviews the number had dropped dramatically due to the ravages of smallpox. Today, most people – though not all – know which of the roughly thirty lineages residing in Old Massett and Skidegate they belong to (Old Massett Village Council Heritage Resources Department 2006).[3] This is a stark change from Blackman's field experience three decades earlier, where she noted the effects of external intrusions on Haida kinship:

> Missionary emphasis upon nuclear family units and the government's Indian Act affected the status of women by gradually eroding matrilineal descent. Although today matrilineal descent is still acknowledged to exist by the older generation and is traced for certain purposes, bilateral kin terms prevail, lineage exogamy is no longer practised, and most younger people do not know their lineage membership. Moiety affiliation is generally known and functions on ceremonial occasions, though moiety exogamy has also broken down. (Blackman 1992, 48)

One of my interviewees remembered her youth as a time when people knew if they were Raven or Eagle, but not the name of their specific lineage. Today, Haida lineage names are spoken frequently in public and private, and much social interaction centres upon lineages. Lineages hold annual dinners or picnics to create occasions to gather together as a lineage. Skidegate also organizes a basketball tournament annually where the teams are lineage based, and there is a "clan march" for the Haida Heritage Centre annual celebrations. Lucy Bell has organized museum visits called "*Naanii/Jaadaa*" trips where pairs of older women (*naanii*) and younger women (*jaadaa*) from lineages in Old Massett spend time together looking at Haida collections in museums, based on the idea that knowledge should be shared intergenerationally within a family.

Both financial and emotional support are expected and received from one's lineage. At the time of my arrival on Haida Gwaii the family members of a man who had undergone an organ transplant in Vancouver, some five hundred miles south, were keen for one of them to stay with him during his recovery. But such costs fall outside their medical coverage, and Vancouver is one of the most expensive Canadian cities to live in: a long-term stay in the city, plus travel to and from Haida Gwaii, would be very costly. In response, family members provided two woven cedar hats – one in a Stetson style, one in a traditional Haida style – for a raffle in order to raise money. A number of the family members sold tickets to their friends, co-workers, and in-laws, raising hundreds of dollars to cover travel expenses. Similarly, members of a lineage may pool their financial resources in order to send lineage representatives to feasts and funerals being held off-island.

To the satisfaction of many of the older people, Haidas are showing greater awareness of and more actively affirming the particular lineage to which they belong. A telling example of this occurred at Chief Matthews Elementary School in the village of Old Massett, where one night parents assembled to watch as the students told the audience in

Haida and English which lineage they belong to and what crests they are allowed to wear (figure 4.1). Red corrugated cardboard banners hung around the room displayed stencilled lineage names and the proper crests. Parent volunteers were sought for a project to make permanent, cloth banners for the following year. A program book was also distributed listing lineage memberships of the students and who was preparing to be adopted into a particular lineage. The students sang Haida songs as proud parents videotaped and clicked away with their cameras.

A project entitled *Haida Memories*[4] undertaken by Lucy Bell and funded by the Virtual Museum of Canada's Community Memories program shares similar goals. An online exhibition, *Haida Memories,* contains over four hundred photographs, most of which have been scanned and digitized from the personal albums of people in Old Massett. The photos are grouped largely along lineage lines, with additional categories to further illustrate the complementary division into Ravens and Eagles, the land, and Haida ceremonies.[5] The interpretive content on the site is limited, which allows it to stand at a distance from interlineage disputes over land, titles, or resources. The exhibition is, rather, a place to go to become familiar with one's own lineage and with the lineage and *k'waalaa* networks in Old Massett more generally. As noted earlier, not only is it necessary to know who is Raven and who is Eagle for the purposes of organizing potlatch or feast work, but it is also extremely important for the purposes of dating. Older people continue to keep their eyes on burgeoning romances, imparting knowledge about genealogical connections when needed.

Being able to recite one's lineage history is a valued skill older Haidas fear is being lost. The common practice of addressing any elderly person as *nanaay/naanii* (grandmother) or *chinaay/chinnii* (also spelled *tsini/tsinnii,* meaning "grandfather") was, suggested one *naanii,* confusing smaller children over who is a relative and who is simply elderly. Her concern likely reflects the younger generation's lack of genealogical knowledge more than linguistic conservatism, particularly given multiple translations of *tcinga* (root *tcin*) as "grandfather," as "ancestor," as a term of respect used for an old man, and as a supernatural helper (Durlach 1928, 68). Another factor people identified as a threat to the amount of time family members spend together, and by extension a challenge to the person-to-person transmission of genealogical knowledge, is the plethora of non-Haida entertainment like television and the Internet.

Figure 4.1 Chief Matthews Elementary School students singing Haida songs, wearing their own hats and Eagle or Raven capes from the school, 2005. The banners represent the matrilineages of the students.

> [My grandmother] was a great one for teaching us how to dance and sing. She said, "Always remember who we are." She would tell us the histories of all our people, and tell us over and over again. "Remember your family history," she would say. We didn't have a written language, so we had to depend on the old people telling us. (Flossie Lambly, quoted in Jensen and Sargent 1986, 57)

Today, whenever family connections are recited, there is sure to be an elder person who praises the effort and encourages others to do the same. At the May 2006 Celebration – a biannual gathering of Tlingit, Tsmishian, and Haida dancers in Juneau, Alaska – the Kaigani Haida from Alaska invited those attending from Haida Gwaii to a dinner in honour of the Alaskan high school graduates. During the evening, one of the Haida men in our party stood to thank our hosts. He began by telling the gathering who his mother and grandmother were and where they came from in Alaska, and expressed confidence that some among his hosts were his relations. The making of this connection pleased and was encouraged by the hosts: people nodded, clapped, smiled, and enquired about familial connections later on in the dinner. A shared history conjures ongoing responsibilities that come with being a member of a lineage – as well as the responsibilities that come with being a member of an opposite lineage.

These overt expressions of kinship can be made sense of in multiple ways. Strathern (2005), for example, stresses that alongside the apparent "demise" of the Euro-American family – owing largely to divorce – there are strong desires within reconfigured families to create relationships and a sense of kinship. Are performances of Haida genealogy and kinship then an indication of family well-being, or of challenges to well-being? The situation of Haida families often seems to involve a paradox: as the Haida nation grows in strength politically, culturally, and financially, it continues to be stressed by unemployment, substance abuse, and family violence.[6] Institutionalized racism bears much of the guilt, but older people are quick to identify "conveniences" such as televisions and grocery stores as equally contributing to the breakdown of Haida families and Haida ways.

It was said to me that today "families are so dysfunctional, they're functional." In people's efforts to function, or their evaluations of what is functional and what is dysfunctional, pre-colonial values and patterns of Haida kinship emerge. As a consequence of alcoholism, for example, many children are being raised by grandparents or spend weekends in the homes of lineage aunts and uncles. Similarly, while remembering her youth, an elderly woman lamented that "the problem today" is "that everyone helps everyone else." She wanted to return to a system where lineages handled things privately, always ensuring family members were taken care of. For her, a lineage-based system represents the appropriate and respectable way of handling crises in particular. In this light, lineage grandparents, aunts, or uncles assuming parenting duties is a solution anchored in Haida kinship values.

Another approach to encouraging familial behaviour was voiced by Barb Wilson, who worked for Gwaii Haanas National Park Reserve and Haida Heritage Site. Barb makes her home in Skidegate and has focused her professional and personal efforts on improving the health of Haida Gwaii. She concentrates on land and resource rehabilitation in recognition that her ancestors, once laid to rest in trees, caves, or mortuary poles, all returned to the environment that supported them. Their bodies became the earth again, molecules of minerals and organic nutrients. She sees a very literal connection between her ancestors and the land. The plants, animals, and people support each other. Humans are afforded food, shelter, fibres, and tools from their environment, and in turn should refrain from overharvesting or polluting these resources. Ideally, people and land should be granted the same degree of respect, which means people must defend the integrity of their families with the same tenacity they devote to environmental causes or land rights struggles. Barb views the breakdown of families, accompanied by poor mental, physical, and spiritual health, as a process paralleling the breakdown of the land as a result of overlogging, overfishing, pollution, and introduced species. The healing of the land is dependent on, and incomplete without, the healing of the people, and vice versa. Indeed, many Haida view damage done to the land as a personal affront or personal injury.

When the Haida guest in Alaska communicated his genealogy, and when Barb Wilson identified people with and through their land, they both expressed narratives in which individuals and lineages act together to create a sense of self. Many Haida today recognize their *k'waalaa* and lineage system as a particularly enduring facet of their culture. Because the *k'waalaa/gwaay gaang* system dictates social responsibilities as well as providing specific identities for people, its prevalence and perseverance are recognized as key factors in maintaining a sense of what it is to be Haida in a larger world.

Kinship and Personhood

Cultural identity, individual identity, and family identity are deeply intertwined on Haida Gwaii. As a means of understanding how these components work together to construct identities, Carsten's (2000, 2007) efforts to understand the motivations behind adoptees seeking reunions with birth mothers is instructive. During interviews adoptees began with the almost formulaic motivation of wanting to "know where I come from" and to "find out who I am," implying an assumed link between self-identification and kinship of a biological kind. Yet the interviews also display a more complex sense of relatedness, not tied simply to biology but to nurturing, effort, time, and participation in what Carsten calls "unmarked exchanges of kinship" (2000, 690, 696).[7] These are everyday activities such as walking children to school, disciplining bad behaviour, sharing meals, and playing games that contribute to a sense of permanence – a key quality of kinship. Carsten interprets Schneider's (1984) analysis of American kinship and Weston's (1997) analysis of gay and lesbian kinship as systems that create and privilege permanent bonds between people. The dilemma facing the adoptees with whom Carsten worked was how to balance the permanence created by shared blood with the permanence created by shared time, activities, nurturance, and effort. Despite the permanence of blood, adoptees found that the reintegration of birth kin in marked exchanges (birthdays, weddings, reunions, funerals, etc.) lacked significance and meaning as a result of an absence of unmarked exchanges (Carsten 2000).

Unmarked exchanges do not unequivocally produce kinship. Gibson (1985), for example, demonstrates how such day-to-day sharing in the Philippine Highlands produces feelings of companionship, a category of relatedness altogether different from that of kinship. Kinship among the Buid, Gibson reports, requires the sharing of specific substances, but has little to do with the sharing of activities. Abu-Lughod (1999, 62–3) also points out the categorical difference conceptualized by Alwad 'Ali whereby sharing the blood of the patriline creates the basis of kinship, while sharing food creates another category of relatedness described as "sharing a life," 'ishra, that applies to husbands and wives, long-term neighbours, and patron-client relationships. Still, in these examples, notions of kinship and relatedness are based upon ideas of permanence. There is *potential* for everyday interactions to be productive, or "generative" (Ingold 2000), of a category of relatedness. As Ingold argues, ancestry, memories, land, and personhood are not inherited, but rather are "grown" through joint activities (2000, 140–51). Routine events such as deploying hunting skills, walking forest paths, providing nurturance, and cooking and feeding cause beings (and their environment) to converge and develop together.

A critical idea in Carsten's work is her proposal that "we can also look at this steady accumulation of everyday events as the stuff of which, retrospectively, shared memory may be created. If kinship is constituted out of everyday small acts and events in time, this is also a prospective process of co-production of memory" (2000, 697). Just as memories contribute to feelings of kinship, the activities of kinship contribute to the potential memories one can have. Kinship, then, can be a way to know one's past, creating a structure through which remembering occurs. I believe the Haida repatriation process exists within this dynamic, as a series of small acts and special events occurring through time, resulting in shared memories and a heightened sense of kinship. I explore this possibility in more depth in chapter 6, but first it is useful to determine the degree to which Haida practices and beliefs more generally foster the co-production of kinship and memory.

Patterns of naming in Haida society, for example, illuminate how kinship bonds and memory are created across generations. During a Haida's lifetime, she or he may receive one or more "Haida names." As discussed in the next chapter, these names are owned by particular lineages and are presented to an individual at a tea, feast, or potlatch in front of witnesses. The name may have belonged to one or many other people in the past, and often symbolizes a relationship between the giver and the receiver of the name. Someone may give their niece their grandmother's Haida name because the grandmother and niece share particular qualities, perhaps a physical gracefulness, manner of speaking, or love of joke telling. Haida names are a form of property, held within a lineage, and the person presenting the name must be recognized as having the right to extend it to another person. This right usually comes from belonging to the lineage in which the name originated, but may also require that the giver be the senior female of the lineage or a direct descendant of the namesake. In the case of hereditary leaders, there is a twofold process whereby men acquire the chieftainship of a place or village and also receive a particular chief's name.[8]

A name that has been in use for generations is treated with respect, and out of reverence for the name and the act of being given it, a Haida may choose to use the name only during ceremonies or extraordinary events. More often, Haida names are used with increased frequency in all public events as a means of sharing one's pride in, and demonstrating one's connection to, family, place and culture.[9] The social prestige of Haida names stems from both quantity and quality; receiving multiple names over one's lifetime is a sign of wealth (Gwaganad 2004). Nevertheless, people are expected to "live up" to the names they receive and maintain or improve the reputation of names that belong to their lineage. As the hereditary leader of Skedans, the late Niis Wes (Ernie Wilson), explained to me, a name means nothing until you do something with it. In other words, a person cannot rely on a name's history to bring them respect; the receiver must act in ways becoming of the name.

Over time, certain names accumulate a history and carry the legacy of important individuals and their achievements. The effect of reusing names that evoke memories of feats, accomplishments, and characteristics has been explicated by Boelscher (1988) through the metaphor of "telescopic time." Events occurring across time become enmeshed within the name – rather than a specific person – unifying rather than differentiating the members and achievements of each lineage, and collapsing temporal distances between generations.

Repetition of names also occurs with English or Christian names given to Haidas at birth. The famed weaver Isabella Edenshaw, for example, was the mother of Florence Edenshaw Davidson, who shared her life history with anthropologist Margaret Blackman in 1977 and became the subject of the first published life history of a Northwest Coast woman (Blackman 1992). One of Florence's own daughters, Primrose, who is also a highly regarded weaver, has "Isabella" as a middle name. One of Primrose's daughters is named Isabel, and she too is a highly respected weaver, while Primrose's great-granddaughter also carries the name Isabel. It is not uncommon for people to have both a brother and uncle with the same name, or to name their own child after a grandparent. These names, as with Haida names, come to act as mnemonic devices, encouraging the sharing of family connections and life histories. It is perhaps too early to know if this will be part of the same "telescopic" pattern as occurs with Haida names.

What the telescopic model suggests, however, is that the use of names on Haida Gwaii can produce collective memories or histories that exist beyond a single lifespan. They operate in contradistinction to Maurice Halbwachs' analysis of Europeans' treatment of names, where he supposes

> that the dead retreat into the past ... because nothing remains of the group in which they passed their lives, and which needed to name them, and their names slowly become obliterated. The only ancestors transmitted and retained are those whose memory has become the object of a cult by men who remain at least fictitiously in contact with them. The others become part of an anonymous mass. (Halbwachs 1992, 73)

In actuality, much remains of ancient and historic Haida populations, including patterns of kinship relations, names, artefacts, lineage crests, and a strong belief in the continual presence of deceased ancestors themselves. There is nothing "fictitious" about the connections created through names.

The most notable way Haidas align themselves with their ancestors is through the use of lineage crests, which are synonyms with "lineage" in Haida dialects: *gyaaging.aay/ gwaay gang* (Skidegate/Old Massett dialect). Each lineage has the rights to a set of crests that they can wear on clothing or jewellery, as a tattoo, on drums or paddles, on house or memorial poles, even incorporated into business logos (figure 4.2). The most common crest forms are animals – bear, beaver, raven, eagle, killer whale, frog – though there are also other natural forms such as clouds, a tree, a rainbow, supernatural forms such as the sea creature *tcamoos* (an animal representation of a submerged tree stump, or snag, in the water), and objects such as a fish-drying rack. Crests originate in historical encounters with the natural world and supernatural beings. Once a crest is the property of a lineage, those belonging to that lineage have the right to wear and display it; certain crests are even more exclusive, with rights to chiefly or high-ranking property being limited to the chief's immediate descendants. At birth, a person inherits the right to wear and display the crests associated with their matrilineage.

Leaders of lineages have the ability to give a person or group outside the lineage the right to use a particular crest. Interestingly, fathers can give their children the right to use their crest, but those children cannot pass on the use of the crest to their own offspring (Boelscher 1988, 38; N. Collison 2006, 62). Some crests can be found among multiple lineages, others are specific to one particular lineage. Lineages can also attempt to claim the right to use a crest through potlatching (N. Collison 2006, 62).

Crests are not fixed in how they may be designed. Individual artists design variations of crests to suit their aesthetic taste, and people likewise exhibit their crests with their own individual style. At a headstone moving I attended, three sisters wore matching tunics with identical killer whale crests to show they not only belong to the same lineage but have a particular relationship to each other (figure 4.3). Wearing one's crest, either formally through regalia or informally through casual clothing and accessories, is a source of pride.

Since the 1970s, a growing number of Haidas have been wearing to formal occasions regalia that almost always features crest designs. Regalia, especially when donned by a group of people, is admired as beautiful and respectful. In fact, transformative qualities are often bestowed on the wearing of regalia, which is thought to promote self-assurance. Young dancers in Skidegate, for example, were encouraged to bring their button blankets or vests to dance practices so that they would stand taller and experience the increased confidence that comes with being in regalia. "You know who you are," I was repeatedly told, "when you are in your regalia." Wearing and displaying crests reinforces individual identity through reference to corporate identities such as

Figure 4.2 Vince Collison of the Haida Heritage and Repatriation Society at the End of Mourning ceremony in Skidegate, 2005. His drum has an eagle crest painted on it.

Figure 4.3 Tunics with matching crest designs worn by sisters to a headstone moving hosted by the Williams family in Old Massett, 2005.

lineage, *k'waalaa*, and nation. The crest designs on the blankets and bent-wood boxes made for repatriation similarly demonstrate the desire to identify people as part of lineages, *k'waalaa*, and the Haida nation.

This connectivity is further expressed through the impressive amount of "informal" crest wear sported by Haidas on an everyday basis. "Hoodies" and jogging pants with "Haida" or "Haida Nation" and raven or eagle designs are produced by artist James Sawyer. His garments are happily received as Christmas and birthday presents and worn on all occasions by people of all ages. Artist Reg Davidson has an extensive line of clothing featuring various embroidered or silk-screened crest designs: long-sleeved shirts, t-shirts, women's blouses, leather jackets, winter coats, fleece vests, and undergarments. Haida entrepreneurs have modified popular motifs – Adidas, Hot Wheels, the Nike "swoosh," university logos, army camouflage – and inserted Haida-oriented phrases, eagle feathers, "Watchmen" (three men in tall cedar hats often carved at the tops of poles), or other identifiable features from Haida culture.

The range of non-clothing items sporting crests is vast, providing significant opportunities for the expression of self. These items include oven mitts, Christmas stockings, business card holders, canvas bags, trivets, watches, water bottles, bumper stickers, and greeting cards. The designs on these objects may be the work of Haida artists or other artists working in formline style and may be the same objects that provide tourists with treasured mementos of their visit to British Columbia. While rules govern what crests Haidas may wear, non-Haidas may wear any crest as merchandise. Crests that are part of art made for non-ceremonial functions essentially stop functioning as crests when taken outside the Haida social system. The artworks become forms of cultural or artistic expression. Property owned by a lineage, however, does not cease to represent or belong to that lineage. Charlotte Townsend-Gault (2004) carefully navigates the significance of seemingly trivial objects that are disposable and ephemeral yet bear crests. She argues that the abundance of aboriginal-motif objects in circulation in the province of British Columbia serves to create both a presence and an absence: the bodies of aboriginal peoples and symbols of aboriginal sacred values are made present through crest decorations on various objects, yet at the same time the objects evoke among non-aboriginal people a recognition of their lack of knowledge about aboriginal peoples and their social values and systems. Townsend-Gault provocatively suggests that the extension of crests in this way has the effect of putting the non-aboriginal buyer/receiver always in debt, unable to return the gift with anything comparable.

For Haidas, such merchandise provides an opportunity to fill their surroundings with their crests and other familiar aesthetic imagery. While the production of regalia, masks, and finely crafted objects for ceremonial occasions has increased to fill the void created by ethnographic collecting, mass-produced consumer goods provide affordable, readily available, and functional objects for expressing identity within non-ceremonial settings. Whether displayed during formal or informal occasions, crests are constant reminders of what belongs, "in the double sense of being owned and being part of" a lineage (Boelscher 1988, 29).

Weston (1997, 36, 117) argues that this dual sense of belonging arises from feelings of "shared history": the physical presence of parents and siblings during one's childhood and adolescent years; shared experiences of tight economic times; resettlement in new home towns; long-term individual support (i.e., providing child care, fixing automobiles, house sitting, lending money); and (very frequently among gay and lesbian families) shared experiences of alienation. In contrast, Carsten documents the difficulty facing Scottish adoptees in creating personal narratives of "who they are" or "where they come from" because of an absence of shared histories with their biological kin. Adoptees made it clear to Carsten that they were not searching for "another mother," but were instead seeking to place themselves within a continuum that included their biological kin as the past, their life with their adopted kin as the present, and their children and grandchildren as their future. In Pierre Nora's (1989) sense, the adoptees shared neither history nor memory with their birth families.[10]

In comparison, Haidas perceive their matrilineages as enduring social groups, pre-existing the individual and consisting of already formed relations that individuals benefit from, contribute to, and continuously affect. Marilyn Strathern (2005) draws upon Roy Wagner's work to consider what a clan is and what its role is in shaping a person's identity. Strathern's ethnographic fieldwork with the Melpa in highland Papua New Guinea supports Wagner's claim that the clan extends beyond people, to actions:

> As a virtual body, the clan contains all the persons and actions, past and future, that constitute it, and clanship means for any one individual both the possibility of living through all these others and the possibility of benefiting from its numerous connections; not the clan as a discrete unit, but the clan and its relationships with others is what envelops persons. (Strathern 2005, 187n22)

Haida lineages, and their notions of how personal identity is formed through lineage membership, mirror this process. The "others" with whom a Haida lineage has a relationship include the land, supernatural beings, animals, and other people living and deceased. The continuity of Haida kinship comes not just from people's current activities with their lineage and opposite k'waalaa, but also from knowing that their family has interacted with other families on Haida Gwaii for thousands of years. Haida senses of self often stem from being able to fulfil the complement of social responsibilities and duties – including continuing to interact with and have responsibility for their ancestors – that are a result of belonging to a lineage.

Kinship, Memory, and Identity: Time, Reincarnation, and Relatedness

As Haidas understand it, their ancestors are not segregated from the living in death. While they no longer have a physical form, their presence is at times still seen, felt, or heard, usually at the level of individual experience. There is casualness in the relationship between the living and the deceased: a familiarity and two-way interaction. Artists often blamed their ancestors when a tool went missing, while other people also explained missing or unexpectedly moved personal effects as the result of their ancestors' interventions. Such stories were related to me in good humour. Haida recognize that their ancestors have not lost their sense of humour in death, and neither have they lost their sense of compassion. Haida find that it is not unusual for the recently deceased to accompany a relative or friend for a few days or even a few months, their presence felt while the friend or relative is, for example, driving in the car or doing housework. When adults shared stories with each other relating how they had felt the presence of an ancestor, their experiences and explanations were supported and validated by their peers. Such experiences can cause initial apprehension or unease in a person, though these feelings were always assuaged by friends or family. When doors opened without any sign of a person nearby, adults would remind younger people that it was "just someone coming to visit" – perhaps their *naanii* or *chinaay* (grandfather). Adults also simply became accustomed to such experiences, as a particular ancestor might tend to spend time in their workshop, or repeat the same trick on them. Haida Heritage and Repatriation Society (HHRS) committee member Leona Claw spoke of hearing singing in treetops and children playing on the beach during repatriation ceremonies when no children were present. In the former case she heard in the singing a deceased friend's voice, which brought comfort. The children's laughter, it was suggested to her, was the happy playing of the repatriated.

There are more formal aspects to the relationship between living and deceased. Platters of food will be prepared and offered to ancestors by placing the platters in a fire during ceremonies. When I attended a potluck meeting with the Skidegate Repatriation and Cultural Committee (SRCC) in November 2005, they also prepared a plate of food for ancestors and placed this outside for them. The provision of food serves literally to feed the ancestors, but also to pay them respect. As well, as I discuss further in chapter 5, the deceased's close lineage relatives will host a headstone moving or End of Mourning feast that officially remembers the deceased, signals the end of public mourning for the family, and provides the necessary means for the deceased to journey to the Land of the Souls. In short, the well-being of the living is nurtured by their ancestors, and the well-being of ancestors is reliant on the acts of the living.

The interactions between ancestors and descendants generally should not leave one feeling sad, burdened, or scared, so when these feelings do arise it may be taken as a signal that something is not right, or that something needs attention. The ancestors themselves are often credited with sending these signals, affecting people's feelings in order to raise their awareness. Sue Gladstone from the SRCC noted the persistence of ancestors: when they have a plan for you, they will persist in sending you signals until you recognize those signals and are able and willing to take action. It is in this manner that Haida credit their ancestors for signalling that repatriation was possible and required.

The agency of deceased ancestors was communicated to me using a variety of examples. The deceased, like the living, can act independently or communally. Melinda Pick, who serves on the SRCC, was taught that Haida children pick the parents they will be born to. This idea is also present in Florence Edenshaw Davidson's memoirs: she recalls her husband indicating to whom he would be born in his next life, and indeed returning as promised (Blackman 1992, 133). Individual deceased family members are suspected of playing tricks or sharing space in someone's home or workshop, while the crackling, hissing, and popping noises of a fire are deemed to be the ancestors as a group saying *haawa'a* (thank you) for the offerings of food put into a fire. Similarly, when a water pitcher cracked audibly in the hands of women washing the grave plaques for the repatriated remains during a ceremony in Skidegate, it was interpreted as the ancestors communicating with the conglomeration of living Eagles and Ravens.

The individuality of ancestors continues in their rebirth. The identity of the person reincarnated into a child is sometimes determined at birth; in other cases the children themselves reveal their ancestral identities during play with each other or in conversation with others. As a reincarnate, a new child brings with him or her the skills from the former life. Haida feel it is important, therefore, to provide that child with the opportunities that will enable her or him to use those skills. Children are not limited in any way by their experiences in a former life. As they grow, they acquire new skills, tastes, and character traits that will become part of their personal identity. They are not supposed to replicate the life of someone else; they are to make their own mark on the world. Each child is a unique individual, and at the same time is the reincarnation of another person. As a result, adult relationships with children can be multilayered, as a woman's daughter may be the reincarnation of her mother, for example, or a grandson may be the reincarnation of an uncle. Blackman records this type of relationship between Florence Edenshaw Davidson and her father:

> Charles Edenshaw adored his new daughter [Florence]. "My Dad used to favor me," [Florence] says of their relationship. This was perhaps in part because she was believed to be the reincarnation of his own mother Qawkúna. *"Hada, ding awu di ijing"* ('Dad, I'm your mother') were Florence's first spoken words. (Blackman 1992, 53)

During my fieldwork, a granddaughter of Florence confessed a special affection for one of her own granddaughters as she is the reincarnation of Florence, a much beloved *naanii*. Other Haida today are not aware of the specific ancestor they are the reincarnation of, but still know themselves to be reincarnated.

In *Time and the Other*, Johannes Fabian (2002) uses relationships between the living and the dead to demonstrate how anthropologists have accepted the concept of "coevalness" but only as it applies within a culture, rather than between cultures (viz., between the culture being studied and the culture of the anthropologist). Although he uses this analysis in a different context, Fabian's point emphasizes how our very notion of time can affect our ideas of the possibilities of kinship:

> To cite but two examples, relationships between the living and the dead, or relationships between the agent and object of magic operations, presuppose cultural conceptions of contemporaneity. To a large extent, Western rational disbelief in the presence of ancestors and the efficacy of magic rest on the rejection of ideas of temporal coexistence implied in these ideas and practices. (Fabian 2002, 34)

Haida cosmology and beliefs very clearly describe the coexistence of the living and the deceased. Swanton recorded instances of people identifying blue-flies, *dï'dʌn* (also spelled *diidaan*), as old friends who, despite death, still remember them, and stories of reincarnation where the grief of the living prompted a deceased man to return to them:

> While working out a canoe at Masset, a man named Saqdō'dji was killed; but when he arrived at Tā'xet's [Ta'xiit] house,[11] he looked back and saw his friends[12] weeping. That determined him to jump down, but at first he was afraid of "killing himself" against the sharp tree tops. Finally his

friends bothered him so much by weeping, that he did not have a good time, and he threw himself down. He seemed to strike something hard. Then he heard someone say, "Wash him, wash him!" and, opening his eyes, he found himself under a stump partly burned out, where his new mother had gone to bring forth. He knew himself, but could not speak. When seven or eight years old, he went to the place where he had formerly been making his canoe, and found his tools just where he remembered to have hidden them. (Swanton 1905a, 36)

More recently, Haida elder Gwaaganad remembered the distrust of artist Bill Reid in Haida "last-minute" organization. As Reid was raised off-island in Victoria, Gwaaganad suspected "that he didn't have the trust that we had, the knowledge that we have that our ancestors are always around to help us and guide us" (Gwaganad 2004, 68). Reflecting on her own attitudes, she continued:

And you have to have faith in that. Before I do a speech, long before I got asked a year ago to do this, and almost every time I thought of it, I asked the ancestors to come and help. And I believe that it's basically something of what they want you to hear that's coming from me. (Gwaganad 2004, 68)

When Reid made provocative statements about the inferiority of contemporary Haidas to historic Haidas, Gwaaganad rejected such a notion on the grounds that she and her ancestors are inseparable: "we are our ancestors. Our ancestors are here. We're here because of our ancestors" (2004, 70). More telling is Gwaaganad's persistent recognition that Bill Reid, too, is part of this cycle of family, ancestry, and inheritance: she invokes the many Haida names he was given, acknowledging those who bestowed the names on him; she acknowledges his place within his clan and his clan's achievement at honouring him in death; and she ties him to his grandsons and the artistic talents all of them have been gifted with. When Ingold examines how hunter-gatherer groups conceptualize generations, he proposes, "life is not compacted, as the genealogical model implies, into a linear sequence of procreative moments suspended in time." He continues, "the life of every being, as it unfolds, contributes at once to the progeneration of the future and to the regeneration of the past" (Ingold 2000, 143). The past is not disconnected from the present, and significantly, it has the potential to be both coterminus and historic, to both reflect and influence the present.

Thus, in addition to Carsten's argument that time invested in a relationship is essential to the development of kinship relations, and that the ability to place oneself within a generational continuum (over time) is important to a sense of personal identity, a sense of contemporaneity – coevalness – is required to fully appreciate the depths of Haida relations. Furthermore, in accepting coevalness, any analysis of Haida repatriation needs to consider the ancestors whose remains are held within institutions as more than historic actors, and to reconsider them as continual members of Haida society. By making repatriation synonymous with reparations or restitution, the time frame begins with the colonial era. A richer understanding of the Haida repatriation process comes instead from situating it within Haida notions of reincarnation and the continual regeneration of lineages.

Irene Mills of the SRCC is hopeful that as more ancestral remains are brought home, those ancestral spirits will become rested and feel well enough to return as new members of the Haida community, bringing with them the old knowledge they have. "Old knowledge" includes Haida words or phrases, ways to use resources, and Haida names. Not only will the ancestral spirits need to be healthy and ready to come back for this to happen, but Irene feels the current community will also need to be ready and able to foster and reap the benefits of such knowledge and skills.

The potential for people to be born with memories adds an important new dimension to Carsten's suggestion that the production of kinship and memory are intertwined. While Carsten's scheme privileges contemporaneous experiencing as a foundation for the production of kinship and shared memory, new possibilities for imaging this relationship exist within Haida society. Nika Collison remembered her fellow committee member, Jenny Cross, raising the possibility that, because of reincarnation, they could be repatriating themselves. Not only does the building up of memory occur through the repetition of names, shared life experiences, and shared lineage histories, it also occurs as a result of reincarnation, inherited from previous generations. In each case, there is a strong correlation between kinship as a means of acquiring memories and kinship as a structure for remembering.

Time, and perhaps Haida scholarship, will be required to determine the extent to which collective memory is shaped by memories acquired through reincarnation. But there is one more possible lense through which to view the co-production of kinship and collective memory: the

link between respect and remembrance and the ability for acts of remembering to be simultaneously acts demonstrating respect.

Respect through Remembrance

Haidas engaged in acts honouring their ancestors are often behoved
to do so by the notion of "respect." Although "self-respect" is central to
understanding respect on Haida Gwaii, this should not be taken to
mean respect is an individualized attitude. The force of "respect" comes
largely from knowing that one belongs to something bigger than oneself. Haidas see themselves as part of a continuum that began with
Foam Woman and Djila' qons and will continue to exist after them.
Accordingly, one should act in ways that will make both ancestors and
successors proud. Respect is contingent on knowing who you are as an
individual, but also in knowing that your identity as an individual is
largely determined by your relations – the interdependence of persons,
families, and communities.

The transmission of names, the recitation of genealogies, and appropriate usage of lineage crests are equally acts of remembrance and acts
of respect. The same can be said of the repatriation process. The ancestors who had been exiled were remembered, in the dual sense of being
brought to mind and of being reintegrated into the realm of Haida social relations, through the actions of their descendants working to bring
them home. Making blankets, grave markers, boxes, meals, singing
songs, and giving speeches – actions that impart respect – cannot be
separated from acts of remembering. The remembrances offered as part
of repatriation activities draw from and expand upon Haida mourning
practices, a topic I cover in more depth in the next chapter.

Sergei Kan's analysis of Tlingit[13] mortuary potlatches underscores
the gravity of attending to and remembering ancestors. He writes:

> The Tlingit believe that the dead could not only help but harm the living
> with illness and death, if the latter did not remember, honor and help
> them. As long as the dead were remembered by their living matrikin and
> could participate in their potlatches, they remained immortal and sat close
> to the fire in their noncorporeal houses (Swanton 1908: 462). The forgotten
> ancestors, on the other hand, moved further and further away from the
> fire, suffered from hunger and cold, while their "houses" in the cemetery
> crumbled. Ultimately, the continuity of the matrilineal clan, as a cultural

category, depended upon a human ability to *remember*. (Kan 2004, 290–1, emphasis in original)

Likewise on Haida Gwaii, forgetting is a sign of disrespect and alienation, antithetical to the expectations of kinship. Moreover, for Haidas it is socially destabilizing. As Kan (2004) points out, within the Pacific Northwest death does not erase social identity; rather, it modifies the distribution of kinship obligations and expectations between lineage and opposing moiety members. Neglecting and forgetting one's ancestors poses harm to those spirits and reveals the living's apathy and disregard for personal well-being, family well-being, and social identity. In the next chapter, I explore the Haida notion of *yahgudang* (respect) and consider how it is aligned with selfhood, social status, and cultural continuity. As a concept, *yahgudang* has two qualities: it is both an act of paying respect and an indication of a person's fitness for receiving the respect of others. Repatriation committee members focus largely on the first quality of *yahgudang*: they seek to pay respect to their ancestors. However, the second quality of *yahgudang* ("fitness for respect") has been strengthened by the process of repatriation and has influenced Haidas' perceptions of themselves as family members and as a nation.

5 The Values of *Yahgudang*:
The Relationship between Self and Others

Based on fieldwork and research conducted with First Nations in coastal British Columbia and Alaska (including Kaigani Haida) throughout the1950s, Philip Drucker (1963, viii) believed that the only exceptions to the assimilation of Northwest Coast cultures were a handful of preserved artistic skills and "the people's pride in their identity as Indians." The latter he characterized almost as though it were a vestigial organ, having a continual presence in the body, but being of little efficacy or importance. Yet for Haidas, "pride" is closely aligned with the pervasive and highly valued cultural ideal of "respect" or *yahgudang*. During my fieldwork, I repeatedly heard older generations express their wish for the younger generations to have (i.e., to act with) self-respect: to be drug- and alcohol-free, to heed their parents, to eat the foods provided by the islands' ecology, to attend to their families, and to follow cultural protocol. Although self-respect is central within the ideal of *yahgudang*, the concept is equally and simultaneously a measure of the "relationship between self and others" (Boelscher 1988, 11). As a measure of relationships between self and others, *yahgudang* has a specific role in shaping social relationships, including those at the heart of repatriation.

Yahgudang, as mentioned above, has two components: "to pay respect" and equally "to be fit for respect." Haida notions of respect, which are tied to social status and wealth, also need to be considered within Haida notions of ownership and protocol surrounding usages of property and wealth by individuals and lineages – especially in the public sphere. *Yahgudang* shapes how material and immaterial property is used to delineate individual and collective wealth and status, to express support or disapproval towards another person, to validate important rites of passage or political alliances, and to mourn deaths and attend to deceased bodies. When repatriation committee members turned to the concept of *yahgudangang* they were honouring their obligation to care for the bodies of their deceased relatives, but the nuances of *yahgudang* mean that those who show respect will also grow in respect. Hence, in the case of repatriation, there is an outcome for the living as well as for the deceased.

I open this chapter with a discussion of the principles underlying *yahgudang* and consider the ways *yahgudang* draws together kinship and status, and how it is used to communicate personal and familial integrity, status, wealth, and well-being. Although acts of *yahgudang* can consist of words and/or deeds, my focus is the use of objects to express *yahgudang*. The ways *yahgudang* was enacted and performed with objects historically during times of death and mourning provide a means for understanding the presence of particular artefacts and practices within the repatriation process on Haida Gwaii. It is not my intent to conflate history with authenticity; rather, my goal is to situate the repatriation process within a cultural archive involving specific types of practices with artefacts and within broader patterns of object use and meaning making. Focusing on the importance of property and material culture in demonstrations of *yahgudang*, and especially within the repatriation process, brings to the fore the central roles of property and material culture in the creation of shared experiences and collective memory within Haida society.

What Is "Respect"?

"Respect" is a word much used within repatriation debates but rarely defined. There is an assumption that everyone shares an essential understanding of the word and thus can agree upon what actions constitute "respect" (Krmpotich et al. 2010, 279, 382n8; Vilaça 2005) and, conversely, what actions constitute "disrespect." Repatriation discussions stand to benefit from cross-cultural inquiry into the parameters, definitions, and nuances of "respect." This inquiry is poorly achieved through dictionaries alone. The Oxford English Dictionary[1] provides a range of meanings for the term "respect," many of which address its relational qualities. Respect happens between two or more entities, or is a function of how those entities are physically or ideationally positioned in relation to each other.

The most careful ethnographic analysis of *yahgudang* is Boelscher's *The Curtain Within* (1988). Her model illuminates the multiple meanings encompassed within this cultural value, including its intimate connection to social status and the obligations and expectations of lineage and moiety relationships. Having respect for one's self is identified by Haidas as the root of respect more generally. Without self-respect, people are unable to truly have respect for others. Blackman (1992, 141–2) describes this sense of respect as used by Florence Davidson:

> "Respect for self," a phrase that recurs in Florence's life history, represents a traditional behavioural ideal in Haida culture. The concept embodies proper speech, proper etiquette, proper behaviour, respectability, and self-assurance. It is a theme that not only weaves through Florence's life, but prefaces her account. Her concern for proper speech is indicated in her warning that she would not relate "what's no good." The admonition "respect yourself" was used on her by adults to elicit proper behaviour as she was growing up.

Fitness for respect is earned, and respect for others is shown in Haidas' interactions with other people, beings, and property when Haidas adhere to the expectations and obligations associated with their social rank and their position within a lineage.

Within Haida discourse, there is always the potential to acquire, lose, or regain *yahgudang*; it is never a fixed quality. Instead, a person's or lineage's *yahgudang(ang)* is continuously reinforced or compromised when their actions are either sanctioned or contested by the Haida public as constituting *yahgudang(ang)*. Evaluations of an individual can influence the reputation of a lineage and vice versa, while disparaging words directed towards a lineage can be used as a personal insult. Historically, *yahgudang* was most frequently associated with people of high class or *yahgid* (nobles), and it was the behaviours of high-class people that were the standard for measuring *yahgudang* (Boelscher 1988, 70–1). As the majority of Haida society occupied a social position within the *yahgid* sphere, with only a small proportion belonging to a "commoner" class and an even smaller proportion classified as "slaves" (Blackman 1992; Boelscher 1988; Murdock 1936; Suttles 1958), the behavioural protocols that made a person fit for respect represented, to a large degree, cultural norms and aspirations.

Abu-Lughod (1999, 166) proposes that "social and economic systems cannot reproduce themselves in a particular form without the actions of individuals, and individuals are guided by ideas, especially cultural notions of morality and virtue." Historic ethnographic material elaborates upon parents' desires to give potlatches in their children's honour to build their children's status and thus their fitness for respect (Blackman 1992; Boelscher 1988; Murdock 1936; Swanton 1905a). Through implicit and explicit teachings, lineage members also worked to ensure their kin were well prepared to represent them in more public spheres. Remembering her youth at the turn of the twentieth century, for example, Florence Davidson recalled the lessons and reprimands of her grandmother to speak sparingly lest she develop the unfavourable behaviour of talking all the time, to sit down while drinking water to demonstrate feminine behaviour (only men drank standing up), and to always have a presentable appearance in order to attract a husband (Blackman 1992, 91–4). Each of these traits was interpreted by her elder relatives as demonstrating respect for herself and respect for those around her. Florence also recalled her mother telling her "to respect yourself more than that" when she threatened to run away to avoid her arranged marriage (Blackman 1992, 96). Her mother warned her that neither complaining, self-pity, nor speaking harshly about her future husband reflected the status of their lineage and therefore the respect Florence was obligated to show herself, her family, and others.

Today, behaviours that are identified as demonstrating *yahgudang* continue to include generosity, cleverness, avoiding gossip or slander, dressing well and maintaining a tidy personal appearance (especially when travelling), heeding the advice of elder family members, observing rituals, and refraining from boasting. Bringing food to and visiting with elder relatives is frequently identified by Haidas as an act of *yahgudang*, as is offering prayers and food to deceased relatives. The ideal of respect is further manifested when people harvest only as much of a resource as they need, intentionally honing their skills so that they can extract resources with minimal impact and ensure future availability.

Generosity, especially towards family members, is a virtue relating to *yahgudang* that is strongly encouraged and favoured by Haidas. To be called "stingy" is an attack on one's character and is used as a way of chiding children. One woman showed her disapproval of her current lineage chief by commenting to friends, "Some chief he is – he's never brought me fish." In this sentiment, she was articulating the belief that people in positions of respect should act accordingly, that is, should be generous with their wealth. It continues to be inappropriate on Haida Gwaii to boast about one's wealth, though conversely it is inappropriate to admit to financial hardship. The former in particular can bring bad luck – specifically a loss of fortune – while the latter is unbecoming of *yahgid* behaviour. Instead, as Florence Davidson related in her memoirs and as Irene Mills said to me in conversation, when a person unselfishly and unabatedly shares their wealth with others, it is believed that that wealth will return to them in some way. Even in times of financial difficulty, people are willing to give generously of their money, resources, and time to help others, and do not consider it a "loss."

Today, as in the past, actions and sentiments intended to demonstrate *yahgudang* are frequently mediated by lineage and *k'waalaa* relationships. A young Haida woman explained to me that it was important always to offer your best foods or most finely crafted objects to members of the opposite *k'waalaa* to convey both your regard for them and your own wealth and abilities.

The reach of kinship into the ideology of *yahgudang* is visible in the metaphors used to instil a sense of respect for cedar. Historically, stands of cedar were the property of lineages. Western red (*ts'uu* in Haida) and yellow cedar (*sgaahlaan* or *sgahlaan*) trees provide wood for houses, canoes, poles, tools, masks and boxes, and fibre for mats, sails, baskets, clothing, and regalia. Cedar was and is instrumental in daily and ceremonial life and has aptly been called the tree of life (Stewart 1984; see also Turner 2004). Boelscher (1988, 22) draws attention to Haidas' referencing of cedar bark as "every woman's elder sister" (i.e., a close lineage member), elaborating that "women were the ones who prepared and wove cedar bark. Like an older sister, cedar bark deserved respect, helping her 'younger sister,' woman, by providing material for her clothing and her household gear." The metaphor of kinship is meaningful for Haidas, as it conjures the sense of reciprocity believed to adhere between cedar and humans; cedar provides resources for survival, and humans in turn contribute to the survival of cedar by offering prayers of thanks to cedar, harvesting bark without damaging the tree, and instilling these values and practices in each successive generation.

Another manifestation of the influence of kinship relations can be seen in Haidas' reluctance to talk about the history or experiences of another lineage, especially in any formal way. It is appropriate and respectful to speak directly only about one's own lineage. My understanding is that this aversion is related to the disapproval of gossip, though it may also be linked to the ownership of stories and people's care to abstain from narrating stories to which they have no rights. Many stories are like crests – the property of lineages. Lineages frequently maintain their own accounts of historic events, shaped by their perspectives and how the history continues to influence their lineage. The link between speech acts and *yahgudang* is so integral that Boelscher's *The Curtain Within* focuses on public discourse to analyse and understand the specificities of respect on Haida Gwaii.

One way this relationship can be conceived of is in terms of belonging. As Boelscher (1988, 29) argues, all things "belong" to either Eagles or Ravens, "in the double sense of being owned and being part of." This double sense of belonging applies equally to objects, resources, and people, including repatriated ancestors, who are both the responsibility of lineages and have a responsibility to contribute to the well-being of lineages. Likewise, *yahgudang* represents a reciprocal relationship between individuals and collectives. The dynamic of *yahgudang* is such that how well one's lineage (including people, resources, and property) and one's affines are taken care of is a reflection of one's self. People are taught therefore to respect the land, to respect elders, to respect their family, to conduct themselves in respectful ways, and to respect those with whom they are working.[2]

The combined influence of kinship and public evaluation in identifying a person's actions as *yahgudang* can be seen in the following memories shared with me during fieldwork. A friend remembered travelling by bus as a young boy to visit his sister on the mainland in the 1960s. His parents dressed him in a suit and ensured he was well groomed when he departed on his trip. After days of fun and play, the return trip home was, for him, an extension of his relaxed, personal holiday. But he remembered how appalled his parents were when he disembarked from the bus wearing casual clothes and looking dishevelled. In their minds, the return trip was a public outing and required a certain decorum. The attention shown by his parents reflects the desire among Haidas to be viewed (and for one's children to be viewed) as high class, having wealth and self-respect, in the eyes of others. In this case, it was not just the eyes of opposing lineages they sought to impress, but also the eyes of non-Haidas. Parallel stories were related to me on separate occasions by Lucy Bell and Candace Weir from the Haida Heritage and Repatriation Society. Both women recalled the advice they received from Claude Jones, a Massett elder, to always dress formally, either in regalia or tailored clothing, when they were travelling with the Haida Repatriation Committee. Seeing them as ambassadors for their families, their villages, and the Haida nation, Claude advised them to dress respectably as a demonstration of their respect for the people working in museums and their own selves. It can also be understood as a means of demonstrating the wealth and capabilities of themselves as individuals, of their families, and of the Haida nation as a whole.

Within the prescribed behaviours of *yahgudang* is a paradox. Haidas are encouraged to give freely of their wealth, to put the wishes of their elders before their own, and to put the well-being of their families before their own interests. And yet it is through these acts of selflessness that people come to be favoured, improve their social status, and gain wealth. One effect of this paradox is the layering of politics within all Haida actions. "Political" in this sense, however, needs to be understood as always related to the familial and the moral. *Yahgudang* thus needs to be understood as a mechanism for political action as well as for morality and cultural continuity: it is a politico-moral ideal. Therefore, through the use of *yahgudang* as an interpretive strategy, what we usually consider the "politics" of repatriation is transformed into a much more localized negotiation of identity and control. *Yahgudang* is not apolitical, but the dichotomy it privileges is not one of colonial/ colonized relations; it is one of lineage/non-lineage relations.

In the remainder of this chapter, I establish a precedent for the use of particular objects within the repatriation process by focusing on the power of objects to express *yahgudang* within and between lineages in various social situations, including times of grieving and mourning. It is not simply the presence of particular kinds of objects that indicates *yahgudang*, but rather how a person adheres to the traditions of ownership and display of tangible and intangible property that marks their fitness for respect and their respect for others. *Yahgudang*, then, is part of the creation and internalizing of a cultural archive on Haida Gwaii, linking contemporary performances to a longer tradition.

Rights, Responsibilities, Property, and Respect

The role of material culture and family property within social interactions is clearly expressed by Nika Collison, a curator and co-chair of the Skidegate Repatriation and Cultural Committee:

> While Haida art fulfils many roles, *it is [its] social function that is its truest responsibility.* Whether painted, carved, tattooed, woven or appliquéd, the "art of the clan" signifies lineage, rank and history through the depiction of crests and oral histories and through finely made objects. (N. Collison 2006, 59, emphasis added)

In giving art a social responsibility, Collison reminds us that Haida objects are more than museum objects or works of fine art to be gazed upon. The presentation, destruction by the owner, gifting, and creation of property can manifest competition, changing statuses, allegiances, rights and privileges, wealth, grief, and gratitude. Collison identifies the intrinsic role of objects in conducting acts of obligation, nurturance, reciprocity and, by implication, *yahgudang*. Objects can be documents of a lineage's status and wealth and symbols of a person's self-respect, respect for others, and respect for their ancestors' traditions. The combination of object and intentions in certain settings strengthens the place of *yahgudang* within the cultural archive.

Respect for traditional behaviours or a "pride in their identity as Indians" has not persisted unfailingly on Haida Gwaii. Throughout the nineteenth and twentieth centuries, various factors challenged the cultural institutions and traditions involved in displays of self-respect. The paucity of traditional Haida objects in the wake of ethnographic collectors (discussed in chapter 2) and the adoption of Christianity by many Haida created an environment where visages of supernaturals stopped being danced, where eulachon grease and herring roe were no longer served in large communal feast dishes, and where lineage and moiety histories and membership were less frequently expressed through material culture. Differences in status based on access to property were further dissipated by wage labour, which enabled people from every Haida social class to amass economic wealth. At first, new economic wealth was used to acquire symbolic wealth through potlatching, although later many of the forums and objects people used to express their regard for others and their pride in themselves, their lineages, and their traditions were reclassified as backward or immoral. The amount of property and wealth that could be given away (or destroyed) in the presence of witnesses, thus improving the status of the host and his/her lineage, was restrained by capitalist and Christian ethos (Blackman 1973, 52). The potlatch ban coupled with the surveillance of missionaries and Indian agents during the first half of the twentieth century further meant Haida ceremonies surrounding life events – births, deaths, namings, headstone movings, marriages, adoptions – were conducted in private more often than public. A lack of collective spaces for enacting – and thus remembering – the principles of *yahgudang* can threaten the continuity, or lead to the invalidation, of *yahgudang* as a central Haida philosophy, particularly as public evaluation is a critical component of determining *yahgudang*.

It is difficult to determine with certainty the influence these changes had on the underlying values of property use. Blackman (1973) and Boelscher (1988) both argue that the result has been a tendency towards continuity of function even where external forms may have changed (see also Thomas 1997). During the twentieth century, for example, there was a rise in the use of silver and gold jewellery carved with crest designs among Haidas at the same time as these objects entered the tourist art market. The use of bracelets to display lineage crests was in many ways an adaptation to the cultural values of the Church and Indian agents, who saw precious metals as acceptable forms of adornment (silver dollars and gold coins provided ample metal to hammer and carve a bracelet) and jewellery making for the tourist industry as an acceptable means of earning a living (an example is provided in Raibmon 2006). Blackman (1973) also documents Haidas' adoption of gravestones to carry out the functions of memorial poles and grave posts. Costing even more than carved cedar grave posts, tombstones were highly effective status symbols and historic records of individual and lineage identities, having been carved with names and crests, raised through status-affirming potlatches, and demarcating lineage spaces within village cemeteries. My experiences on Haida Gwaii suggest that the importance of tangible and intangible property to denote identity, belonging, and respect for others has surpassed the use of objects to denote status and personal fitness for respect. However, there is a growing industry of raven's tail weaving, regarded as high-class weaving, suggesting that the use of objects as markers of status and fitness for respect may very well return to prominence in the near future.

The objects of greatest concern to Haidas and that can be maximally used to express *yahgudang* and status are those that fall within the Haida idea of "property." Traditional Haida concepts of property are founded upon receiving or achieving sets of rights.[3] Haidas distinguish between individually owned property and lineage-owned property. The former includes cars, clothing, household appliances, tools, personal effects, fishing boats, and the like. This category of property seems to be grounded in the object itself, which may be alienated from or by the owner. The Haida language contains specific pronouns to indicate whether something is alienable or inalienable:[4] the pronoun *nang* distinguishes alienable property, while pronouns such as *dii* (my) denote inalienable property. All of one's family members are referred to using the latter pronoun, for example, as are lineage crests and body parts. Alienable wealth is secondary in value or importance. The primary source of Haida prestige stems from having access to lineage-owned property.

MacDonald (1983, 5) defines Haida wealth as involving the "right of access to both natural and supernatural resources," with these rights ultimately stemming from one's lineage and being exercized through the chief. MacDonald notes that all lineages have "a founding ancestor and an accumulated history which [is] the basis for claiming these rights and privileges. Linking the lineage with the ancestral and supernatural sources of power [are] the songs, dances, crests for use in carving, and names belonging to the lineage" (1983, 5). For example, Swanton noted two supernatural sisters, "The-Singers," who live in the sky and on the land, as a source for songs used and owned by people:

> An old Kloo man said that his uncle saw The-Singers coming through the air in a canoe, and learned three songs from them. If it were bad weather, he would go out and sing them, when it would become fair. When a man had died and food was to be sent to him through the fire, the song-leader went off in a canoe, took medicine, and got a new song from The-Singers. All songs used by human beings were acquired from them; and they, in their turn, acquired them from the notes of birds, which are really songs, and which The-Singers can understand. (Swanton 1905a, 31)

This story describes *how* property came to be possessed by persons and lineages, but the meaning of ownership and its role in demonstrating respect is not made clear. The significance of ownership is raised by Meuli (2001, 192), who characterizes ownership as the "outer layer" or "outer skin" of an object. He proposes that ownership conditions our encounters with objects – affects *how* we see an object – and therefore it colours all of our other responses to the object, even as we work our way through the many other layers of meaning. In chapter 2 I conveyed Vince Collison's frustration that the people of Chicago seemed to forget that the Haida poles in the Field Museum belonged to Haidas; he was surprised at the amount of ownership they took over the poles. For Vince, the removal of the poles to the American Midwest could not erase their inalienable ties to Haida lineages.

Within Haida society, highly valued property is, de facto, property with ties to a lineage or kin: its value is determined by kinship relations. While this is significant in its own right, it also emphasizes how ownership of artefacts by museums can impede or problematize the nature of Haidas' relationships to these objects. Lineage property is only rarely alienated: it is as much a symbol of lineage identity as it is the substance that allows a lineage to claim and express *yahgudang*. Likewise, museums rarely occupy a social position that would, according to Haida cultural protocol, sanction them to be the possessors, caretakers, or handlers of lineage property – including bodies.

Haidas' concern that ownership be respected is evident within Haida myths and oral histories. Breaches of the rights to and privileges involving property as determined by lineage membership appear in Job Moody's telling of the history of Jiigwah town, *jiigwah 'llnagaay*, a story that remains popular to this day (Enrico 1995, 160–8). A canoe steersman, *qing gaaying*, was party to a noose-fishing excursion for trout. *Qing gaaying* was wearing a hat with a cormorant crest on it, and each time he lowered his fishing pole into the pool, the hat would fall off his head and into the water. Moody explains within the story, "He wore a cormorant hat although he was a Raven. That's why it kept falling in the water" (Enrico 1995, 161). That the steersman cannot keep the hat on his head shows the impropriety of wearing another lineage's crest; the supernatural woman in the creek reminds him of this by causing the hat to repeatedly fall off and land in the water.

Ownership on Haida Gwaii is not static or atemporal. Rather, rights and property are susceptible to being acquired, shared, lost, and stolen, as the history of property on Haida Gwaii attests. The opposing lineage histories that debate the chieftaincy of 7iidagnsaa at the village of Kiusta capture the importance of lineage ownership (in this case, of a village), the effects of circumventing the system of ownership and inheritance, and the implications for a person's being recognized as *yahgudang*. The contested histories were recorded by Boelscher in the late 1970s, over one hundred years after the original event took place, attesting to the ongoing importance of these concepts.[5] The story is also an effective means of demonstrating that current actions frequently have a history – and a politics – and it is a skilful Haida who can knowingly navigate such histories and politics in appeasing ways. To be able to do so is a sign of *yahgudang*.

Within this history, the K'aawas Eagle lineage tells of the ownership of the village by themselves, and its leadership by one of their own, 7ihldiinii. 7ihldiinii was presumed lost at sea when he did not return from a fishing trip. There was a dearth of legitimate males to be chief in his place, so a woman became acting chief. Upon 7iidangsaa's arrival to claim the village as his own, the townspeople made him wait in his canoe while they discussed the situation. The woman, 7ilskandwaas, recommended 7iidangsaa be allowed to land and to live only at the end of the village, "a symbolic denial of 7iidangsaa's claim to chiefship," as chiefs' houses were historically located in the centre of villages. The K'aawas further stress that the townspeople only decided to "let him stay ... they didn't *give* him the village" (Boelscher 1988, 41–2).

7iidangsaa often narrated his own history of becoming chief of Kiusta, particularly to newly arrived white settlers. During Boelscher's field-work (1979–81), the reputation of 7iidangsaa continued to be affected by the historic ill-regard in which various lineages held his actions:

> 7iidangsaa's ambitiousness and entrepreneurship, the fact that he ac-quired and displayed wealth in the external world without securing the approval and support of his lineage-mates alienated him from his own peers. While his overt display of wealth and power was admired by White prospectors and traders, it contradicted Haida norms of chiefly behaviour, namely yahguudaang, or "fitness for respect." (Boelscher 1988, 43)

The variable respect associated with this name demonstrates the fluidity of *yahgudang*: the actions of the historic 7iidangsaa appear to be largely overshadowed by the positively received actions of his suc-cessors. The current 7idansuu (as the name is also spelled) is Jim Hart, who inherited the name from his mother's brother Morris White in 1999.[6] An internationally acclaimed artist, Hart's reputation is posi-tive in his hometown of Massett. People approved of his potlatching, that he had raised poles, and that despite having a home in southern British Columbia, he travelled home to Haida Gwaii often. An elder in Skidegate also confided that 7idansuu looked like a proper chief, par-ticularly when dressed in his button blanket: his posture, poise and manner of speaking, she believed, were becoming of his title. People's evaluations of his comportment and his actions testify to 7idansuu's own fitness for respect, but they also attest to Haidas' ongoing concern with the ideals of *yahgudang*.

These examples depict the environment in which status-laden tangi-ble and intangible property on Haida Gwaii has been exchanged, per-formed, and evaluated through time. On Haida Gwaii, highly valued property is acquired either through unique encounters with supernatu-rals or through the potlatch. Histories are essential in the creation of value and status, and the property gained in these arenas influences a person's/lineage's social standing thereafter. Symbolic wealth enables participation in these exchanges and is the outcome of these exchanges.

Symbolic wealth is also used as evidence of and justification for *yahgu-dang*. Potlatches serve as opportunities to display the objects consti-tuting or symbolizing a lineage's wealth and history (coppers, masks, regalia, and even houses and poles) with the intent of impressing others and thereby reinforcing – if not improving – social standing. Potlatches provide idealized spaces for hosts and guests to perform rights, status, and *yahgudang* through their behaviours. The manner in which people are invited, whether or not invitees attend, how they eat, what they wear, the order in which they are served, the order in which they are invited to speak, where they are seated, the kinds of goods that are given away in payment for services and witnessing all attest to hosts' and guests' *yahgudangang*.

The concern with life histories and memories as expressed by Paul Connerton (1989) brings us closer to comprehending what it is about a history of transactions that makes objects – or, I would argue, repatri-ated remains – suitable as means of communicating respect for self and others. Connerton articulates clearly how it is that objects can function as symbolic and social capital:

> Objects of symbolic, as distinct from financial, capital are as it were locked into the whole life history, and therefore the memories, of those who pos-sess them. For part of the point of what is possessed is precisely that it cannot be managed by leading a life independently of the specific de-mands of what is possessed. And part of the point of what is possessed is that it is not independent of the past context in which it was acquired. Objects attesting to nobility must be objects which cannot be acquired ei-ther by proxy or in haste. (Connerton 1989, 87)

Within Haida society, it is the history and relationships an object has shared with other beings, whether supernatural or human, that trans-form them into tools for expressing and inspiring respect. The history of transactions on Haida Gwaii is simultaneously histories of family, and reciprocally, histories of self.

Objects that have been part of a lineage's history for many years not only accumulate social capital, they also inspire feelings of respect and pride. Conversely, recently made objects marked with lineage crests can evoke a sense of history and the concomitant feelings of *yahgudang*. In addition to people feeling a sense of *yahgudang* from the property of their own lineage, the emphasis of *yahgudang* on respecting traditions has carried over to a broader sense of pride. As Lucy Bell commented,

"I always felt better after working on a blanket for the ancestors. Or working on [cedar] flowers with the *naaniis*... just that feeling of pride, from working on that. That always helps when you've got problems." The blankets are symbols of respect stemming from an adherence to tradition and family-orientated objects, while the making of cedar roses with elder women is an act that demonstrates respect for the women, who are themselves symbols of history, tradition, and matrilineality.

The power of Haida objects to arouse feelings of respect is evident in their correlative power to demonstrate disrespect or a lack of *yahgudang*. Button blankets, for example, can be worn inside out as a visual and highly public display that the wearer disapproves of the actions of a potlatch's host.[7] Disapproval of a host can also be shown by refusing a gift offered at a potlatch, while guests may feel slighted by their host if they are not given enough food (or the proper kinds of food) to eat (see also Boelscher 1988; Jonaitis 2006; Murdock 1936). During my field-work, potlatch hosts faced retrospective criticism from their guests if their events were seen to be too lavish, especially if the intent of the potlatch or feast was to honour someone else, in which case the host was suspected of improving his or her own position rather than focusing on the honouree. Alternatively, in the story related above of the controversy surrounding 7iidansaa's claim to the chieftancy of Kiusta, the head female in the village shows her disfavour towards 7iidansaaa when she relegates him to a house at the end of the village, an object/space lacking rank and an improbable location for the house of a chief (Boelscher 1988, 78–9).

As much as there is a political component to potlatching, the political success of a potlatch relies on the host's power to affect people at an emotional and sensory level. A parallel phenomenon is described cogently by Marilyn Strathern (1999a) as she examines the ability of specific kinds of artefacts to make physical and affective the notions of ownership, entitlement, and obligation. Strathern reflects upon the significance of Hagen social activities for herself as a cultural analyst and for Hageners as social actors. She emphasizes the process of reification whereby the meaning of giving gifts – and indeed of giving a particular gift to a particular person – becomes embedded in the object that is the gift:

> What I reify here is of course an understanding about sociality, and specifically about a rather particular, and particularly gendered, set of social relations. *What I see in the gesture I then see over again in the wealth items themselves.* These gifts had a further compelling effect on this ethnographer for

the reason that they seemed to compel responses from people who saw them. They were generally handed over in a public context to critical and judgemental recipients before a critical and judgemental audience. The scrutiny of form drove home the fact that, *ipso facto*, a form can only appear with its appropriate properties – or else it has not appeared. A return gift is not a return gift if the items are too few or poor; prestige does not emerge from a display if the display fails. (Strathern 1999a, 15, emphasis in original)

At a more mundane level, the everyday use of lineage crests by Haidas is an omnipresent and visceral statement about identity, entitlement, and *yahgudang*. Crests have come to be symbols of history, perseverance, and appropriate Haida behaviour as well as symbols of rights and identities. Hence, it is fitting and important that the repatriated ancestors be identified through the use of crests. When used appropriately, crests articulate continuity, belonging, and a respect for lineages, their members, and their property. In this light, it is unsurprising that Haidas identify crested objects such as button blankets as being especially powerful vehicles for expressing respect for one's self and others (figure 5.1).

Given the history of button blankets and their absence from public displays of *yahgudang* for over half a century, the wearing of button blankets for any occasion is an important display of pride and respect for Haida cultural values and practices. This respect for cultural protocol and ideals is at the heart of *yahgudang*. In conversation with me, blanket-maker Joyce Bennett related how the wearing of regalia on occasions of death or mourning is a statement of respect irrespective of lineage or *k'waalaa* ties.

JOYCE: I found the most dramatic place to see button blankets is at a funeral. Or headstone moving.

CARA: Why is that?

JOYCE: Because it just shows – I think for a person that died, it just shows so much respect I think. To me, anyways, that's what I feel. And when you wear it – like I remember, we've done so many headstone moving feasts in our family – I remember my *naanii*'s, my uncle's. And because more and more people are making them, more and more people can wear them. When they come out full force, especially when there's a funeral if the family requests everybody wear regalia, it's really, really beautiful. Like remember when we went to –

Figure 5.1 A Haida high school student receiving a button blanket during a ceremony in Old Massett to honour primary, secondary, and post-secondary graduates, 2005.

CARA: Chief Cumshewa?

JOYCE: Chief Cumshewa's funeral, and everybody was in regalia. Didn't it look beautiful? Everybody walking to the cemetery, and it was such a cold, cold day, but people still walked and it was beautiful. Everybody that had a button blanket or a vest wore it and it's out of respect for that person. It's the same thing at the headstone moving feast: the walk to the cemetery is so beautiful when everybody is wearing their button blankets. Even to make your button blanket with plastic buttons, it just has – your blanket just comes to life – it doesn't matter what kind of buttons you have on. It just shimmers, when you walk, or when the sun hits it, or in the snow. (2 April 2006)

There is no single reason button blankets connote respect. Joyce's comments refer to their aesthetic qualities, but worn or aged button blankets will still be received as a demonstration of respect for the deceased and his/her family. Often older blankets are inherited and are direct material examples of lineage continuity and belonging. As crests are the focal point of blankets, the qualities ascribed to displaying one's crest can be ascribed to blankets. A blanket identifies its wearer as belonging to a lineage, and thus a *k'waalaa*. In so doing, it immediately places the wearer in a relationship with the deceased and the deceased's family. The wearing of a blanket is a commentary on this relationship between self and other. If the other is from a different lineage, then the practice of using one's best to indicate that the other person is valued holds; if they are from the same lineage, then the wearing of a blanket attests to the status and cohesion of the lineage. As the deceased's reputation is dependent on that of his or her lineage, what the lineage does on the occasion of an individual's death affects both how the individual will be remembered and how the lineage will be perceived. The more completely a lineage fulfils the social expectations surrounding death, grieving, and mourning, the higher the esteem in which they will be held by others. During the rites surrounding death – funerals and End of Mourning or headstone moving feasts – the expectations of the deceased's lineage and lineages of the opposite *k'waalaa* are brought to the fore, as are Haida notions of respect.

Death, Mourning, Obligation, and *Yahgudang*

In his treatment of historic Tlingit mortuary potlatches, Kan (2004) emphasizes the roles of the deceased's matrilineage and patrilineage (i.e., opposite moiety) in providing "love and respect" for the deceased and his or her matrilineage. He explains that the matrilineage's use of regalia with crests or lineage property such as songs and names during times of mourning emphasized their unity, erasing individual distinctions of rank, gender, or age and reinforcing the connection of the living to the deceased who shared in the same prerogatives (2004, 287). The patrilineage, in contrast, showed "love and respect" through various means such as attending to the polluting parts of the body, feeding the grieving matrilineage, and offering words of condolence and remembrance of the deceased. He argues that even those components of memorial potlatches that represent competition between moieties and within lineages – the inheritance of the deceased's regalia and intangible property, the donation of money and gifts to be redistributed to guests, the seating of guests in particular locations – can be connected to the idea of extending love and respect, as these actions emulate the traditions and values of people's ancestors (Kan 2004, 291).

The link between competition, emulation, and love and respect helps to clarify the dual role of *yahgudang* as it is expressed through the use of property at Haida funerals and headstone moving feasts – instrinsic events within a Haida cultural archive. As Kan points out, competition is present within certain elements of Tlingit memorial potlatches as hosts work to honour (if not bolster) the reputation of the deceased, and as they locate themselves in relation to the deceased and to each other through their contributions to the feast or the payment they receive at the feast. But Kan brings up two important factors. First, he argues that the competition of memorial potlatches needs to be read within the parameters of love and respect in Tlingit society or, I would argue, within the context of *yahgudang* in Haida society. This corelates with the second factor, which is that although exchanges occurring as part of death rites symbolize and negotiate power and status, people engaged in these exchanges *feel* emotions as part of this experience (Kan 2004, 298). The cultural archive, then, is not so much about the exchanging of goods as the shared experiences of performing and using objects in particular ways and with specific intentions.

Similar to Strathern, Kan attributes both the competitive and the affective power of these exchanges to "wearing the regalia of their ancestors, performing their songs and dances, and giving and consuming objects created through hard work" (2004, 298). The result is an internalization of "fundamental cultural values as personally held orientations" (2004, 298) and the continuity of social relationships between the living and the deceased, and by extension the maintenance of a cultural archive. The experiences of feeling love, joy, and grief influence Haidas' sense of having power or status in the future by reaffirming their sense of individual and lineage well-being and performing the unity, functionality, and capabilities of themselves and their lineage.

As with the practices of the Tlingit described by Kan, Haida funerals and headstone movings all feature performances and exchanges using tangible and intangible resources that reflect, respect, and produce relationships between the living and the deceased and between lineages and *k'waalaa*. Swanton, writing on Skidegate pre-Christian burial rites, details the responsibility and obligation of the deceased's matrilineage and his or her opposing *k'waalaa* to perform rites/rights such as singing songs, dancing, or remarrying. He describes the use of particular garments, objects, and actions to demarcate the rank of the deceased or the emotional state of the deceased's relatives. Although Swanton is reporting practices from more than a century ago, the detail of the account and the values conveyed by that detail make it worth quoting at length:

At Skidegate, after a man died, his body was set up on a box in the rear of the house, his face painted, and a dancing-hat placed upon his head. Then his friends[8] came in and passed by, and, if he were a chief, they sang a crying-song, the men in this case joining with the women. Before singing for the dead, the song-leader went off in his canoe, gathered medicine, and procured a new song from The-Singers. After his return, the friends of the deceased called together all of the same clan, and they danced in one house. When it was over, all of the dancers received tobacco. Those of the opposite clan then came in and smoked, after which each of his friends cut off a corner of his piece of tobacco and put it into the fire, when it went to the Land of Souls. A "crying-fire" was built as follows: Ordinarily one end of each fire-stick was laid upon a row of stones so that they sloped towards the door, but now the stones were moved over so that the sticks sloped inward. After the body had "sat up" from four to six days, they put it into the grave-box. If he were a chief, they wrapped his body in a dancing-blanket. His near relatives and friends cut their hair close to the head and put pitch on their faces. When a great chief died, the whole town sometimes did this. These signs of mourning were called *xA'ndawa*, which is the modern phrase "as well." The body, enclosed in the grave-box, was then carried out through a hole (made for the purpose) in one side of the house to the grave-house. There it remained, at least until a council had been called, the successor determined upon, and a potlatch made to raise the grave-post, after which it was removed, and placed in the latter. If a simple memorial column were raised, the body remained in the grave-house. The latter, however, was itself sometimes put up at this time. Occasionally it approached in size the habitations of the living, and had a small house-pole in front of it. Afterwards, in either case, the grave-boxes containing his friends were usually added. No persons of different clans could lie together. For about ten days his wife fasted, sometimes abstaining from food absolutely. She treated herself like a slave, and used a stone for a pillow when she slept. Every day for ten days she took a bath and put the water away in a safe place. During the same time she did not wash her face, but only her fingers, before eating. When she first broke her fast, she called in several children of the opposite clan to eat with her. This feast was called "causing one's self to marry." The object of it was that she might marry some one next time who had still more property, and that she herself and her new husband might have long lives and be lucky. (Swanton 1905a, 52)

During my fieldwork, Haida elaborated upon the expectations of each *k'waalaa* following a death. Members of the opposite *k'waalaa* from the deceased were expected to prepare and dress the deceased and stay with the body to prevent any harm from malevolent spirits, and to prepare the funeral dinner or tea to ensure that the deceased's own lineage members were free to grieve and console each other, unencumbered by the demands of hosting a funeral. Blackman (1973) clarifies that the reciprocal relationship expressed during times of death is, more specifically, between the lineage of the deceased and the lineage of the deceased's father (normally belonging to the opposite *k'waalaa*). The lineage or other family members of the opposite clan of the deceased may choose to commission a memorial pole from a carver of the opposite *k'waalaa* of the deceased. When members of the opposite *k'waalaa* meet these expectations, they are recognized with gifts of money or goods. Friends from either *k'waalaa* often bring food to the home of the deceased's family while family and friends provide hours of continuous companionship so as not to leave mourners by themselves.

These actions are particularly poignant in the context of repatriation, as they elaborate upon the roles of kinship, objects, and performance in responding to death and enacting mourning, and to the idea of respect in relation to death and mourning. How well the deceased's lineage and the deceased's father's lineage (i.e., of the opposite *k'waalaa*) carry out the obligations of hosting a funeral and headstone moving, or fulfil the social expectations associated with grieving and mourning, reflects the degree of their respect for the deceased as well as their own fitness for respect. This is not to say peoples' responses to death are mechanical or calculated. People are deeply affected by the loss of family members and friends, and they are deeply affected by their ability – or inability – to honour someone upon their death. Lineages will save money and resources for years in order to host a headstone moving befitting of the love and regard they had for the deceased. The closeness of this relationship is evident in a passage from Swanton describing historic Haida interments. The bodies of high-ranking people could be both protected and near by placing them in grave houses or in cavities atop memorial poles, while other bodies were protected by bringing the bones into the home:

> In olden times the bodies of those who died far from home were burned, and the bones alone brought back. In either case [those who died away from home, or deceased people of lower rank] the bones were brought into the house and kept where they would be safe. The living liked to have them around. (Swanton 1905a, 54)

It is unclear from Swanton's account how long the bones would be kept in the house. His documentation of the use of grave posts and grave houses by high-ranking lineages, and even of the use of grave boxes buried under leaves behind the homes of lower-ranking lineages, suggests that the bones were not permanently kept within the home. The matter of proximity remains significant, however, as it resurfaces in multiple ways within the history and process of repatriation. As noted in chapter 3, the repatriated remains were reburied within the villages of Old Massett and Skidegate rather than in the infrequently visited village sites from which they were collected in order to protect them from being disinterred again by collectors. The distance of the remains from Haida Gwaii after they were collected was also identified as the cause of the ancestors' distress. Yet some people feared proximity with these remains. The disinterment of these bodies, their unusual experience of being kept off-island without ongoing care and respect, and the uncertainty over whether they had ever been properly mourned and feasted led some Haidas to feel that the remains were susceptible to malevolent spirits, and people feared the negative consequences of handling them and bringing them back into the village. My understanding is that when families have had the chance to grieve their loss and feast the deceased such that the deceased experience relief and are free to join the Land of the Souls, the proximity of the bodies poses less threat or concern for people. In contrast, people remembered their grandparents' unease about and avoidance of the abandoned village sites because of the bodies of smallpox victims that lay unburied there.

The emotional impetus, stemming from *yahgudang*, to provide lasting care for the deceased is a critical element of the emotional distress caused by the collection of Haida ancestral remains. The secret removal of remains to museum storerooms stands in stark contrast to the ensemble of social and public activities and ongoing interactions with the deceased described by Swanton and witnessed by myself during fieldwork. Indeed, after the insult of having ancestral remains removed, Haidas felt a second wave of disrespect when they learned how the bodies were kept within museum storerooms. The general Haida population do not share the museum community's scientific appreciation for the remains as specimens (see also Dumont 2003; Gulliford 1992; Peers 2004; Pullar 1994). Haidas expressed frustration that the advancement of scientific knowledge was claimed as a justification for retaining human remains when, to the best of their knowledge, very few studies were conducted and still fewer results published or used for the benefit of their villages. Curators, archaeologists, and physical anthropologists have implemented measures to preserve human remains, such as climate-controlled environments or limiting access to bona fide researchers, which reflect a respect for data and the potential for future research to enhance knowledge of health issues, population movements, and land use – all of which are of interest to aboriginal communities. Yet, for many indigenous people such demonstrations of respect fail to recognize indigenous perspectives in which the dead are not entirely dead; they continue to interact with and exert an influence on the living and the world. For various peoples, the dead continue to be social actors and require the same degree of attentiveness and respect as the living. Aboriginal scholars and commentators have observed that the dismissal of this world view replicates the racist sentiments within which the remains were collected in the first place, and directs this racism equally towards the living and the dead (Thornton 2002; see also Hill 2001).

Pearle Pearson, a member of the SRCC, when asked how she would explain the importance of repatriation, responded:

> I'd tell them that I'd want my grandfather – great-great-great-grandfather to come home where he belongs. Not stuck in a drawer somewhere. That's where they were – they were in drawers. Just crammed in drawers. Because the Haidas believe in respect for the dead. They have to be buried properly. (1 May 2006)

Remembering when they returned with their ancestors' remains from the Chicago Field Museum, Pearle reflected, "When we landed in Sandspit, when they [the ancestors' remains] came off, it was quiet. Everyone was quiet. There were all people waiting for us. Silence. A lot of respect. Box after box after box. There were a lot." To a degree, the physical movement of the ancestral remains from museums to Haida Gwaii relocated Haida ancestors from a place of neglect to a place of respect. But Haidas indicated to me that the dearth of respect shown their ancestors over the years required additional acts of respect in compensation, such as offerings of food, the wearing and bestowing of regalia, and the use of cedar materials to wrap and cushion the remains in transit.

Within museum collections, and without material or ceremonial signifiers, the social identity of ancestors as deceased, honoured kin was concealed. Incomplete or unelaborated museum records also suppressed the individual and familial identities of the remains held within their facilities. Nevertheless, within the parameters of repatriation it was still possible for Haidas to identify with the deceased as ancestors belonging to both *k'waalaa*. The bentwood boxes made for repatriation were decorated with crests from every lineage, while the designs used for the blankets resonate with Haida village and national emblems that contain both Eagle and Raven elements. Diverging from the usual practice of segregating roles and responsibilities along *k'waalaa* lines, caring for the remains became a shared responsibility among people from both *k'waalaa*, as everyone needed to simultaneously attend to their own *k'waalaa* ancestors and the ancestors of the opposite *k'waalaa*. Describing repatriation as a "community" effort, then, is effective only insomuch as the Haida community is imagined as being the sum of two *k'waalaa*.

At times of death, demonstrations of respect are not limited by *k'waalaa* or lineage affiliation, but rather are guided by the social roles of moiety interdependence. It is the adaptation of these social roles that enables Haidas to most closely adhere to the traditions of their ancestors, and thus respect those ancestors. In this light, it is also possible to imagine the repatriation committees as a corporate group acting as an opposite *k'waalaa* to their villages, doing the work so others may be free to mourn. In carrying out the various aspects of the repatriation process, the committees were engaged in the kinds of behaviour bereaved families normally engage in to convey *yahgudangang* to their ancestors.

The SRCC extended this role even further when they hosted an End of Mourning feast in June 2005, described at the outset of this volume, to mark the return of all known Haida remains from within North America. Little distinguished this event from the other End of Mourning feasts I attended during the course of my fieldwork. The collectivized End of Mourning to honour the repatriated ancestors contained all the elements that make this kind of ceremony successful in commemorating the deceased, relieving grief and, most importantly, allowing the spirits of these ancestors to rest peacefully "on the other side" while the work of bringing home other ancestors continued. People offered food and prayers, danced and subsequently burnt spirit masks, sang the spirit song, made speeches, and gifted witnesses. SRCC members recalled that it was Rose Russ who recommended each lineage in Skidegate take on one task for the day to help relieve the burden of the SRCC and to showcase their abilities to work as lineages. Although the Old Massett committee attended the End of Mourning in Skidegate, they have refrained from hosting a similar feast of their own due to the continued presence of ancestral remains in European museums and potentially elsewhere. Both scenarios demonstrate the tendency for lineages to be units of action, and the appropriateness of doing so. With their actions, the repatriation committees mimicked the fitting – read respectful – conduct of lineages, whether in choosing to host an End of Mourning feast or to address the ongoing dishonour felt by families by not ceasing the period of public mourning. Although the repatriation committees take on the responsibilities of every lineage when they travel off-island to bring home their ancestors, the choices I have just described suggest that lineages are not willing to relinquish their autonomy or responsibilities to "the community" or the nation. This could be interpreted as an indication that Haida are seeking to re-assume their lineage responsibilities, to re-establish their lineage autonomy from an external body – be it the Department of Indian Affairs, the Canadian nation, or the Haida nation.

Conclusion

Haida protocol instructs Haidas on the appropriate uses of objects and property, and as a result is a means of learning ways to show respect (or disrespect) through one's use of objects, whether it be wearing regalia, respecting clan and lineage ownership of property, or adhering to norms of personal deprivation or indulgence. In this chapter, I sought to connect the material culture of repatriation with a cultural archive centred on object use on Haida Gwaii, particularly as these both relate to the notion of *yahgudang*. Critically, the politico-moral lens of *yahgudang* allows us to better understand the values underlying repatriation and the processes of meaning making on Haida Gwaii. In the next chapter, I consider the mnemonic potential of objects on Haida Gwaii in order to emphasize how the physical work of repatriation contributes to another quality of lineageship: the creation of opportunities for shared experiences and thus the development of shared or collective memory.

6 Haida Structures of History and Remembering

I am sitting at Mary Swanson's kitchen table in January 2006. The table is the first thing you encounter upon entering Mary's home. Beyond it, a sofa is positioned beneath a large picture window affording views of Masset Inlet. Hudson's Bay tea was keeping warm in a large pot on the stove, and her grandson Ernie's argillite carving tools were spread across the kitchen table. Mary left her recliner to sit with me and Ernie at the table. I was there to speak with Mary about her involvement with the Haida Heritage and Repatriation Society, and Ernie was glad to join us to learn more from his *naanii* and to contribute to the conversation. At one point, he was trying to remember a particular relation's lineage, providing information to his *naanii* and hoping for clarification. Her response, not uncommon for people of her generation, was, "I really can't say on that." Ernie translated for me, saying, "Naanii don't care for that – me talking about it," to which Mary clarified:

> MARY: No, I really don't know. Because I don't live over there [Skidegate].
> Like you see, all I want to know is our family, what we're doing. I can't
> make it my business in Eagle clan, because it's not my business to do that.
> ERNIE: And I should be looking on my maternal side anyways.
> MARY: Everything needs to be done within the family. You can't interfere
> with Eagles, the Ravens [Mary and Ernie's *k'waalaa*] can't. That's like
> what I was telling Cara [earlier in the interview]. See, Leona lost two
> cousins and her aunts on the opposite clan are supposed to be there
> for them, looking after her and her family. And then everything settled
> down, then they pay them because they're there for them and helping.
> That's how it used to be, now today it doesn't happen. Everyone's just so
> helpful to each other. We're trying to get back to protocol, but it doesn't
> seem to be happening. (13 January 2006)

That same afternoon, I asked Mary who made the silver bracelet she was wearing. I had admired it on several occasions (I have never seen Mary without it), appreciating how "deep" the carving is, the design being rendered ever more visible from the black tarnishing that develops in the engraved lines over time. Mary told me the bracelet was carved by a member of the York family. She moved from the surname to the store it was purchased from in Prince Rupert on the mainland of British Columbia. She never provided the name of the store, but mentioned the store owner's first name, and likewise the store owner had called Mary by name, drawing her attention to the bracelet in question. Mary had made purchases at the store before: she had bought a gold bracelet for her daughter upon her graduation, and was wearing another bracelet from the store as well as the one I had admired. Mary's account then moved back to the Yorks, remembering the carver's father's name, before settling on the name of the carver himself. She was disappointed that she could not remember the carver's Haida name, nor his nickname. She remembered the price of the bracelet as well as her initial decision not to purchase it – but then she had noticed it had two of her crests (wolf and moon) carved on it, which drew her back to the bracelet. She spoke of a desire for a gold bracelet of the same width, before remembering her mother purchasing gold bracelets from Bill Reid at a very good price for Mary and her sister, although her sister's was stolen. Finally, she returned to the crests, telling me, "Our wolf came from Alaska. Our grandfather was Raven, so he had wolf, so we got to have that. But our grandmother had Lady in the Moon, carved on her – or tattooed on her wrist. My daughter Crystal has that same name, *Kuun Jaadaas*."

Bracelets are worn by Haida women on a daily basis,[1] though bangles are also worn. Bracelets are fashioned from silver, gold, and copper, of widths of one-quarter inch to two inches. Usually they lie against the arm just above the wrist. Most are incomplete ovals – formed into a C-shape allowing a gap to slide the bracelet on or off. A smaller number are hinged with a clasp. As works of Haida art, bracelets are admired for the depth of the engraving, the skill of the artist in executing tight cross-hatching and parallel lines, and the aesthetic appeal of the design itself (figure 6.1). As personal objects, bracelets are appreciated when they feature one's crest, are a first attempt at carving by a family member, were made by a relative or friend now deceased, recall a particular event (like a graduation or birth of a child), were received as a gift, or are fine works of art. As with other types of jewellery, some women will have special bracelets they wear when dressed in regalia or formal

Figure 6.1 Two bracelets admired and photographed by Ruth Gladstone-Davies, SRCC, during a 2009 research visit to the British Museum. Left: AM 1981,12.2. *Right*: AM 1981,12.1.

attire for a special function, while others wear their "best" bracelets every day. It is not uncommon for women to wear more than one bracelet (see also Blackman 2011, 52–3).

Bracelets can be read within a structure of colonialism (Edwards et al. 2006; Gosden and Knowles 2001). Missionaries and Indian agents actively discouraged enactments of Haida culture, confiscating dance masks, rattles, and regalia and preaching against the practice of painting one's face with lineage-owned designs or tattooing one's body with crest designs. In contrast, they allowed and encouraged the making of bracelets carved with crest designs, made of precious metals and containing a value within the colonial economic structure as commodities and as a means of providing a livelihood.[2] Bracelets became objects of familial identity for Haidas themselves (see also Bunn-Marcuse 2011) and by extension objects of cultural continuity – some might even say survival. Given the relatively recent production of bracelets, it is more apt to say that it is not so much the bracelet as an object but the crest as an identity that has continued or survived.

Such an interpretation, however, was rarely the focus of women's narratives about their jewellery. Fundamental to each bracelet is its crest, and each bracelet becomes entangled in structures of kinship:

CARA: So the bracelets, the blankets, the tattoos are all the same thing – an expression of the same thing, just in a different form?

JOYCE BENNETT: Yep. All of who you are. It's all of who you are. And where you come from. (2 April 2006)

Crests have survived because kinship has continued to be performed through actions such as the giving of bracelets as gifts to mark life events and belonging. Women's bracelets are layered with memories of particular achievements, life events, and carvers, of giving and receiving bracelets, and of the same crests being worn or displayed by other family members. Bracelets support marked exchanges as well as unmarked exchanges. For instance, Mary's own bracelet reminds her of her daughter's graduation as well as the fact that both of them wear bracelets and can wear the same crests. In the same way, Joyce Bennett kept the bracelet her father carved for her daughter's Vanessa birth; but this tiny bracelet is as likely to prompt a story of Vanessa's days as a youngster, or how Joyce and her father would walk the beach together looking for agates, or how Vanessa's eldest daughter resembles other members of the family. Vanessa's eldest daughter also wears a bracelet, and has done so since her first year of life. In the memory work provoked by bracelets we begin to see how kinship not only influences the designs carved into them, but how kinship can also structure memory practices and history. Looked at another way, kinship affects the material forms as well as the ways people interact with or encounter the objects that are part of a Haida cultural archive.

Alison Brown, Laura Peers, and members of the Kainai Nation (2006) shed light on the potential for kinship to structure history. In their work repatriating historic images to the Kainai tribe, Brown et al. (2006) came to recognize that for the Kainai, history is predominantly family history.[3] This stands in contrast to Brown and Peers' original conceptualization of history considered largely in terms of the colonial process and the anthropological project. Their Kainai counterparts consistently considered history as part of the Blackfoot clan structure: "it has become very clear that for the Kainai people the clan and the local community are the focus of history, and are the social structures through which one experiences and understands history" (Brown et al. 2006, 149).

Themes such as colonization, assimilation, cultural transformation, and cultural survival were provoked by the historic photographs shown to Kainai, but in tandem and as a corollary to clan history; these themes were remembered as processes that affected families.[4]

In chapter 3, I acknowledged that Haida repatriation efforts *could* be interpreted within a post-colonial framework focused on politics and indigenous rights, but that to do so imposes sets of meanings and prioritizes particular relationships that are not supported by the ethnographic evidence. Nadia Seremetakis offers the following caution about how we interpret events, relationships, and objects:

> Artifacts are in themselves histories of prior commensal events and emotional sensory exchanges, and it is these very histories that are exchanged at commensal events and that qualify the object as commensal in the first place. *At the same time, the historicity of the commensal artefact can be effaced, forgotten or denied by current cultural, economic and commensal codes.* Recovery of the artifact's commensal depth, in this context, reanimates alternative codes and other relations of shared experiential substance. (Seremetakis 1994, 11, emphasis added)

Seremetakis' ideas are put into practice by Brown and Peers themselves, who recognize that two "alternative codes" were at work. For Brown and Peers, the alternative code for reading history was family-structured history, whereas for Kainai politically structured or nationally structured history was the alternative framework. As non-Kainai, Brown and Peers did not have the "shared experiential substance" of Kainai clanship that the Kainai participants had the option of invoking.

Likewise, Haidas' words, actions, and objects for repatriation favour a framework of Haida kinship and the associated politico-moral value of *yahgudang*. Maurice Bloch (1996) proposes a metaphorical relationship between mnemonic devices used by people and their senses of self and history. The mnemonic devices he investigates in the Phillipines, Madagascar, and Yemen all rely on values of kinship and recreate kinship structures. But Brown et al. and the Haida case at hand demonstrate that this relationship need not be metaphorical (see also Feely-Harnik 1991 and Saunders 2004). Whereas the crests sewn on blankets, painted on boxes, and carved in bracelets or on poles create opportunities to be reminded of particular lineages and events, there are also material qualities to these objects that can prompt remembering.

Bracelets, as objects that are worn on the body, can travel with people and be co-present at a wide range of events. As we see in Mary's reminiscences, her silver bracelet led her to think about wanting a gold one of similar thickness, but also that she and her sister received gold bracelets from their mother and that her sister's gold bracelet was the target of thieves. If one's sense of history and autobiography are known through shared experiences and embodied memories, then heeding the structural possibilities of kinship helps clarify what distinguishes a Haida cultural archive and the ways in which Haida repatriation efforts are being integrated into their collective history.

Seremetakis (1994) encourages us to examine how history is experienced by paying particular attention to the ways in which the senses and memory are intertwined, each creating and recalling the other, specifically through the presence of artefacts. She argues for a history that recognizes the interconnection of the senses and memory, where tastes, smells, tactile qualities, sounds, and sights can be indicative of transitions and continuums. She suggests we recover the "commensal depth" of artefacts, the multiple shared experiences and shared sensations that underly memories, history, and relationships.[5] Seremetakis uses the metaphor of sedimentation to describe the process of acquiring commensal depth: repeat embodied performances involving objects instil upon those objects memories composed of emotions, history, and sensory experiences (see also Edwards et al. 2006).

Commensality is at the heart of cultural archives. It is a prerequisite for sounds, images, objects, stories, places, and experiences to enter a cultural archive and for that archive to be recognizable and resonate. The repatriation process has included crested items, such as bentwood boxes and button blankets, as well as non-crested items such as local foods, cedar mats, and cedar roses, both of which emphasize that the construction of the repatriation process incorporated familiar tropes precisely because they emphasize the shared material and embodied experiences that structure family relationships (figures 6.2, 6.3). Furthermore, the objects and associated performances of the repatriation process contribute to a larger process of building a Haida cultural archive grounded in kinship structures.

Repatriation and the Creation of a Cultural Archive

The bentwood boxes holding repatriated remains garner significant attention from Haidas and non-Haidas alike. They recall "traditional" Haida material culture as represented in oral histories, museum

Figure 6.2 The experienced hands of weaver Jii̱x̱a, Gladys Vandel, demonstrating how to prepare cedar bark during an outing with the Nygstle Society, 2006.

collections, and art galleries, and embody indigenous technology and ecological knowledge. When painted or carved with a crest, bent boxes become even more recognizably "traditional." The relearning of bentwood box making can be taken as an indication of cultural revitalization, but repatriation committee members are hesitant to isolate bentwood boxes in this manner. Heeding Seremetakis' caution, I see the current code of revitalization as bearing the potential to overpower the code of kinship and *yahgudang*. The impetus to make bentwood boxes was not a desire for the return of particular types of objects, but rather a desire (particularly on the part of elder advisors) to *act* respectfully, to act as family or, synonymously, to act as Haidas. In conversation, Lucy Bell, Candace Weir, and Vince Collison offered the following explanation:

VINCE: In a lot of ways I think Lucille put it best when she said, "This could be my grandmother, this could be part of my family." As soon as you

Figure 6.3 Jenny Cross, Skidegate Repatriation and Cultural Committee, preparing cedar bark to weave mats and roses for repatriated ancestors. Photograph by Jack Litrell, courtesy of SRCC.

put it in that kind of context, I think it makes a lot of sense. You do
what you can to give them a respectful burial because they had such
an undignified –

CARA: Unburial?

LUCY: I think that way of looking at things really helped us over the years.
Just trying to figure out how are we going to get them, or what are we
going to put them in, or somebody on the committee wanted to take
pictures of the transferring and when we were preparing to take them
home. And all we had to say to ourselves was, "What if this is my *naanii*
[grandmother]? My *chinnii* [grandfather]? Would I want pictures of him
being put in the casket?" And answers come very quickly when you
think of them as your direct relatives. (22 December 2005)

The desire to act as family – to act as Haidas – is strengthened by visual
signals such as crests and historically based objects such as bentwood
boxes. These sights and objects foster pride and, when joined together,
a crest and object create a marked object in a sense: a strong statement
of skill, continuity, and purpose that recalls lineage histories and rights
and the practices and traditions of earlier years. In the past, intricate
carvings and paintings of crests and abstract designs decorated the
bentwood boxes and chests that were owned by chiefs and people of
high class and were used for storing valuables and, often, for interment.
Today, bentwood boxes are remembered for their connection to people
who were both fit for respect and wanted to demonstrate respect to
their kin and to the deceased.

As commensal objects, boxes accumulate, or become sedimented
with, people's experiences and memories. There is an interaction between people's bodies and the four-hundred-plus boxes made for repatriation. People experienced planing wood, kerfing planks, steaming
and bending wood, and painting crests (figures 3.3, 3.4, 3.5). They laid
their ancestors in boxes and carried them to the graveyard. People saw
boxes in their surroundings, walked around them, danced past them,
and ate a meal beside them (figure 6.4). Significantly, as crested objects,
boxes always have the potential to be mnemonic devices that prompt
remembrances of a lineage, or that enter the object into a lineage's history. As Poignant and Poignant (1996, 12) observed in Nagalarramba,
Australia, repatriated photographs of people's ancestors created "continuities of self and family" by making "genealogies visible." I find this
an apt description for what crests do: they focus the commensality of
objects on the intersection of self and lineage.

Figure 6.4 Finished bentwood boxes stacked in a canoe, Skidegate. Photograph by Nika Collison, courtesy of SRCC.

Another set of valued and meaningful objects produced for repatriation and marked with crest designs were the small button blankets made for the remains by elementary school children on Haida Gwaii. Button blanket making flourished with the arrival of wool broadcloth on the Northwest Coast, fell prey to assimilationist policies, and was revived in the late 1960s and 1970s (Jenson and Sargent 1986). The experience of making the repatriation button blankets becomes intertwined with other significant events occasioning the making and use of button blankets. Blankets were and are used at historic and contemporary potlatches where Haidas receive names, dance to impress and have fun, transfer chiefly titles, and legalize adoptions. Many of those children who helped sew blankets for the first repatriation in the mid-1990s just received their own blankets from their families in commemoration of their graduation from high school. Blankets are worn to feasts, protests, and government negotiations as formal attire and as political statements. It is observed that people stand taller when wearing a blanket, and feel prouder. Women turn their bodies and dip their shoulders to showcase their crests and their beauty while dancing. Even small children help mothers, aunts, and grandmothers sew on the hundreds of buttons. People still remember with laughter fathers sewing on last-minute buttons in the car en route to their daughter's graduation. And people still remember with reverence the power and beauty of blankets worn to funerals and End of Mourning ceremonies.

Button blanket and regalia maker Joyce Bennett recollected making button blankets for each of her four children upon their high school graduations. While cutting fabric, sewing crest designs, and adding buttons, Joyce said she went through the full range of emotions, remembering the times she was proud, enraged, enamoured, made to laugh and made to cry by each child. As Carsten (2000, 2007) suspects, there is an accumulation of memories of marked and unmarked exchanges underlying the relationship of mother and child. These memories pull the event of graduation – marked by the gift of the blanket – into a history of family. Whether as layers sedimented upon an artefact, in this case a blanket, or as meaningful components that comprise biographies, there is a reciprocal process at work whereby Joyce draws upon the memories of family to create objects that, in turn, mark recipients as family and encourage family as a structure for identity, history, and memory.

The use of blankets – objects that require time and effort to construct and that mark people as belonging to a family – within repatriation helped to ensure the ancestors would feel respected. Their making and use also resulted in shared, embodied experiences, contributing to Haidas' sense of being kin by acting as their ancestors had: sewing blankets, burying family in blankets, and using blankets to connote respect and identity. As with bentwood boxes, the use of blankets marked the repatriated ancestors as honoured kin and helped to ensure peoples' memories of them would be just that: as respected members of lineages from their own or their opposite k'waalaa.

In addition to the objects made specifically for repatriation, there are objects encountered as a result of repatriation. The Haida representatives who travel to museums for repatriation always request time with the Haida objects within the museums' collections. A network of memories and shared embodied experiences develops between Haida and these objects when they see and touch the button blankets and bentwood boxes made by their ancestors, when they dance old masks or blow into flutes to hear their pitch, when a weaver's fingers feel the precise execution of warp and weft in another weaver's hat. Vince Collison described these experiences as helping to increase the relevance of objects that are inalienably connected to them through kinship, but separated from them in time and space. "The reason we wanted to dance a lot of these pieces," offered Vince, "is we felt they were more relevant if we got to dance them."

By comparison, poles – iconic symbols of Northwest Coast art and culture – are represented as archetypal mnemonic devices in the literature (Barbeau 1990; MacDonald 1983; Stewart 1984; Swanton 1905a). Characterized as historic documents, poles cannot be "read" to discern the events they memorialize apart from their original contexts. The commemoration of events and people through poles depends upon prior knowledge of what each crest and figure was intended to signify. Stewart (1984, 76) clarifies: "poles stood as visible proof of declarations that had been witnessed and validated by all those attending the ceremony of their raising." Once raised, a pole becomes a public monument, a visual and material reminder of people, alliances, events, and rights. This is its conscious, intended purpose. The object at this level parallels the durability of the lineage: ideally it physically outlasts an individual and connects past and present kin in the celebration of a lineage member's achievements (and thus a lineage's history), in the recollection of intra- and inter-family relations, and in the continuity of crests and images.

As poles have the ability to commemorate the achievements of someone with a particular name or to commemorate the achievements and rights within a lineage's history, a pole is always performing on behalf of its raisers. Its raisers must have performance consciousness (Dening 1996), as the claims being made through the pole are thereafter subject to public and personal scrutiny, comparison, and memory. Regardless of one's presence or absence at a particular pole raising, the longevity and public nature of a pole forces shared experiences to a degree, but the nature of these encounters is not easily controlled.

In addition to marking chieftainships, celebrating the construction of longhouses, or remembering deceased relatives, contemporary poles are also being carved as a means of commemorating village and national events. There is a series of poles standing at the K̲aay Llnagaay Heritage Centre and Haida Gwaii Museum site that represent each of the southern villages occupied during the 1800s, and whose inhabitants migrated to Skidegate to resettle after the epidemics. There is also the *Migration Home* pole standing in front of Chief Matthews Elementary School in Old Massett (figure 6.5). The Haida Heritage and Repatriation Society led a fund-raising effort and commissioned this pole to exhibit in Hamburg, Germany, as part of Expo 2000. The pole was created with both a local and an international audience in mind (see Jonaitis and Glass 2010 for a history of indigenous and non-indigenous relations as

Figure 6.5 *Migration Home* pole standing in front of Chief Matthews Elementary School in Old Massett, 2005. The pole was commissioned by the village of Old Massett and carved by a team led by Reg Davidson.

evidenced in poles). While in Germany, it was used as a testament to Haida creativity, craftsmanship, and cultural continuity and as a point of departure for talking about repatriation. While non-Haidas proposed that the pole remain in Germany as a gift to the host country, Haidas never intended this pole to stay overseas; it was essential that the pole return to Haida Gwaii, just as it is essential that their ancestors return to Haida Gwaii. For its Haida audience, the pole is intended to remind them of the repatriation efforts, people's determination to return their ancestors' bodies to Haida territory, the history of artefacts leaving Haida Gwaii, and the potential for such artefacts to "migrate home."

Poles aid the memory and come to signify more than the political and/or social function of the occasion at which they were raised. Meuli (2001, 128, 130) posits that "the mnemonically-intended art [of the Northwest Coast] acted as an aide-mémoire physically, but the information that it allowed observers to 'recall' was (and is) the information that is socially relevant in a contemporary context." In talking about poles, Haidas spoke of which child they were pregnant with when it was raised or the precariousness of pole raisings, as this skill is still being remastered. They remembered fashion styles, what they wore, and what was playing on the radio when a pole was raised. People also compared different styles of potlatches and the efficaciousness of hosts. For children, poles can be playmates, fodder for stories, or didactic objects – a means of learning community history in relation to crests and figures. Thus, the commensal depth of poles includes the daily interactions and unconscious responses people have to the poles in their environment, particularly since the poles are there as a background (and sometimes foreground) to everyday experiences, such as driving through the village, taking out the garbage, or picking up the mail.

In such reminiscing it is possible to see how peoples' memories of poles bring together phases of their own and the object's social life (see also Hoskins 1998). In response to a question about his early memories of carvers and artists, artist Gwaai Edenshaw[6] responded:

One of the clearest memories – everything else is just fragments and pictures, like I can remember woodchips and standing on the pole, but those are just snapshots when I was really young. But my dad worked on a pole – we lived in a boat shed and he had this pole – seven years I think he worked on it. It was his first pole by himself. It was just a fixture in our household! It was neat to have it around. I remember at that time, I was really scared to touch it – I thought it was a piece of art and I would scrape it with a button or ruin it. It's so different from now, because I have no qualms about leaping over a pole or walking on top of it to get a better look at it. (29 December 2005)

In Gwaai's description, we might imagine the softness of woodchips, the smell of sawdust, and the rhythmic chopping of an adze or the penetrating buzz of a chainsaw – important tools at different points in the carving process. Gwaai's comments about walking on poles remind us that, for carvers in particular, these are not solely visual objects; they are made. For all their publicness, poles might spend their first years as a massive, cut log sitting in someone's front yard, the outer wood turning grey in appearance. Once brought into the carving shed, the outer layers of wood are strategically removed and the wood again looks yellowish and reddish, moist. Gwaai's first encounter with the pole his father was carving was as horizontal furniture as much as a "heraldic column," as early European sailors described them. He continues to experience poles horizontally through his life as a carver, as robust cedar that supports a person's weight as he or she walks along its length, able to touch and explore the carved indentations, smooth planes, and symmetry of the crests wrapping around the pole. Gwaai almost chides himself as he remembers his reverence for the pole in their house based on a misperception of its material vulnerability. Memories of fear give way to memories of leaping over poles – of being comfortable in his physical interactions with these objects. Gwaai, when part of a team carving a pole, attaches importance to the crests and figures that tell stories and commemorate events; but there is another material, mnemonic aspect to poles that supports remembering his childhood, his father, his emotions and values, and his craft as a carver.

Haidas' association of personal memories with these historic documents supports Pine's (2007, 106) suggestion that official commemorative sites or monuments are frequently incorporated "as something much closer to personal, everyday memory," while everyday things have the potential to become imbued with "bigger" memories. In fact, the major challenge facing Carsten's scheme is determining where marked exchanges end and unmarked ones begin. As predicted by Pine, a number of everyday objects – aprons, dish cloths, tea cups, knit hats, mugs, screwdrivers – work alongside "official" objects such as poles. The *Migration Home* pole does more than provide an official document recording the history of Haida repatriation: it connects people's life events to that history. Lucy, for instance, remembered not being able to oversee the raising of this pole because of the imminent birth of her daughter. The pole also contributes to the Haida cultural archive by fostering the desired shared experience of daily visual (and perhaps also tactile) encounters with poles in the village, and the building of an aesthetic landscape. There is a material and sensorial remembering of kinship and history evident in Haidas' reminiscences that bridges Carsten's sense of the co-production of memory and kinship through marked and unmarked exchanges, and Seremetakis' emphasis on the role of the material and sensual in remembering. If commensality speaks to a shared history of experiences with objects, on Haida Gwaii commensality is heightened where history is further understood as an element of kinship.

There are still other kinds of objects within the repatriation process bearing no crests at all – foods, their preparation and consumption – that can help elucidate the connections between kinship structures, remembering, and the creation of a cultural archive. Food's intensely synaesthetic qualities predispose it to sedimentation, to becoming affiliated with multiple and potentially diverse memories.[7] Sutton (2001, 160) argues against any inherent ephemerality to food, and Haidas consider food essential to any gathering. Gifts of food can create and perpetuate long-lasting social relations between persons, as the gesture of the original gift is recalled long after the material decomposition of the food itself (see also Jolles and Mikaghaq Oozeva 2002). Moreover, shared tastes, smells, textures, appearances, and sounds combine to produce collectively known flavours, trigger memories, provide comfort and a sense of familiarity, provide basic sustenance, produce discomfort or trigger the body to expel various substances, signal readiness for cooking or serving, mark occasions as routine or ritual, or symbolize transnational flows of commodities (cf. Wilk 1999). In addition to signaling national, ethnic, class, or gender identities, the production, consumption, or gifting of food can also create and maintain identities of kin relationships, of grieving or mourning, of respect or neglect (see, for example, Conklin 2001; Counihan 1999). The presence of food is expected, desired, and required at Haida feasts and (as Haidas will joke) in any informal gathering as well. Guujaaw, artist and past president of the Council of the Haida Nation, writes, "Haida Culture is not simply song and dance, graven images, stories, language, or even blood. It's all of these things and then [...] It's a feeling you get when you bring a feed of cockles to the old people, and fixing up fish for the smokehouse [...] Along the way, you eat some huckle-berries, watch the kids grow up ... attend the funeral feasts" (Guujaaw 2006, 3; un-bracketed ellipsis in original).

Each Haida family has their own way of "putting up" foods, whether it be k'aaw (herring roe on kelp),[8] other seafoods, game, or berries. The method of preparing k'aaw I describe below is that of Irene Mills, in whose home I was staying when the much-anticipated delivery arrived. In both Skidegate and Old Massett, k'aaw is a preferred food. It is enjoyed in seafood stews, fried in a pan with soy sauce, eaten fresh from the sea or brined. We prepared brine in a large plastic tub, adding coarse salt to water and stirring until a potato floats. We rinsed the k'aaw in fresh water and left it to dry slightly before dunking it in the brine and then hanging it to remove any excess brine (figure 6.3). Some of the kelp strips were the length of an arm, making it necessary to cut them in half or thirds for storage purposes. When the k'aaw is harvestable, there is more than any nuclear family could eat, so Irene vacuum-packs her k'aaw so it can be stored in the freezer or insulated and shipped to her mother and other family who live off-island.

Preparing k'aaw is time intensive, and one never knows exactly when a harvest will arrive on the doorstep. Irene's came after dinner one evening, and we immediately set to the task of preparing the k'aaw. Her brother, who lived nearby and had also received k'aaw, came to the house with his wife and daughter to both share his k'aaw with Irene and to freezer-pack some for himself and family. In assembly-line fashion, polyethylene bags were cut to size and dated, while the k'aaw was rinsed, brined, hung, halved, and then packaged.

The events of the evening were contextualized later that evening as we rested after our labours. Reflecting on the night's work, Irene shared memories of putting up fish with her family in other years, waiting into the night for the fishermen to come in with the catch, and setting to work preparing the fish for canning no matter what the hour. She recalled how, when preparing fish, each person is given a task – usually the same one year after year, until they inherit or advance to a new task – making the participation of the extended family a prerequisite in order to cover each step of the process. The significance of cooperating in the process is captured in Joyce and John Bennett's belief that "the family that prepares food together, stays together." The preparation of k'aaw is an activity centred on family that encourages Haidas to remember their kin, their kinship obligations, and their shared experiences.

The commensality of food preparation extends further as people deliver delicacies to elder lineage members, encourage the serving of

Figure 6.6 Hanging k̲'aaw to allow the excess brine to drip off before vacuum-packing, 2006.

"traditional foods" such as smoked fish rather than store-bought foods as a sign of respect for the land and Haida ways, or ensure there are ample leftovers to be taken home after a feast – a sign of the host's generosity and a means of caring for the elderly or less fortunate. Food obligations frequently reflect lineage and k'waalaa relationships and are always incorporated within the notion of yahgudangang.

As exchanges that happen seasonally and reinforce cooperation among kin, food preparations are best understood as marked exchanges within Carsten's scheme. And yet the outcome of food preparation is the potential for innumerable unmarked exchanges in the sharing of food or reminiscing, as well as additional marked exchanges such as hosting feasts and preparing family meals for special occasions. Having memories of putting up foods is becoming increasingly important as a number of Haidas live off-island or have less time to hunt, fish, and gather due to the demands of employment or schooling. Irene remembered her young grandson, exhausted but eager to participate in the late-night fish preparations, and she confessed her own eagerness to have him watch and help where he could, so the experience of putting up fish would be something in which he shared and of which he had memories. Just as people who live off-island may miss the landscape or the tides, they may long for particular foods: "Haida soul food," as Natalie Fournier termed it. In sending k'aaw to her relatives off-island, Irene was sending them a piece of home, a chance to once again savour particular flavours and textures. These flavours are known because of the memories of past sensory experiences, of eating, of preparing brine or slicing fish, of potlatch feasts and family lunches, of being on the beach and knowing when the tides and winds will be right to get the best harvest of scallops, crab, or clams.

Unsurprisingly, food has been a material necessity throughout the process of repatriation. Raffle prizes consisting of freshly baked pies and bread have been used to raise funds. The Haida Heritage and Repatriation Society hosts lunch-time fund-raisers selling sushi made by volunteers using locally caught crab, prawn, and salmon. The Skidegate Repatriation and Cultural Committee hosts seafood dinners featuring Haida dancing, locally caught fish and shellfish, and a slide show presenting the goals of repatriation to raise funds by appealing to summer tourists.

Aside from its role in fund-raising, food also plays a role in perpetuating a collective sense of Haida identity among Haida Repatriation Committee members. They playfully tease each other for packing home-canned salmon, defended as "real food," in their luggage on repatriation trips. The food offered in fires for the ancestors draws upon this same familiarity – the shared textures and flavours of Haida Gwaii (figure 6.7). As much as possible, the foods offered into a fire are the same kinds of foods that the ancestors would have eaten during their lifetimes: huckleberries, salmon berries, halibut, salmon, eulachon grease. This requires the committees to bring foods such as salmon and k'aaw with them when travelling to museums. The production and consumption of foodstuffs for repatriation create opportunities for individuals to locate themselves within a history – quite often a family history – of shared experiences centred on fishing, canning, clam digging, feasting, hunting, berry picking, being gifted with eulachon grease, harvesting k'aaw, gathering scallops, or bringing food to elder relatives.

Whether it be the joint experience of cooks seasoning halibut stew, carvers bending cedar, or Haida hands sewing buttons onto blankets with the emotions of love, nostalgia, anger, frustration, respect, or pride,

Figure 6.7 Jenny Cross (centre) and Dolly Garza (right) preparing food for burning for repatriated ancestors, End of Mourning ceremony, 2005. Photograph by James McGuire, courtesy of SRCC.

the effect is one of creating a collective frame of reference and an ability to know one's family across time through shared, embodied experiences – in other words, through a cultural archive. Myriad objects and acts could be explored in this vein: painting crest designs, listening to the spirit song, fishing, cooking, serving food, dancing, wrapping up bones, singing, supporting fund-raisers, praying, speaking Haida, speaking English, putting cedar "Haida roses" in graves, eating together, sitting alongside family members, walking to the graveyard, visiting with friends, dressing in regalia, exploring museum collections, orating lineage and clan affiliations, and the list goes on. While each of these actions can be isolated as part of the repatriation process, their significance comes from their presence in other facets of Haida daily and ceremonial life. Moreover, many of these shared experiences are further interpreted through the Haida ideal of *yahgudang* as it is expressed in private and public spheres, in marked and unmarked exchanges, between individuals, lineages, and *k'waalaa*. Thus, these actions join a material and embodied landscape of memory and kinship already in progress.

Creating Collective Spaces for Narration

Kirmayer (1996) proposes using the metaphor of a landscape in which people dwell to conceptualize the creation of public spaces for retellings. People do not perceive this landscape in exactly the same way.[9] Individuals revisit certain places in the landscape with greater frequency than others, and being in one location will influence how one sees or travels to other narratives and memories. Kirmayer is using the notion of landscape metaphorically to describe the mechanics of memory. His metaphor echoes the mnemonic practice of imagining rooms and locating information within their architectural and decorative features (Yates 1966), although movement through Kirmayer's scheme is less intentional or directed than the practiced recall of orators in Roman times. Although Kirmayer is using landscape as a metaphor, the concept of a cultural archive aids us in hypothesizing how material landscapes can literally shape where and when reminiscing and commemoration occur. Building up a material landscape for commemorating, remembering, and retelling narratives of repatriation enhances the ability of repatriation narratives to be incorporated into, and in turn help structure, collective memory.

A variety of spaces – some impermanent and changeable, others permanent – served to prompt narratives about repatriation. In Skidegate, a stockpile of bentwood boxes grew at the canoe shed – an eye-catching feature that enabled Andy Wilson to speak with hundreds of people about the work the committees were doing. Village cemeteries became marked by wooden crosses and cedar grave plaques that continue to communicate that the people buried there were repatriated from museums and private collectors, and are now home to stay on Haida Gwaii. The *Migration Home* pole, commissioned by the village of Old Massett to symbolize the repatriation of their ancestors and artefacts, journeyed to Germany for exhibition and then returned home and was erected in front of Chief Matthews Elementary School. The display of posters advertising repatriation fund-raisers and repatriation merchandise, including clothing, travel mugs, and canvas bags decorated with the repatriation logos, has a presence in everyday, unmarked exchanges in restaurants, businesses, and homes.

Through the combination of feasts and reburial ceremonies, clothing, household items, and public monuments, the process and outcomes of repatriation have materialized within village, family, and personal landscapes. The addition of repatriation-centred objects within the landscape of memory on Haida Gwaii provides potential connections between repatriation, feasting, gifting, tourism, carving, funerals, or other frameworks used within collective memory. People's memories of repatriation enter structures for remembering already in existence (Halbwachs 1992). The ability of community members to share in the collective narrativization of repatriation increased as the process became associated with an increasing number of people, places, objects, and events.

Still, linking individual memories with collective structures for remembering is not always predictable. When I asked various Haida friends and acquaintances who had not served on either repatriation committee whether there was anything within their surroundings or environment that reminded them of repatriation, I received a mix of responses. A few people thought that there was nothing around their village or in their daily life that triggered memories of repatriation. Frequently, answers were tinged with the person's perspective on the value of repatriation of either ancestral remains or artefacts. One person, for example, offered the opinion that wasted money and repatriation were reminders of each other. The wearing of clothing with the repatriation logo was identified as a time when the events of repatriation were remembered. Being in a museum also brought repatriation to mind, as did seeing people carving within the villages, carrying on Haida aesthetic and professional traditions. Sue Gladstone of the SRCC, speaking of the role of repatriation within Haida collective memory, suggested that within the Haida community people's connectivity to the repatriation process varies. Those more directly involved in the process were likely to have a greater number of memories linked to a wider spectrum of places, times, and activities. Demonstrating her point, I was with a group of people who were talking about fishing when their conversation about the robust stature of a living Haida man led one person in the group to an impromptu reminiscing about the size of one repatriated Haida ancestor whose skeleton indicated he too was an imposing figure, comparable to or even bigger than Haida men today.

The challenge many Haidas are posing to themselves is to do more than just remember. They want to return in their actions, values, and philosophies to "normal" Haida life. As Nika Collison observes in the documentary *Stolen Spirits of Haida Gwaii* (McMahon 2004), one of the important qualities of the repatriation process is that Haidas are asked to make button blankets, cedar boxes, or cedar roses not simply for the sake of maintaining skills, knowledge, or cultural identity, but as a means of communicating a relationship with, and respect for, their relatives.

Through the repatriation process, Haidas sought to activate relationships with their ancestors, particularly those who had been alienated from Haida Gwaii, but more recently they have also sought to personalize relationships with Haida children who have been adopted out to non-Haida families or families living off-island. Significantly, in both repatriation and the welcoming home of adoptees, the interactions between persons were supported through the use of objects, environment, language (often as song), and food. The creation and use of multisensory collective spaces such as feasts, where objects provoke the remembering of history and the creation of embodied memories, have proven significant in the construction of commensality. Seremetakis (1994), Stoller (1989), and Sutton (2001, 2006) all emphasize the indispensable role of the senses in memory and hence the centrality of embodied memory to, and the synaesthesic quality of, collective identity.

I am reminded of older museum methods that interpreted touch as an integral aspect of learning from objects. Classen and Howes (2006, 201) document the attitude taken by curators at the Ashmolean Museum at the University of Oxford in 1702: "touch provided an essential – and expected – means of acquiring knowledge." Considering the effects of physical contact with artefacts on museum visitors, they continue:

> By touching a collected object the hand of the visitor also encounters traces of the hand of the object's creator and former owners. One seems to feel what others have felt and bodies seem to be linked to bodies through the medium of the materiality of the object they have shared. (Classen and Howes 2006, 202)

More than "seeming" to feel what others have felt, shared experiences of objects *do* allow people to feel in common, to connect through an object. What the Haida repatriation process demonstrates is how particular groups (in this case families and source communities) have a heightened interaction with the makers and users of objects in response to a cultural archive of shared prior experiences of places, tastes, smells, actions, sounds, events, people, motions, and skills.

The activities of repatriation have facilitated a cultural archive as Haidas create objects to denote honour, and rebury their ancestors, and as they come into contact with the objects made, worn, danced, eaten, and held by their ancestors. This in turn broadens the range of shared experiences or shared history Haidas can draw upon in their constructions and affirmations of kinship relations. Crested objects, such as poles and bracelets, establish a visual connection between individuals and lineages, and are foci for narratives about family and history. Wearing a crest and identifying oneself through a crest are shared experiences, just as the flavours of food, the feel of a northwesterly wind, the view of a landscape, the witnessing of a potlatch, and the warmth in a bracelet just removed from an arm are shared experiences. These shared experiences create the commensal depth in artefacts and performances, and while this commensality is deeply embedded across the Haida nation, it is deepest within a family. The effect of years of repatriation efforts and reburial feasts has been the sedimentation of acts of kinship and respect, in objects and in people's bodies.

At the outset, the individual parts of the Haida repatriation process were chosen because the associated objects and performances were widely known and approved of as indicators of kinship. After ten years of returning ancestral remains to Haida Gwaii, repatriation as a whole has become a performance of kinship and its obligations. On Haida Gwaii, the cultural archive is being augmented by the repatriation process but, at its core, is structured upon kinship.

In the next chapter, I consider people's reminiscences of repatriation more closely. If, as Climo and Cattell (2002, 12) observe, "the individual consciousness by which we recognize ourselves as persons, and the collective consciousness by which groups identify and organize themselves and act with agency, arise from and are sustained by memory," I ask how narratives of repatriation become part of Haidas' collective memory and cultural archive, and thus part of Haida identity. How Haidas tell their stories, particularly the story of repatriation, highlights how knowledge, experience, and place create feelings of continuity and allow a cultural archive to be communicated. At the same time, these narratives reflect the importance of *yahgudang* and kinship in the ways people make sense of history and of themselves.

7 The Place of Repatriation within Collective Memory and Identity

At a 2003 reburial feast marking the return of remains from the Field Museum, a Haida man pronounced, "What we have seen today will be spoken of long after we're gone." This sentiment reflects a wider belief that the acts of repatriation will continue to be part of the collective dialogue on Haida Gwaii. It further reflects a desire that the work and accomplishments of repatriation become part of Haida history. Additional statements made during repatriation feasts have expounded on the Haida qualities of strength, perseverance, and adaptability. Haida ancestors are remembered as having embodied these attributes. But these qualities are equally important to how Haidas want to see themselves and want others to see them today.

In his essay "Ilongot Hunting as Story and Experience," Renato Rosaldo (1986) brings us into his investigation of the stories people tell about themselves. How people tell their stories, he argues, is based on shared knowledge, experiences, places, and a sense of what is important. Shared experience, knowledge of (and in) places, and a shared sense of what is important are the same ingredients identified as the basis for collective memory: commonly held narratives produced as a result of remembering with and through other people, settings, events, emotions, and experiences. Collective memory is a means of knowing oneself and communicating relatedness with and to others (Archibald 1999, 2002; Casey 1986; Climo and Cattell 2002; Kirmayer 1996). Indeed, Connerton (1989) argues that shared memory is a requirement for a sense of society. Where shared experiences prompted by repatriation help Haidas to know and feel they are related as kin, sharing stories and memories of repatriation contributes to the building and reshaping of a broader collective Haida identity. It is critical to understand why making kinship is an important aspect of Haida repatriation, but the enduring effects of Haida repatriation efforts can also be seen in the ways Haidas are adjusting and reframing their personal and collective memories of repatriation to confirm social and cultural identities.

Incorporated within collective memory and narratives, the process and cultural archive of repatriation has become enmeshed with broader social and cultural processes occurring in Haida society. In initiating the repatriation process, generations of Haida learned for the first time that their ancestors were being held off-island, while the eldest generation was confronted with this avoided or unacknowledged memory. Following through with the repatriation process provided this fact of removal with a space in which it could be remembered and reminisced about, creating dialogue and history. But the process of repatriation also provided a space in which narratives of loss could be amended by narratives of control, kinship, responsibility, and *yahgudang*.

Repatriation has become a powerful symbol for contemporary efforts to re-emphasize lineageship and *k'waalaa* in Haida identity and sociality. It has come to stand as a counterpoint to the period in which Haida families were economically dependent or were threatened by disease and assimilationist policies such as residential schooling and the loss of status. Repatriation has also become a powerful component within contemporary efforts to revitalize people's sense of pride in their Haida identity and to re-emphasize the fulfilment of kinship obligations within the spectrum of esteemed behaviour. Haidas see an essential need for pride, which they view as a response to assimilationist measures and the damage they inflicted upon Haidas' sense of the value of their language, knowledge systems, moral code, and spiritual beliefs. Both villages' repatriation committees came to recognize the ability of repatriation to facilitate individual and community healing by providing a space in which traumatic historic events *and* corrective contemporary measures could be remembered and vocalized with the support of the community. In opposition to stories of loss or leaving, repatriation serves as a story of ancestors coming home. It counters stories of loss with actions of reclamation.

In this chapter, I investigate the ways Haidas are retelling, commemorating, and communicating the history and meanings of their repatriation efforts. The retellings I explore here rely on the spoken and written word far more than the embodied and material performances in chapter 6, but the broader construction of a cultural archive remains important. If, as Laurence Kirmayer (1996) argues, collective memory can only exist where there are spaces for collective retellings, the emplaced and material facets of a cultural archive bare on the construction of collective memories and histories. In configuring the repatriation process as a space for collective remembering, we see more clearly how narratives of repatriation intersect with and shape Haidas' sense of self and their collective memory and identity. By providing safe spaces in which painful histories could be remembered, and by amending those histories with acts of respect, love, care, and honour, repatriation has altered how individuals can remember their family members and their own actions as kin. Thus, while the repatriation process was designed to extend respect towards others, it has had the effect of displaying contemporary Haidas' fitness for respect.

New Memories, Shifting Narratives

Addressing narratives of loss – in terms of both verbalizing experiences of loss within public discourse and challenging notions of loss – has been one of the pivotal outcomes of the repatriation process to date. The predominant narratives addressing loss, crisis, or dysfunction during my stay on Haida Gwaii frequently coalesced around the multigenerational experience of residential schooling that lasted throughout most of the twentieth century. Residential schooling came on the heels of the creation of reservations, growing access to alcohol, and major economic shifts. Despite the presence of the Haida language and cultural knowledge among the older generations, it was still a turbulent time where Haidas imagined their ancestors needed to choose which of their traditions to retain and which to sacrifice in order to survive and protect their children. In tandem with loss of control over their children, many Haida families during this time also lost their economic independence. These conditions have been part of many Haidas' everyday decision making and life strategies for over a century (Parkin 1999).[1] Haidas observed that each situation exacerbated the other, with impoverished families unable to prove to Indian agents that they could provide for their children if they remained at home, and with estranged young adults leaving residential school and adopting alcoholism as a coping strategy – men in particular fell into cycles of unemployment and alcoholism. In conversation, Irene Mills succinctly expressed ideas I'd heard in a number of homes:

> They slowly started losing their confidence that they could provide for their families. And I'm speaking of men. It was because they felt they were

of no use to their community anymore that you started having problems with alcohol. And of course residential school had an impact on that as well. So if you take a people out of their home and what they're used to, because you're trying to assimilate them, [and then] they're not working the land and they don't have the language that they used to, the words that they use for the different activities – whether it's berry picking or fishing for salmon or halibut, or getting abalone or clam digging – then it's one less thing that then they have in their collective memory. So once you start reducing the collective memory in the food gathering, and using the natural resources, [you take] that independence away. (11 May 2006)

In learning of their ancestors' remains in museums, Haidas added the loss of deceased family members' bodies to the already present narratives of loss of control, children, language, cultural traditions, and cultural treasures.[2]

The pain of losing one's family members to collectors was expressed by Mary Swanson as she recollected the sadness people felt over the removal of their family members' bodies from Haida Gwaii to places unknown.

I told him [a caretaker] when my dad owned the mill – he brought it over from Howkaan, Alaska, this was in the twenties. Anyways, when all the elders stopped in for tea or coffee, they used to talk about these remains that were taken off the island. No one could say anything because they couldn't speak English, they couldn't stop them. So I told him some of the elders used to cry when they talked about it. It was really sad for some of them, knowing that some of their relatives were taken off the island like that. (13 January 2006)

By forgetting this information – or more, aptly, by disallowing it from being remembered within family and village collective memories – an older generation avoided transferring the attendant pain to following generations. The information lay dormant, unspoken and unacknowledged, in a protective gesture aimed at minimizing its ability to cause harm. Robertson (2007) documents a similar reluctance of elder generations in a Catalan community to remember the period from 1936 to 1950. While younger generations are eager to reintegrate people's memories from this period of civil war into their history, elder generations refer to this time as "*la miseria*," marked by painful memories of hunger they would rather not re-experience through remembering. Elder generations were also reluctant to discuss partisanship during any time period or in any form, as such discussions not only evoked memories of being under suspicion but also feelings of fear.

Russell Thornton (2002) argues that when human remains and cultural objects held in museums were collected in the wake of traumatic events, their retention within the perpetrators' institutions and their embedding within the perpetrators' narratives prevents individuals and groups from achieving a sense of closure. Thornton writes of the ability – and the necessity – of repatriation to provide closure on traumatic historic events for Native American nations. Associated objects held in museums are more than reminders of injustice; the objects continue the offence against the surviving generations. Because people are unable to forget or amend the past, trauma becomes inherited at the level of the collective (Thornton 2002; see also Duran and Duran 1995; Duran, Duran, and Brave Heart 1988). Thornton insists that remembering, rather than separating or dissociating contemporary communities from history, is at the core of resolving inherited trauma. He is careful to clarify that closure does not equal forgetting. Through repatriation and other commemorative events such as the Year of Reconciliation to mark the Sioux Uprising or the Cherokee Trail of Tears Association's annual ceremonies to remember the deaths and displacement of their ancestors, Thornton (2002, 20–1) posits, individuals and groups are able to put an end to the effects of traumatic historic events.

The lines between repatriation and historic trauma are neither clear nor unidirectional, but research investigating the influence of traumatic experience on collective memory and narrative construction provides a useful analytical tool for considering how Haidas are using these narratives to communicate individual and collective identities. In using memory theory grounded in trauma, I do not mean to identify Haida people as victims; rather, Haidas use repatriation within three different narrative strategies to *counter* this memory of loss. The strength of traumatic memory studies is that they provide models that incorporate both individual agency and socio-cultural influences in the construction of social identities.

In repatriating their ancestors' remains, contemporary Haida sought to rectify historical indecencies that had continued on into the present. The commemorative actions and objects of Haida repatriation efforts re-remember Haida ancestors and transform them from persons displaced and disrespected to reintegrated, treasured, and respected members of families and society. When Haidas engage in and support repatriation efforts, they are creating spaces in which they themselves can be remembered as having acted as family members *should* act.

In explaining the importance of repatriation, Pearle Pearson of the SRCC emphasized that she wants her "grandfather – great-great-grandfather – to come home where he belongs. Not stuck in a drawer somewhere." Although individual names are rarely attached to the human remains held in museums, Pearle was still very clear about her relationship to the Haida remains held off-island. She knows her family members to be among them, and thus the story of repatriation is a personal one for her. She also remembered seeing, while on the trip to repatriate remains from the Field Museum in Chicago, which village names were listed with each set of remains, giving her a sense of which lineages the remains are part of. Her efforts working with the SRCC to honour her own ancestors (and, appropriately, the ancestors belonging to other lineages) shift the story she is able to tell about her great-great-relatives. She does not have to forget their removal, but she no longer has to grieve their absence: she can instead speak of her efforts, and the efforts of her village, to bring respect to her ancestors. Pearle remembered when they brought the remains home and took them off the airplane: "There were all people waiting for us. Silence. A lot of respect." Significantly, her community's participation in this way affirms her own narrative that her ancestors were deserving of respect and that repatriation afforded them this respect. Pearle's ability to incorporate the acts of repatriation within her own biography as a demonstration of family well-being is supported by the ways her community acted and continues to remember the events of repatriation. At the same time, her biography – constantly being reshaped in response to the accumulation of life experiences – reinforces the collective narratives of healing, autonomy, and Haida family values prevalent in contemporary Haida discourse.

The slippage that occurs between personal biographies and collective narratives of repatriation is apparent in the ways Pearle remembered her time serving with the committee.

CARA: What has been the biggest impact for you, being involved in this work?

PEARLE: When we went down into this room, where all the remains were. Then. What a feeling that was. There were so many of them. Babies. And huge – there was one that we thought the man must have been 6'6" at least. We saw a piece of the leg, up here [indicates femur] – long. He must have been a giant. I can't explain the feeling I had.

CARA: But you knew that they had to come home?

PEARLE: I knew they had to be a relative of mine from way back. (1 May 2006)

HHRS member Candace Weir similarly moved between collective narratives and individual memory, interleaving aspects of her personal life with the history of repatriation – a practice common among committee members. Responding to Vince Collison's observation that Candace Weir had become the Haida Heritage and Repatriation Society's song leader, Candace responded that that was something that happened in more recent years. Leading the singing, she continued,

> was new – in the beginning. I mean, I knew it, but it wasn't so easy. It was dealing with the whole process. I was thinking of it when Christian's cousin just moved home and we were in Victoria at her place for dinner and I thought, "Okay, I know these songs," but to sing the lead alone, I was really too shy to sing them at first. That was ten years ago. Now I don't really like to do solos, but I can. It's a lot easier. The whole process, that whole ten years of what was involved in my whole life really helped. Repatriation was part of something that helped my circle enclose, come together a bit more. Lots of other understandings along the way. I felt fortunate in the Massett end, having the elders there. I felt if we didn't have them there I wouldn't have got even half the learning. I think we were alone on the first trip, just the Massett group. But every time, we had the elders there, the same core group of elders, which was so important. Over the years, three have passed on. They'd have been with us too, I'm sure. We've had that same group of tough *naaniis* right from day one. Meetings. We had biweekly and then it was weekly meetings for over ten years. Fund-raisers. They'd be out at fund-raisers. And just every event. And then our trips. That's where I got my little reignited flame and my whole candle lit, was from their teachings. (22 December 2008)

When I asked Candace if participating in the repatriation process and her contact with the *naaniis* had influenced her choice to become a language teacher, she replied:

> I think that's where it all started. Ten years ago, lots of different things happened: with the language, working with the elders, singing. It just helped. That was a big part. And then with that core group of *naaniis*, establishing rapport with them and getting to work with them on different things ... I got a gift through the process from one of the *naaniis* who passed away. We use the butterfly as our logo but she gave me this little glass butterfly plate that I still have, when we were working on this. And then there was the trip I stayed behind because she was passing away. It

was past the point of going away. [I went back and forth:] I'm going, I'm not going, I'm going, I'm not going. I had to write a letter [to the HHRS] to say, "This is it. I can't go," as much as my heart wanted to be there and my first reaction was to be there, but at the same time I was glad I was here. But prior to that she had given me this nice, pretty butterfly plate. It's at my house because I have everything ever given me along the way. (22 December 2008)

Candace as well as her friend and committee-mate Lucy Bell remembered the ways fund-raising, travel, correspondence with museums, and coordination of museum visits affected each woman's social life, marriage, children's lives, and health. But the women also remarked that it could be difficult for them to see the work of their committee as historic, inspirational, or marked in any way. They reflected that they were simply too close to it; it had become part of their normal, everyday lives.

In contrast, Candace's husband and fellow HHRS member Christian White observed that repatriation "pretty well changed a lot of our history. It made history. So, in a way, a lot of our history would be different right now if it didn't happen." I understand this to mean that as the process of repatriation becomes interwoven with existent narratives in Haida communities, it has the potential to refocus these narratives. As a result of repatriation, Haida have gained new memories and additional vantage points from which they can navigate the terrain of collective memory. Both of these things influence how narratives are told, heard, and remembered. The manner in which Christian integrated the outcomes of repatriation within his sense of his family's history explicates this idea:

Well, for myself I understood that repatriation was going to be a lot of work, to accomplish what we had to accomplish. I leave it up to our elders to give us guidance on the spiritual part of it. I just felt like I had to do my part. I could see how everybody was quite passionate about bringing these ancestral remains back. It really brought quite a few of us close together over those years – working together and with the remains. It seemed like it was a real community effort for the people that were on the inside of what was going on. We could understand the spiritual significance, I guess, and also that it was important for healing. I was brought up always feeling a sense of loss. I think some of it was a little bit of the loss of the culture, but at the same time we were reviving it. I think a lot of it was at the loss of our livelihoods. We lost a big part of our livelihoods. We came from being almost the wealthiest people on the coast to being like the welfare state. My family felt that loss, in that part. (19 November 2005)

Christian's narrative illustrates one way in which a sense of loss is being voiced within Haida narratives, and one way in which people are contextualizing repatriation within their personal narratives to counter experiences of loss. He identifies repatriation as a means of personal healing – an idea that finds firm support among fellow committee members, or those "on the inside."

Abstracting from her own life, Irene reflected on how participating in repatriation activities – activities that are part of a cultural archive – can influence the lives of Haida youth as well as non-Haida individuals:

Whether it's painting a line on a box or it's sewing a button on – it goes back to the kids learning from a really early age, in their community, in their home, and then carrying that with them the rest of their life – knowing they had a hand in something that was so important to their nation. Because it helped their nation – even if people may not be conscious of it – healing those wounds that have been inflicted on us that we're not even aware of. Whether it's the small pox epidemic. Things slowly start working within our nation, [and] I believe people just feel better. And it's like the people who aren't Haida who participate ... They try and discount their involvement by saying, "I just painted a box," and I say, "No, you didn't just paint a box – you helped us by painting a box." Because we're all really busy and we can't all be experts at everything, so we encourage that kind of community participation, whether they're Haida or not. What happens is they feel better because they had no control for so long and they felt bad about what happened to our people, and it made them feel better just to help us that little bit. So it helped the island as a whole and then visitors who come here, it impacted their lives by saying, "I couldn't change what my ancestors did, but I can help you when you need help getting your ancestors and making things right." (11 May 2006)

In Irene's village of Skidegate, the repatriation process was often aligned with another event: the physical destruction of persons as a result of epidemic diseases and events predating residential schooling. During reburial feasts and the End of Mourning in Skidegate, prayers and food were offered simultaneously for the repatriated ancestors and the victims of smallpox. Skidegate Repatriation and Cultural Committee members said it was not an easy decision to include the victims of smallpox within these ceremonies because there are Haidas who have not yet fully grieved for these deaths, and have not yet incorporated this near-extinction of families into their sense of self-identity and history. The public space of repatriation and of an End of Mourning ceremony, they hoped, would work together to provide a safe space for remembering and retelling, geared as they are towards bringing emotional relief for both the living and the deceased.

The documentary *Stolen Spirits of Haida Gwaii* (McMahon 2004) vocalizes a connection between the loss of family members to smallpox and their loss to ethnographic collectors and scientific research. The film created a space for collective retelling that has the potential to become a historic document or site of commemoration in its own right. Although directed and produced by non-Haidas, it has been taken up by a number of HRC members as "our documentary"; a sense of ownership over this award-winning film is palpable among repatriation committee members from both villages, who during interviews would teasingly respond to my questions about the history of repatriation with "Watch our documentary!" At times, they would use a person's familiarity with the content of the documentary as a gauge of her or his knowledge of the repatriation process, and during conversation they would often mention the film's director, Kevin McMahon, with respect. Shortly after the film won two Gemini Awards,[3] a public screening was held at the Tluu Xaada Naay longhouse in Massett as part of a fund-raiser for the Haida Heritage and Repatriation Society. The DVD is also available for sale at the Haida Gwaii Museum giftshop.

A central idea of the documentary is that Haidas want what they once had: control over their lives, families, beliefs, and cultural practices. The repatriation process is framed as a reassertion of Haidas' abilities to control their lives and re-enact and adapt their traditional beliefs and cultural practices within contemporary contexts. In contrast, the late nineteenth and much of the twentieth centuries are described by Nika Collison as a "blip" in Haida history – an uncharacteristic period of dependency and assimilation. In the documentary, the late Ethel Jones, who worked with the HHRS in Massett, likewise evaluated the period when Haida remains were being taken off island. Speaking to the camera, she hesitates, then explains that Haidas were "being Indians" at that time, not knowing what white people were doing to them or on behalf of them (see also Harkin 1988, 104, on the presence of Native passivity within ideas of loss). It is helpful to compare Ethel's analysis of this earlier time with an analysis of contemporary Haida society given by Niis Wes, the late Ernie Wilson, hereditary leader of Skedans. In the same documentary he comments, "gradually [we're] getting back to normal Haida life. For a long while it was squished, now it's slowly coming back" (McMahon 2004). Niis Wes' words conjure images of land masses rebounding after the weight of a glacier melts away. Although smallpox, Indian agents, missionaries, residential schools, and collectors seeking remains have disappeared from Haida villages, people are still recovering from their weight.

HHRS co-chairs Lucy Bell and Vince Collison (2006) have written of repatriation as a means of revitalizing people's *pride* in their culture, rather than as a revitalization of the culture itself. Potentially, the dislike HHRS committee members expressed for cultural revitalization narratives is grounded in an anxiety that the inhumanities of the colonial experience will be forgotten or removed from the collective narrative if the twentieth century becomes glossed over as an exception. It is critical to acknowledge that, for Massett repatriation committee members in particular, repatriation narratives do not erase the destructive impacts of colonialism even when those narratives are focused on positive, kinship-oriented actions or continuity. Lucy was also one of the few people to talk about the capacity for repatriation to create hardships; she acknowledged that it taxed elements of her personal life and would challenge readings of the situation that celebrated her daughter's "opportunity" to travel and see so many museums and cities in order to repatriate her ancestor's remains.

The narratives of repatriation in Old Massett explicitly include, rather than ignore, traumatic events. They are characterized by the surmounting of challenges and the presence of challenges awaiting attention. There persists the question of cultural treasures – including family property – held in collections throughout the world. Vince Collison stressed that the continued presence of historic Haida artefacts in non-Haida museums repeatedly reminds repatriation committee members of the injustices of colonialism. It is in this light that the HHRS' decision to delay an End of Mourning ceremony may be viewed. Although an End of Mourning ceremony or headstone moving does not require forgetting, it does shift the context in which people remember from that of active mourning to that of relief or a releasing of grief, an end of public mourning. The HHRS intends to refrain from hosting such a ceremony until all of their ancestors' remains and cultural treasures return to Haida Gwaii.

There is a complex narrative of frustration, sadness, and anger at the presence of Haida objects in museum collections *and the absence* of Haida objects on Haida Gwaii.[4] In a segment from *Stolen Spirits*, carved goat horn spoons in the collections of the Field Museum become a reminder of absence and loss as Mary Swanson handles the spoons gently and with intellectual and emotional interest, but also with lament:

> My grandfather used to carve the big spoons like this so we were able to use it. Then we had a house fire. Everything burned up. Mmhmm. Now we just see his work in museums. But I'm really emotional today to see all this beautiful work because none of us is using these spoons today. No one. (McMahon 2004)

Regardless of how museums incorporate these objects into scholastic or popular narratives about human or national history, Vince maintains that as objects of Haida history they hold greater significance for Haidas. (Despite this tension, Christian White of the HHRS pointedly reminded me that the relationship between museums and Haida people continues to develop, strengthened by the shared experience of repatriation in which Haidas and museum staff work at extending and receiving respect and minimizing alienation between Haida, their ancestors, their objects, and museums.) The absence of material culture from the landscape or cultural archive on Haida Gwaii stands in contrast to the presence there of new materials made for the repatriation process. The latter are not a substitute for the former, but create different collective spaces for remembering and forgetting and provide the material evidence to support new memories and narratives.

Given the degree of displacement present in Haida experiences and narratives of loss, I see similarities with David Parkin's (1999) efforts to understand the role of memory and narrativization in the self-identification of refugees. Parkin powerfully describes conditions of crisis, isolation, and displacement among refugees as catalytic forces that can dismantle or erode identity while also compelling its reconstruction. He writes, "The recoverability or otherwise of personhood from an objectified state may, then, depend not just on the severity of trauma but on how much memories of life before trauma can become an acceptably realistic link with the present, bridging the gap between past loss and future potential" (Parkin 1999, 315). Finding "an acceptably realistic link" is also the crux of Laurence Kirmayer's approach to understanding memory and trauma, whereby the social contexts of retelling, as well as the content of the retelling, find validation among one's social community. Haida repatriation narratives enable significant links to "memories of life before trauma," creating continuities between past, present, and future populations.

The material richness of the repatriation process and cultural archive has the ability to recall this period of material wealth and technical knowledge, further supporting Parkin's call to consider how objects can be catalysts for reconstructing identities following traumatic events. Within the repatriation process, for instance, cedar was used extensively, as were the techniques of weaving, kerfing, and steaming cedar. The ability of cedar to connect people to another epoch is powerfully evoked in artist April Churchill's sensation of having her ancestors guide her movements and help her in the creation of a woven cedar mat for the repatriation process (Bell and Collison 2006, 142). But mass-produced, everyday objects likely to be grabbed from a shelf or out of a cupboard also play a role connecting past and present. Those objects sold and raffled off during fund-raisers and marked with the repatriation committees' butterfly logos, recall historic, cultural knowledge unaffected by Christianity or Western rationalization (figure 7.1). The butterfly design was adopted when Haida elders recalled their ancestors' knowledge that the appearance of butterflies in spring signified the wandering spirits of family and friends who had died away from Haida Gwaii and whose remains could not be brought back (McMahon 2004; SRCC 2006). Vince Collison from the HHRS explained their butterfly design was chosen from many entered into a competition they hosted. The design is by Ron Dallyn, inspired by a story recalled by his mother-in-law, Margaret Hewer, in which the butterfly is a wandering spirit; she linked the story to the repatriation committee's travel to far-off places in order to bring their ancestors' wandering spirits home once and for all. "Margaret was there when we started and has since passed on, but every time I see that logo," Vince said, "I think of Ron and her" (email message to author, 16 June 2013). In addition to Vince's very personal memory, the information latent in the butterfly design and the relearning or reactivation of this knowledge create a tangible connection to the past.

Despite Haidas' confidence in their relationship to their ancestors and their homeland, there exists anxiety about being (or becoming) estranged from the language, knowledge, and practices of this historical epoch. If Haida are seeking to affirm their contemporary identity in a set of principles and values that are not based on an identity as wards of the state (an all-too-common Canadian narrative), then the period

Figure 7.1 HHRS logo (left) designed by Ron Dallyn and SRCC logo (right) designed by Brad Collinson.

prior to smallpox and the current period in which repatriation is underway act together to suggest identities or periods of dependency are aberrations. The standard constituting "normal Haida life" stems from remembrances of a time before smallpox. In contrast to the twentieth century, the first half of the nineteenth century is recollected and historicized by Haidas as a time of great economic and artistic achievement, highly functional according to traditional protocol and values, and with minimal negative interventions from colonials (Davidson 2006).

The period in Haida history prior to smallpox has become a time that can be remembered as life before trauma. It is longed for as a time of achievement, wealth, autonomy, and knowledge. As Harkin (1988) argues, this period may be more aptly told through narratives of "gain" than "loss." Narratives of loss, he contests, occur when history begins, problematically, with colonialism. For Haidas, the period prior to smallpox represents a standard of cultural fluency – including linguistic fluency – on the opposite end of the spectrum from cultural estrangement and the endangerment of the Haida language.

Continuity, Identity, and Memory

A number of Haida who shared their stories with me were not only interested in ideas about continuity but also had means of measuring continuity in nuanced and holistic ways that push back against art-historical and anthropological readings of cultural contintuity based on particular kinds of artistic production.[5] They measured continuity through a wider range of social practices and assessed continuity based on their own experiences. Nika Collison and Irene Mills from the SRCC, for example, encouraged me to consider the preparation of meals for repatriation feasts as equally worthy of attention as the making of bentwood boxes (see also Crosby 2004). The former is a skill that has never been lost, while the latter is a relearned skill prompted by repatriation. In drawing attention to the practices surrounding food production, they were proposing another set of objects and memories upon which to focus and legitimize collective memories. Significantly, this set of objects reflects continuity rather than loss, perseverance rather than reintegration.

In other cases, Haidas spoke about continuity in ways that were episodic, rather than linear and uninterrupted. Fox and King (2002, 1) describe unsatisfying schemes in which culture is imagined to be steady and linear and where continuity is achieved through the reproduction of representations and beliefs "relatively intact across generations through enculturation." No such confines or prerequisites pertain in the Haida case. Instead, shared experience forms a powerful basis for common identities between temporally distant generations or after lapses in activities.

The complexities of continuity are visible in the following excerpt from an interview I conducted with Jaalen Edenshaw, whose first direct involvement with the HHRS did not happen until 2009. His words were offered in 2006 as part of a larger conversation about the influence of repatriation on the Haida nation and about younger people's engagement with cultural identity:

I always have a hard time with the idea of a "Haida revitalization." The only place that I would hear it for the longest time is schoolbooks and what not: "The Haida culture died and things were brought back by Bill Reid and Robert Davidson" – in these books that were written and so forth. And that bugged me because just growing up – how I grew up – Haida identity has always been at the forefront of my upbringing. We'd be taken out of school for two, three weeks at a time to go fishing, or whatever. That's just how things were. It wasn't weird. I know a lot of other kids never got that kind of opportunity, but even if they weren't doing it on a regular basis, it was still within their vocabulary because it was happening and that's part of who we are. I think as far as being out on the land, that's never changed, except I think our generation does it less than the generations before us. In that sense, "revitalization" – I don't think we're necessarily doing it any more. I think we're doing it less. But I think it's a continuation. All of us, my generation, we grew up with the pot-latches and with dance practice – probably most kids my age at one time did dance practice, have always seen it, and heard the songs. I'd always get mad when people told me, "Oh the culture's dead," then I realized that it was in pretty hard shape at one time. Not that it was ever dead, but there was a period there when it wasn't used as much as it was, or even is today. It hurts hearing older people talking about how there weren't things that we take for granted now, as young people. I'm not even too young right now, but we take for granted potlatches and memorials. That was a big thing when that started happening again and people started doing that. So we are grateful for the elders that held that up. People like to say it was gone more than it was because it's a better romantic story. But it was gone for thirty years or so. That's still a lot of people that were alive, whether they were in their teens then, but everything was smaller. I'm grateful any-way that people like Robert [Davidson] and my dad [Guujaaw] and those people took an interest when they were at a young age, and took an inter-est and started performing. Because if they never did that, then all of that wouldn't have been transferred to us. We wouldn't have it as part of our language. We'd have something else: it would still be Haida, but it wouldn't be this. (18 January 2006)

One of the tensions captured in Jaalen's response is the distance be-tween narratives and experience, or we might also say between nar-ratives and the cultural archive. Because of the distance between the narratives in scholastic books and his own life experiences, he questions the accuracy of this literature. Similarly, Nika and Irene challenged scholastic narratives that privilege artistic production at the expense of other activities like cooking that are equally integral to a cultural ar-chive. Jaalen, Nika, and Irene all engaged their knowledge and memo-ries of recent Haida history to evaluate the literature more carefully. At the same time, Jaalen's own experiences make it difficult for him to imagine a time when cultural practices and protocols were not as wide-spread as they are in the present or were before the twentieth century. In Jaalen's thoughtful statement, he grapples with how experiences have come to be shared among Haidas through time. In some cases, practices have continued steadily; in other cases, they have declined; and in others still, Jaalen identifies periods of activity shared by tempo-rally distant generations.

Jaalen surmised that the reintegration of particular cultural practices reflected the meaning and utility of those practices during various times within Haida history.[6] As Haidas experience different challenges and successes, certain practices are expanded, neglected, or adapted. Thus, rather than imagine Haida cultural practices as steadily declining, or steadily increasing, Jaalen described things as happening in waves. The effect is that Haidas share experiences whether as part of the peaks or of the troughs of these waves. The centrality of shared experience is evident in his final comments: even when Haidas do change or adapt their practices, new ways become "Haida" through their repetition and widespread enactment by Haidas. Furthermore, as individual experiences are made known to others through narratives, practices enter into people's vocabulary and become "part of our language."

There exist collective spaces where Haida experiences of repatriation have been explicitly narrated in an attempt to characterize, if not also memorialize, the repatriation process: articles within the *Haida Laas* journal and newsletter; an exhibition at the Haida Gwaii Museum; the documentary film *Stolen Spirits of Haida Gwaii* (McMahon 2004) that chronicles the return of Haida ancestors from the Field Museum in Chicago;[7] and three episodes across two seasons of the television series *Ravens and Eagles*.

In the newly refurbished Haida Gwaii Museum, a site designed for both Haida and non-Haida audiences, an exhibition on repatriation entitled "*Yahgudangang* – To Pay Respect" (figure 7.2) is embedded within a gallery that features visible storage and narrates the historical development of the Haida nation; the social systems of the Haida, including potlatching and matrilineal descent; the Haida language; and the relationship between Haida beings and their environment. The exhibition represents Haida authorship, particularly given Nika Collison's overlapping roles as then-museum curator and co-chair of the SRCC. In addition to wall text panels, the exhibit contains photographs of Haidas in museum collection areas, performing at different museums, making the artefacts of repatriation, and celebrating the return of their ancestors. The exhibit includes one small and one medium-sized bentwood box (not yet painted with a crest) made by HHRS member Christian White and a small button blanket with the common repatriation blanket design of a raven and an eagle facing each other – their heads, beaks, and wings coming together to form a heart shape – made by students from the Sḵ'aadG̱a Naay Elementary School in Skidegate. There is a touch screen where visitors can choose clips to watch from *Stolen Spirits of Haida Gwaii* and the *Ravens and Eagles* television series episodes on repatriation (Bear and Jones 2002, 2003a, 2003b).[8]

Figure 7.2 *"Yahgudangang* – To Pay Respect" exhibition at Haida Gwaii Museum, including a button blanket and undecorated bentwood box on display, 2010. Photograph by Drew Davey.

The text in the exhibition is factual in tone. It explains the removal of remains from Haida Gwaii, defines repatriation and *yahgudangang*, presents the priorities and work of the Haida Repatriation Committee, lists the numbers of remains returned, informs people of what to do if they discover remains on Haida Gwaii, and presents the integrated role of the community within the process. There is a quote that highlights the significance of Haida objects to Haida people by chronicling an artist's journey that begins with her denial of her native identity during her adolescence and concludes with her finding a sense of identity in the old artefacts exhibited in museums:

> I began to really understand the sophistication of the old stuff when I looked at the artifacts. I thought, "This is what I'm about." ... As I grow older, this becomes more fascinating because I think about how I could have missed the opportunity of discovering it, it has given me an identity.

> It puts more value into my life, being a vision maker, as one person said, being that part of a people that creates visions and pictures in the same way dancers do. (Francis Williams in Jensen and Sargent 1986, cited in "*Yahgudangang* – To Pay Respect," Haida Gwaii Museum 2007)

This quotation is accompanied by the statement: "We do this [repatriation] because our ancestors are our relatives – we are who we are because of them." The exhibit is a potent reminder that repatriation is about "belonging" in the double sense of being part of and beholden to a family. This duality appears in a clip on the touch-screen terminal featuring Vince Collison, who invokes the idea to affirm that Haida artefacts in museums belong to Haida families.[9]

The narrative in the exhibit integrates repatriation efforts focused on human remains with those focused on artefacts. It asserts both the return of human remains and of objects as a matter of moral principle and as a means of reviving pride in Haida identity. The exhibit's narrative simultaneously displaces non-Haida perceptions that repatriation is a political statement by contextualizing it within the frame of kinship and self-respect, and for Haida audiences reinforces the culturally meaningful concept of *yahgudang* as an expression of kinship and self-respect. The difference is slight but significant. Rather than remove politics from the process of repatriation, within Haida understandings of *yahgudang* there is always a sense of morality and politics. It is "identity politics" of a different kind: an encouragement for Haidas to see value in their ancestors and families, in their cultural practices and philosophies, and ultimately in themselves. In this sense, I see the exhibition as a collective effort to educate Haidas about cultural values and to provide knowledge about how, when, and where to enact (and hence reproduce) those values. The politico-moral message underlying the exhibition is that contemporary Haidas are fit for respect in part because they have endeavoured to bring their ancestors home and care for them.

The greatest challenge to individual memories, Kirmayer posits, is an absence of plausible spaces in which to situate one's memories, or when one's memories have the effect of causing a break or discontinuity in the overall narrative. Invalidated by a collective or institutional narrative, such memories can be problematic in the construction of one's own identity and in the way one remembers (see also Crane 1997). Lambek and Antze (1996) suggest that memory is called into question when identity is in question – an apt observation given the potential for narratives to shift both by force and by choice. The extent to which aboriginal nations in Canada have been seeking self-representation within historical settings, and self-determination in political spheres, reveals a conviction that a shifting narrative can affect how the past is known, and that there is a concomitant impact of this newly realized past on the present (see Nicks 2003; Phillips 2003). Parkin (1999) encourages us to consider the effects of alternative collective narratives trumping the prior ones through which people situate themselves: when refugee status, for example, trumps ethnicity; when non-Native narratives trump Native narratives (Crosby 2004), or when national narratives supercede familial narratives (Brown et al. 2006, and see chapter 6).

In an earlier chapter, I noted Haida resistance to including repatriation within treaty writing or other political endeavours. The Haida wanted neither to wait for the tortoise-paced process of political negotiation nor to negotiate for the right to have their ancestors home. The president of the Council of the Haida Nation has also gone on public record positioning repatriation as a moral rather than a political issue (McMahon 2004). Lambek and Antze (1996) provide insight into the effects of this decision on the narrative possibilities that follow:

> Remembering trauma may be personally empowering and sometimes lead to collective organizing. The inscription of trauma narratives may be a necessary, sufficient, and compelling means of establishing recognition. At the same time, such an identity politics can subjugate and immobilize victims in the very act of recognizing their suffering. The reason is that the political gains offered by a victim identity (e.g. "trauma survivor") are accessible only through expert discourses (in law, medicine, psychiatry) which have their own agendas and are themselves instruments of power. By their very nature such discourses deal in causes rather than meanings, events rather than persons, instances rather than entire lives. Thus ... reinscribing personal stories into these public discourses often obscures their richness and moral complexity. There is a vast gulf between the narrative possibilities afforded by notions of personhood, kinship, and morality on the one hand and the dry language of bureaucracy and biopolitics on the other. (Lambek and Antze 1996, xxiv)

Kinship, personhood, respect, and morality, I have been arguing, are at the heart of the Haida's process of repatriation. Indeed, Haida feared the effacement of these aspects if a route of political negotiation were pursued. The repatriation committees have also consistently emphasized that aspect of *yahgudang* which is focused on the respectful treatment of others, rather than its parallel, politicized function of improving one's own social status. The ongoing narrative of repatriation is one in which Haida families are involved in a project to regain the elements of their families.

At this point, I want to return to Janet Carsten's (2000, 2007) concern with the place of kinship in the formation of biographies. Like the Haida, Scottish adoptees identified family (in the Scottish case, specifically biological family) as an important element within their personal histories. Yet the absence of information about their biological families compromised their ability to narrate their own biographies. The adoptees hoped reunion with biological parents and/or siblings might help to construct their personal histories. Unexpectedly, they found that the very reason the information was lacking in the first place – an absence of shared history with their biological kin – meant that including reunited kin within their present and future biographies was also extremely difficult. Carsten explains:

> The people whose stories I listened to were also confronting the ruptures in their own kinship time, the radical breaks in the steady accumulation of everyday practical experiences of kinship that had in turn disrupted the flow of ritually marked kinship time ... The steady accumulation of unmarked exchanges of kinship was missing in relations with birth kin. And this, in turn, emptied such ritual high points of much of their desired meaning. (Carsten 2000, 696)

Carsten's informants discovered that, while they were able to learn facts about their biological family, for the most part this factual history contained little more than information (2000, 692); it lacked the shared experiences and memories, both marked and unmarked in nature, that existed with adopted families.

As a space for retelling and remembering, the process of repatriation connects multiple generations of Haida families through its ability to re-engage them physically and emotionally in various components of a cultural archive. It remedies substantial ruptures in kinship time. It does not solely ask Haidas to commemorate their ancestors; it asks Haidas to reintegrate themselves with these ancestors, to engage in marked and unmarked exchanges with them. While committee and community members alike are hesitant to single out repatriation, it nevertheless presents a concrete set of achievements that act as evidence within a larger, ongoing process of integrating Haida with their ancestors. Repatriation builds collective spaces and joins a landscape of memories already in progress. It contributes to and legitimizes the narratives of family, self, and nationhood Haida are eager to tell: narratives of responsibility, care, accountability, and connectedness to their families – past, present, and future. These are narratives of *yahgudangang*, stories that relate the respect held for others and people's own fitness to receive respect from others. It is worth emphasizing that the place of repatriation within this collective narrative is likely to transform as individuals, families, and the Haida nation continue to reminisce and integrate repatriation efforts into their personal biographies and cultural archive.

8 Conclusions and Beginnings

The process of repatriation is not yet over for the Haida. Ancestral remains continue to be held in museum collections in Europe, while family and cultural treasures exist in innumerable institutions around the
world. During my visit to Haida Gwaii in July 2010, the HRC celebrated
the return of their first ancestor from overseas – from the Pitt Rivers
Museum at the University of Oxford. At the same time, they were pain-
fully aware that another of their ancestor's remains continued to be
held at the British Museum. Just days before, a small delegation of HRC
members, Gaahlaay (Lonnie Young, hereditary leader of the Ts'aahl
clan), Melinda Pick, and Vernon Williams, had travelled to Oxford for
the transfer of the ancestor's remains from the university to the Haida.
Their voyage echoed one they had made eleven months earlier to
study Haida collections at both the Pitt Rivers Museum and British
Museum and to present their request for the repatriation of their ancestor in writing to the Pitt Rivers director, Dr Michael O'Hanlon. On that
earlier occasion they travelled with eighteen other Haidas (Krmpotich
and Peers 2011, 2013). I had been part of the team that organized the
initial collections visit, but had left Oxford to begin a new job in Canada
just before Gaahlaay, Melinda, and Vern returned to repatriate their ancestor. My former colleagues at Pitt Rivers who worked tirelessly to
host the research visit were all in attendance for the handing over, and
I am told[1] there was not a dry eye in the room as the vice-chancellor of
the university received the remains from Dr O'Hanlon, who then entrusted them to Gaahlaay to bring home.

The HRC decided to time the repatriation of their ancestor with a
reciprocal visit to Haida Gwaii by a small delegation of museum staff
involved in the earlier research visit. Curator Laura Peers and her

husband travelled to Canada with the Haida delegates and their ancestor. Peers remembers Vern seemingly wrapping his entire body around
the bentwood box as he cleared Canadian customs at the Vancouver
airport, his demeanour that of a cautious bear, unwilling to let anyone
trespass within that bentwood box. She remembers him nearly sprinting away from the Agriculture Canada desk, not giving them an opportunity to second guess their approval for him to enter Canada with
the uncommon carry-on, nor an opportunity to quarantine or potentially even destroy the remains.

The other members of the museum delegation, myself, conservators
Sherry Doyal and Kate Jackson, and assistant curator Devorah
Romanek, met in Haida Gwaii to share knowledge about the museums'
collections and preventive conservation and, importantly, to join in the
ceremonies for the repatriation of the ancestor.

On the afternoon of the ceremonies, there was a fire, food burning,
and prayers on the pebble beach in front of K̲aay Llnagaay Haida
Heritage Centre led by elder Diane Brown. We stood in a circle with
hands joined and listened to Diane's words in Haida and English.
About half the people present were Haida, but there was also a large
group of youth tourists who were welcomed into the ceremony and
joined the circle.

We moved indoors and were joined by villagers from Skidegate and
Queen Charlotte City for a feast in the heart of the Heritage Centre,
overlooking Skidegate Inlet. The families of repatriation committee
members brought large aluminum foil containers filled with fish prepared in numerous ways, mixing bowls filled with salads, and dozens
upon dozens of freshly baked buns. Visiting museum staff and repatriation committee members alike prepared and delivered plates of
food to seniors at the long dining tables decorated with cedar boughs.
Younger attendees lined up buffet-style to pile up their plates.

After dinner, attendees made their way to the square longhouse with
sunken floor in the Heritage Centre. People gathered on the tiered
benches while concerned Haidas made sure there were enough chairs
for seniors so that they would not need to navigate stairs or bench seating. There was a procession with singing and drumming, at the front of
which was the bentwood box cradled in Haida hands. In this setting,
there was no need for bear-like protection nor sprinting. The box was
carried across the floor and placed on the first tier in the centre. As various people addressed the crowd – Guujaaw, president of the Council of
the Haida Nation, Nika Collison and Melinda Pick from the SRCC, the

museum staff who had supported Haidas in their visits to the UK, hereditary leaders from the historic southern villages – the box remained in its place of honour. After speeches and slide shows featuring images of the museums' collections, the box was carried to the mortuary house – the smaller longhouse around which the expanded Heritage Centre was built. Museum staff were invited inside the longhouse, which was barely tall enough to stand in. The only light came in through the open door. Instead of being ringed with tiered platforms for inhabitants or guests to a potlatch, this longhouse was ringed with shelves. Small bentwood boxes rested on the shelves. Each of my colleagues said their farewells to one box in particular before stepping out the door. They were replaced one by one with Haidas I had come to know in the previous six years; they came in to speak to their ancestor and pay their respects.

Their ancestor remained in the mortuary house overnight, awaiting reburial in Old Massett, a short distance away from where she or he was originally unearthed. Waiting for the *kuniisii* in Massett were repatriation committee members – descendents – who had arranged for a mass, procession to the cemetery, reburial and tea. The next day museum staff were asked to bring the *kuniisii* to Massett. We packed into our rented Toyota Corolla; our belongings filled the trunk and every available space in the interior. We were making the one-hundred-kilometre drive from Skidegate to Old Massett – a drive I had done often throughout my field research – but this time my husband was behind the wheel and my son and two colleagues from the British Museum were squeezed into the backseat. I fastened my seatbelt, and then Nika Collison and her Ts'aahl clan sister Nadine Wilson handed me the low, square wooden box. It filled the space between my torso and the glove compartment.

As I was handed the box, I recalled learning from Haida Repatriation Committee members that they always travelled to museums to repatriate their ancestors' remains; their elders decreed that the *kuniisii*'s care and respect could not be left up to others. Indeed, just one week earlier three Haidas had flown with this *kuniisii* from Heathrow via Vancouver to the small airport across the inlet from Skidegate. My part may only have involved the last one hundred kilometres of a seventy-five-hundred-kilometre journey, but this small act of trust and friendship filled me with pride.

When I first arrived on Haida Gwaii, they were celebrating the return of all known Haida ancestral remains from North America. That was 2005. In 2010, they were celebrating their first successful overseas repatriation. There was always a tension between repatriation as a job that simply needed doing, and the emotional force of what a relatively small group of people was doing on behalf of every clan that makes up their nation. Experiences and memories continue to accumulate. I have not yet had the chance to reminisce about this repatriation with my Haida colleagues. Unlike most of the stories in these pages, which are Haidas' remembrances of ten years of repatriation activities, this final remembrance is my own.

Throughout this book, I have sought to understand the motivations driving Haidas to repatriate their ancestors' remains, and to understand the material and performative aspects of the repatriation process. The best way to do this is to locate repatriation within the broader context of Haida kinship – a fundamental feature of Haida identity that structures social relationships and guides appropriate uses of property, resources, and objects. Kinship affects the way Haidas experience the world and provides the dominant structure through which remembering occurs and history is internalized. In asking what it is that makes kinship, I have argued for a dual process whereby marked and unmarked exchanges accumulate to create shared memories that join people across generations and spaces. As Janet Carsten (2000) explains, there is a co-production of kinship and memory.

Haida kinship structures have been undermined over the course of multiple generations through Canadian federal laws as well as moral systems that privileged patrilineal descent, devalued and even criminalized cultural transmission, and sought to minimize the impact of Haida families on children. These actions posed serious challenges for Haidas' abilities to maintain the social and moral qualities of *gwaay. gang/ gyaaging.aay* (lineage) and *k'waalaa* (moiety) relationships. The removal of ancestral remains from the islands and their storage in museums was felt as a further affront to Haida families, causing grief and sadness across multiple generations. Both personal biographies and collective histories that seek to stimulate pride in a Haida identity need to somehow navigate lapses in familial behavior whether resulting from threats to the physical, emotional, and economic well-being of family members or from an inability to conduct rites of *yahgudang*.

Haida repatriation efforts counteract this legacy and re-instil the preciousness of kinship. They do so by fulfilling the expectations of kinship and by demonstrating *yahgudangang* (respect) for people's own ancestors, for those of other Haidas, and for their own selves. In their endeavours to pay respect to their ancestors, Haidas inadvertently created situations that fostered shared experiences between generations separated by time or space. The material and performative qualities of the repatriation process become particularly important here. Through the construction of button blankets and bentwood boxes, through the preparation of food offerings and feasts, through singing, speaking, and praying, and through the memorialization of repatriation via dance, song, a pole, and a museum exhibition, a cultural archive and a corpus of memories built upon respect rather than neglect developed among committee members and the Haida nation more generally. The acts of honour, commemoration, and love built into the repatriation process repositioned people as fulfilling their kinship obligations – a key factor in determining *yahgudang*.

One outcome of repatriation has been the strengthening and deepening of Haida collective memory and kinship relations as individuals enact common cultural values, reminisce, share embodied sensations and, critically, evaluate and validate each other's experiences and memories. It is difficult to disentangle repatriation as an event isolated from "Haida culture" or social practices. Repatriation is rarely an isolated incident. Where peoples or nations pursue the return of artefacts or human remains from one institution, they frequently need to repeat the process at others. Within communities, nations, and museums, committees are struck and policies and procedures are devised, implemented, and refined. What was once new and unchartered territory becomes part of people's everyday lives. And it is often in the rhythms of daily work that the components of a cultural archive can be identified (James 2007).

By providing a significant number of shared experiences, the process of repatriation created a sense of continuity and commensality between generations. It is in this light that I have read Carsten's argument that the quantity of everyday, "unmarked" interactions shared in common contributes significantly to the ability of "marked exchanges" to create a meaningful sense of unity and belonging. By building up a repertoire of embodied experiences in common with their ancestors, as well as enacting appropriate rites, Haida repatriation efforts were able to reincorporate Haida ancestors into the ongoing familial and social relations on Haida Gwaii.

"Kinship" is part of a discourse used consciously on Haida Gwaii to emphasize cultural continuity and a unique identity (see also Rowlands 2002, 107 on the self-consciousness of culture). Not only do the actions and narratives of repatriation attest to what Haida kinship values *are*, they attest to what Haida kinship is *not* in the eyes of others. Repatriation contradicts majority society's narratives of neglect or incompetence within aboriginal nations. It contradicts majority society's narratives privileging the individual as a jural person and as the locus/possessor/ wielder of rights. It does not automatically follow, however, that this challenge to majority narratives is solely a component of post-colonial or decolonizing identity politics. The primary audience of concern to Haidas was their own relatives (deceased and living) and the families that comprise the Haida nation. Identity politics, in this case, needs to be cast as a predominantly local phenomenon, as an expression of the relationship between self and others, and as an expression of both morality and politics: that is, *yahgudang*. The political and moral relationships being summoned, shaped, challenged, and activated were, first and foremost, those among living and deceased Haidas rather than those among aboriginal and settler societies or colonized and colonizers. The political identities that most frequently mattered to repatriation committee members were those that expressed their knowledge of and adherence to cultural values regulating lineage and *k'waalaa* responsibilities, personal decorum, and respectable behaviour.

Continuity and Identity

There is an interplay between identity, continuity, and adaptability that underlies the story told here. While the current trend is to analyse repatriation within the frame of an identity politics that is focused on indigeneity or post-colonialism as political identities, Haida repatriation efforts show us that community, cultural, national, and individual identities are in tension with each other, without privileging a colonized/ colonizer dynamic as a defining feature (Krmpotich 2012). This is not to deny the politicization of the processes creating identity, continuity, and adaptability, but rather to encourage exploration of the full spectrum of meanings and structures that give these processes force within social, cultural, and political realms. Recognizing and validating the potential for kinship to drive relations requires an understanding of the force of kinship (Geertz 1968; Rosaldo 1984).

Within repatriation discourse, identity and continuity loom large. More specifically, it is often the continuity of identity that acts as the basis for both repatriation claims and the evaluation of evidence for or against return. Within the Haida nation and in other indigenous communities, continuity is not being asserted based on a complete repetition of cultural practices, or the complete transmission of genetic material.

Shared experiences of land surface as one reason for this sense of continuity (cf. Glass 2008; Modest 2012), but another possibility is the shared experience of being mothers, grandmothers, uncles, nephews, daughters, or fathers – in a word, family. It is this sense of the shared experience of being family that Connie Hart Yellowman powerfully evokes as she brings together the Oklahoma city bombing in 1995, the Cheyenne massacre at Sand Creek in 1864, and the repatriation of the Cheyenne victims from the Smithsonian Institution in 1993. She writes:

> On that terrible April day, while I clung to my daughter, I thought about all the mothers who lost their babies in such a senseless act of violence, and how they would never get the chance to hold their babies again. A flashback occurred and I realised that this was all too familiar. Only two years earlier, I briefly held the repatriated remains of a young girl – someone's daughter – who along with hundreds of others died in violence at Sand Creek. (Yellowman 1996, 104)

Kinship involves sets of shared experiences and a cultural archive that inform ways of knowing, ways of acting and reacting, and ways of imagining. In thinking through the force of kinship, we might consider Catherine Lutz's definition for "emotion" as "an index of social relationships rather than a sign of a personal state" (Lutz 1988, 4). It is in the indeterminacy between emotion and kinship, in that index of social relations, that we can better understand continuity, identity, and the force not only of kinship but of repatriation.

Interviews

The interviews listed below were formal conversations driven by the author's questions. They were audio recorded and/or recorded in writing. All audio recordings and written notes were transcribed and provided to the interviewee for her or him to amend, add to, or clarify.

Cited in Text
Lucy Bell, Old Massett, HHRS, 22 December 2005
Joyce Bennett, Old Massett, 2 April 2006
Leona Claw, Old Massett, HHRS, 27 March 2006
Vince Collison, Old Massett, HHRS, 22 December 2005
Jaalen Edenshaw, New Masset, 18 January 2006
Natalie Fournier, Skidegate, SRCC, 4 May 2006
Irene Mills, Skidegate, SRCC, 11 May 2006
Pearle Pearson, Skidegate, SRCC, 1 May 2006
Mary Swanson, Old Massett, HHRS, 7, 21 November 2005, 13 January 2006
Candace Weir, Old Massett, HHRS, 22 December 2005
Christian White, Old Massett, HHRS, 9, 19 November 2005
Andy Wilson, Skidegate, SRCC, 17 April 2006

Not Cited in Text
Git_Kun, John Williams, Skidegate, 25 May 2006
Nate Jolley, Tow Hill, Haida Gwaii, 7 February 2006
Lynn Maranda, Vancouver, Vancouver Museum, 20 September 2005
Bill McLellan, Vancouver, Museum of Anthropology, 29 July 2005
Kimiko Von Boetticher, New Masset, 15 February 2006
Eldon Yellowhorn, Vancouver, 29 July 2005

Notes

1. Introduction

1 Anthropometry did not always require the collecting of skeletal remains. Spencer (1992) and Edwards (2001) document the use of photographic techniques to allow for measurement and comparative study of people and crania without having to remove either from their homes. Boas (in addition to collecting crania) collected measurements from immigrants entering the United States and the children subsequently born to them in the US (Boas 1912; Stocking 1989), while Bashkow (1991) records how physical anthropologists conducted anthropometric measurements and census surveys of living populations as part of larger anthropological field expeditions in Micronesia.

2 Trudy Nicks (1995) offered an early assessment of the task force report only three years after its release. Stephanie Bolton presented a later assessment during a 2005 conference in Edinburgh, Scotland.

3 For overviews of NAGPRA, see Fine-Dare (2002) and Trope and Echo-Hawk (2000). For analyses of the effects of NAGPRA, see McKeown (2002), Killion (2008), and the 2010 special issue of *Museum Anthropology* edited by Nash and Colwell-Chanthophonh on the theme "NAGPRA after 20 Years." See also the National Museum of the American Indian Act, Public Law 101–85.

4 Citations containing only a date indicate an interview with the author. A list of interviews is provided on p. 177.

5 For printed accounts, see Ayau and Tengan (2002), Brown et al. (2006), and Noble (2002). For film productions, see Brody (1994) and McMahon (2004).

6 Case studies investigating the significance of artefact repatriation demonstrate how artefacts and photographs in museums continue to act as

prompts for recalling stories, vocabulary, artistic skills, genealogies, and political histories when reintroduced to source communities (Binney and Chaplin 2003; Cruikshank 1995; Jacknis 1996; Kramer 2004; 2006; Poignant and Poignant 1996). The repatriation of human remains can also trigger memories, both as a result of the remains themselves (Thornton 2002; Yellowman 1996) and via mortuary rituals (Ayau and Tengan 2002).

7   *Voices from the Blue Nile* is available at http://www.voicesfromthebluenile .org.

8   In 1998, a small delegation of Haidas visited the British Museum and Pitt Rivers Museum to open dialogues about repatriating two ancestral remains, one at each institution, and to see the Haida collections. Lucy Bell recalls the formality and atmosphere of these visits in stark contrast with the delegation's experiences in North American museums around the same time. Bell also noted that this visit to the Pitt Rivers Museum predated the arrival of Peers as curator (Krmpotich and Peers, 2013).

2. Departures and Arrivals

1   Standardization of the Haida language is an ongoing process as it transforms from an oral language to an oral and written language. "Gwaaganad" is the most recent spelling of this name; however, "Gwaganad" has been retained when referring to work published using the earlier spelling.

2   "Band" is a legal term in Canada, defined by the Department of Indian and Northern Affairs Canada as "a body of Indians for whose collective use and benefit lands have been set apart or money is held by the Crown, or declared to be a band for the purposes of the Indian Act. Each band has its own governing band council, usually consisting of one chief and several councillors. Community members choose the chief and councillors by election, or sometimes through custom. The members of a band generally share common values, traditions and practices rooted in their ancestral heritage. Today, many bands prefer to be known as First Nations" (INAC 2003).

3   There have been migrations of white settlers on the islands as well, with towns being created, moved, or abandoned as mines, whaling stations, and military barracks opened or closed.

4   Reserves – tracts of land held by the Crown and delineated for the use and benefit of federally recognized Indian groups (INAC 2003) – were created in the 1850s and 1860s in British Columbia in an effort to prepare the new colonies of Vancouver Island, and later British Columbia, for settlers and capital expansion (UBCIC 2005). As early as 1876, a joint reserve commission was organized to address disputes between First Nations and the

government over the creation, reduction, and management of these lands – matters still debated today.

5 Boelscher (1988, 73) draws attention to the separation of foods into high- and low-class categories, particularly in historic times. The former includes foods that require co-operation (salmon, berries) and foods from larger animals that can feed many people (halibut and, historically, sea lion and whale, while deer may be a new food that fits into this category). The latter includes foods that are gathered by scrounging on the beach (shellfish, small mammals, and small birds). My experience during field research was that shellfish such as butter clams, cockles, and scallops were valued ingredients, but also usually involved some co-operation among family members or friends.

6 There are nine provincial and national parks on Haida Gwaii, and fourteen Council of the Haida Nation protected areas (Forest n.d.).

7 Rather than "authenticity," Tourtellot's article notes the "cultural integrity" of the site, evidenced by the positive working relationship between Parks Canada and the Haida. The village of SGang Gwaay was named a UNESCO world heritage site in 1981.

8 Harrison (1925) suspects the earliest European visitor to Haida Gwaii was the Spaniard Bartholomew de Fonte who, in 1640, describes going ashore in a place called "Mynhasset" that bears strong resemblances to the historic Haida villages along Masset Inlet. De Fonte describes seeing canoes "fifty and sixty feet in length and hewn out of single cedar trees" (Harrison 1925, 23). "Massett," however, is not a Haida word. The villages occupying the current site of Old Massett were named K'aayang, Ts'aagwals, Iijaaw, Gadgaaywaas, and Tang xyaangdlaas.

9 The exact number of Haida villages is difficult to determine. While George MacDonald discusses twenty-one inhabited villages on the islands in the 1800s in his *Monumental Haida Art* (1983), archaeologists working in what is now Gwaii Haanas National Park Reserve and Haida Heritage Site document seventy-three town sites, with forty-four of these sites containing evidence of permanent houses (Acheson 2005, 318).

10 In the summer of 2006, Kwakwaka'wakw artist Beau Dick (who was a childhood mate of Haida boys at residential school in Kwakwaka'wakw territory, and later married a Haida woman and raised a family on Haida Gwaii) had a potlatch in Alert Bay to remember a voyaging group of Haidas who died from smallpox while in Kwakwaka'wakw territory. The bodies of these people remained where they fell; thus Kwakwaka'wakw have dubbed the place "Blood Island." In a lecture given at the University of Oxford in March 2007, Vince Collison of the HRC said they were

uncertain whether these remains would be repatriated, but appreciated the ceremony and remembrance Dick proffered for these ancestors. Dick hosted a second potlatch of this kind in Alert Bay in May of 2008, attended by many Haidas, including members of the Haida Repatriation Committee and Haida dance troupes.

11 In linguistic texts, the Haida language is divided into two dialects, North (Massett) and South (Skidegate), or sometimes into three dialects – Skidegate, Kaigani, and Old Massett. Within these categories, however, are further dialectical differences.

12 See also Furniss (1999) for an exploration of how differing approaches to natural resources have shaped Native and non-Native perceptions of each other in the interior of British Columbia. Hugh Brody's *Maps and Dreams* (2004) provides an exceptional insight into differing attitudes towards the resources of the Peace Valley, and British Columbia more generally. John Vaillant's *The Golden Spruce: A True Story of Myth, Madness and Greed* (2005) also seeks to chronicle the mindsets existing within (and against) the logging industry using the rogue actions of one logger-turned-activist on Haida Gwaii.

13 These objects were central during a 2009 visit of twenty-one Haida delegates to the UK. The delegation went for three weeks to do hands-on research with Haida collections at the Pitt Rivers Museum and British Museum (Krmpotich and Peers 2011, 2013, and see http://www.prm.ox.ac.uk/haida.html, which allows for streaming of the film *Everything Was Carved* that documents the project).

14 Other successful Native collectors on the Northwest Coast include George Hunt, working for Boas in Kwakwaka'wakw territory; Louis Shotridge, collecting in Tlingit territory for the University Museum in Philadephia; William Beynon, working for Marius Barbeau in Tsimshian territory; and Charlie Nowell, working for Newcombe in Kwakwaka'wakw territory (Barbeau 1954; Beynon 1941; Boas 1921; Boas and Hunt 1905; Carpenter 1975; Cole 1995; Jacknis 1991; Raibmon 2006).

15 To a lesser degree, tourism had a role to play in the removal of objects from the Northwest Coast. Native people quickly recognized which of their goods were desirable and marketable to tourists and began producing items for sale to the socialites steaming their way up the Inside Passage. Baskets, jewellery made from pounded and carved silver dollars and half-dollars, and Haida argillite carvings were especially suitable for sale as curios and souvenirs. Collectors began to lament the tourist souvenir industry, as they felt the works being produced in this vein drove up prices, endangered their artefact supply, resulted in hybrid (read: "unauthentic")

designs, and did not compare in workmanship to older or locally used objects (Cole 1995; see also Duncan 2000 and Koros 2005; for histories of collecting and the interplay between amateur and professional collecting, see Hamilton 2010; O'Hanlon and Welsch 2002; Schildkrout and Keim 1998).

16 I thank Ken Rea, Oliver Bell, and Jusquan (Amanda Bedard) for drawing my attention to the importance of the fishing fleet – and its loss – to the character of Old Massett.

3. Family, Morality, and Haida Repatriation

1 For background on the establishment of the Marine Protected Area see the Department of Fisheries and Ocean website: http://www.dfo-mpo.gc.ca/media/npress-communique/2008/pr12-eng.htm.

2 This term comes from the premier of British Columbia, Gordon Campbell, who proclaimed in summer 2005 that the BC government would be actively developing new policies and programs with First Nations (Lee 2005). First Nations responded to this pledge with a mixture of hope, distrust, incredulity, and pensiveness.

3 In contrast, among other First Nations in British Columbia, the repatriation of artefacts and remains is being negotiated within contemporary treaty writing. For examples of treaty agreements that include clauses on repatriation of artefacts and remains, see the Maa-Nulth First Nations Final Agreement (2009), the Snuneymuxw Treaty Negotiations Draft Agreement-in-Principle (2003, 60–6), and the Nisga'a Final Agreement (1999, chap. 17, appendix L).

4 Only fourteen historic agreements were signed by Governor Douglas and aboriginal nations between 1850 and 1854, retrospectively designated as "treaties" by the courts, twelve of which secured land for the expansion of Fort Victoria (Harris 2002). The Haida are in phase three of the treaty process, but they have also sought agreements outside the treaty framework. In December 2007, an out-of-court agreement concerning timber harvesting on Haida Gwaii was signed by the Council of the Haida Nation and the British Columbia government (McKinley 2008), and in 2009 a "Reconciliation Protocol" was developed with the province to "seek a more productive relationship and … a more respectful approach to coexistence by way of land and natural resource management on Haida Gwaii" (Council of the Haida Nation 2009).

5 Nika Collison recalled the history of the mortuary house in 2013: "The Mortuary House was built as the first point of business after raising the six poles in the creation of the Haida Heritage Centre, knowing that ancestral

remains would be unearthed during site construction. It was a huge process – they consulted the Skidegate Repatriation and Cultural Committee who assisted in developing an on-site protocol guiding development which required a CHN-appointed Haida archaeologist on site at all times. When bones were unearthed all work stopped. It was determined if they were human or other animal. If human, forensic or ancestral ... For the ancestral remains, if they could be replaced in the area they were found, they were. If the building of the centre prevented it, they were placed in bentwood boxes and into this mortuary house where they remain today. The house does also serve as a repository for repatriated ancestors waiting to be reburied" (N. Collison, personal communication, 31 March 2013).

6 Lucy Bell can be seen telling her story in the documentary *Stolen Spirits of Haida Gwaii*, directed by Kevin McMahon.

7 A number of institutions require that a community or nation's elected leaders demonstrate support for any repatriation request put forward by members of their communities. This protects museums, who may be unfamiliar with cultural protocol regarding ownership, stewardship, or inheritance and thus be unable to determine if those making the request are the appropriate recipients of repatriated materials. At the same time, it minimizes the ability of individuals and families to act independently of governing bodies, or discourages the use of repatriation to further fickle or partisan political platforms.

8 Less formal contributions were also made by island residents and tourists who visited the canoe shed in Skidegate where the SRCC was working on the bentwood boxes. Andy estimated that 150 people – volunteers and employees, tourists and locals, adults and youth – contributed to the making of the boxes.

4. The Structural Qualities and Cultural Values of Haida Kinship

1 Abu-Lughod understands "ideology" as "the stuff of definitions of the world, that which allows people to understand and act" (1999, 276).

2 Members of one's father's lineage were considered particularly suitable marriage partners. Church records in Old Massett from 1877 to 1907 demonstrate that marriage practices from that period did not adhere to a simple pattern of marriage (Boelscher 1988). But these records were made in the decades immediately following a smallpox epidemic, making it necessary to ask how often a preferred marriage partner existed, and whether the pattern reflects a looseness in marriage rules, an adaptive strategy, or both. Drawing upon peoples' descriptions of these marriages, Boelscher

found that people's abilities to *apply* kinship terms convincingly were central to arranging and engaging in a marriage.

3 By comparison, Boelscher (1988, 34) recorded six Raven and five Eagle lineages in Old Massett during her field research in the early 1980s. Fission may happen as a result of power struggles among lineage members, with new sublineages being created. Fusion may occur in the wake of challenges to physical survival, as was seen following the smallpox epidemic, but also when there are not enough females to ensure the continuity of a lineage.

4 *Haida Memories* is available at http://www.museevirtuel-virtualmuseum .ca/Search.do?R=VE_1508&lang=en&ex=on.

5 Much like this virtual exhibit recognizes the value in using *gwaay gaang* as a means of classifying photographs, the Haida Gwaii Museum has incorporated "clan," that is, lineage, as a field in their artefact database.

6 On the prevalence of these experiences and social issues more broadly among First Nations in Canada, see the Royal Commission on Aboriginal Peoples (1996).

7 Akin to Carsten's "unmarked exchanges" are Weston's (1997, xviii) observed moments of "exquisite dailiness" that signal family: wiping children's mouths, subtle manners of physical contact, lowered and raised voices.

8 Today, even though people are concentrated in two villages, the chieftainships of many villages are maintained. Some of these villages are now sites to visit within Gwaii Haanas National Park Reserve and Haida Heritage Site and form summer homes for Haida Watchmen, the Haida wardens working for the Park Reserve.

9 At the Skidegate Haida Immersion Program (SHIP), steps have been taken to encourage the use of Haida names over English names and, at the very least, names derived from the Haida language over Anglicized names. It was determined when I was a student at SHIP that I should have a name based in the Haida language. Otherwise, my presence would have proved a financial burden for students and teachers, who are required to contribute twenty-five cents to a jar any time they use an English name in the classroom. A few of the women in the class decided that I would be *Diila jaad*, Sandhill Crane Woman, though I was reminded that this was not a proper Haida name since it was not accompanied by the appropriate protocol. Its relevance and significance were confined to the classroom.

10 Nora (1989) draws a distinction between memory and history, the former connoting personal interaction and vivacity and the latter depersonalized, often textualized, official accounts of past events.

11 Among Swanton's informants, it was thought that people who died a violent death went to the house of Tā'xet. They believed it was difficult to be reborn from this place (Swanton 1905a, 36).

12 Swanton uses the Haida word *ltta'xui*, which translates as "friend" but more specifically is used by Haida speakers to refer to close relationships within one's own matrilineage (Swanton 1905a, 51, 65). Haida speakers used *Qā'galAñ* to refer to persons within one's matrilineage from any prior generation, living or deceased. For living lineage members specifically, *ta'lAñ* was also used. I cross-checked these words with Haida speakers in Massett and with more contemporary resources than Swanton, yielding the following forms: *taw* (Alaskan Haida Dictionary n.d.) and *tuwii* (Massett) for "friend" or a close relationship within one's own matrilineages; *iitlaa kunast gwaay gaangee* (Massett) for persons within one's matrilineage from any prior generation living or deceased; and *iit tulang xiinagaas* (Massett) for the living members of one's matrilineage.

13 Tlingit territory borders the northern (i.e., Alaskan) extent of Haida territory. The two groups share a lengthy history of social, cultural, economic, and political exchanges.

5. The Values of *Yahgudang*

1 Third edition, http://www.oed.com/view/Entry/163779?rskey=d92cHN&result=1&isAdvanced=false#eid.

2 The relationship between respect, kinship, obligations, and status becomes clearer still in situations where social norms fail to be met. For example, Boelscher (1988, 52) explains "bad luck" as a failure to fulfil obligations to one's kin – an infringement of *yahgudang*. She further explains that when kinship obligations are not fulfilled, a person may be banished or dissociated from their family, thus losing the social status acquired as part of a lineage and the economic, material, and emotional support of the lineage. It is instructive that the qualities in opposition to respect, and the consequences of not acting with respect, include foolishness, destitution, or being unlucky (Blackman 1992; Boelscher 1988).

3 A basic definition of "property" within Euro-American societies views it as involving "bundles" of rights that give an individual exclusive control to use and dispose of things, or to waive such rights as they see fit (Bailkin 2004). Anthropological treatments of the characteristics of property have contributed greatly to a more nuanced understanding of the possibilities of property: it may be inalienable (Godelier 1999; Mauss 1990; Weiner 1985, 1992); it may constitute rights over tangible or intangible things;

its value may be personal, social, or fiscal and result from the materiality, sociality, uniqueness, or reproducibility of the things themselves.
Anthropologists have also frequently set out to describe the disparate
premises shaping property laws and indigenous concepts of property, particularly with regard to models for intellectual property (see for example
Barkan and Bush 2002; Brown 1998, 2003; Cory-Pearce 2007; Culhane 1998;
Harrison 1992; Janke 2003; Leach 2003a, 2003b; Nadasdy 2003; Nicholas
and Bannister 2004; Pannell 1994; Posey 2004; Strathern 1999a, 1999b, 2004).

4 Marianne Ignace (formerly Boelscher) first raised this distinction during
a *Xaad Kil* (Haida language) course she taught in Old Massett through
Simon Fraser University. Jordan Lachler, a linguist based in Alaska who
delivers on-line and in-person *Xaad Kil* courses in Old Massett, refined
my understanding of how these pronouns work linguistically. Linguistic
analysis of these categories, particularly as they pertain to modern objects,
is complicated by the nearly exclusive use of the English language by
Haida today.

5 I am mindful of local concerns, also expressed by Boelscher, regarding the
effect of writing oral history. As Boelscher's ethnography stresses, am-
biguity is a central aspect of Haida rhetoric, and of political and familial
reckoning. Writing, in contrast, fixes certain information and can connote
a status of truth. The positive reputation of the current 7iidansuu clearly
demonstrates how the history of this name continues to be shaped.

6 See Wright (2001, 328, 330) for a history of the transfer of this name.

7 Vaillant (2005) records this action as a means of indicating when a funeral
is being held for a child. None of the people whom I asked about this
practice were aware of it, though all were aware of the practice of wearing
blankets inside out to show disapproval. One woman supposed it may
have been something done in a particular family, which would make her
less likely to know about it.

8 As previously noted, Swanton uses the Haida word *ɬta'xui*, which translates as "friend" but which Haida speakers use more specifically to refer
to close relationships within one's own matrilineage (Swanton 1905a, 51,
65). See p. 186n12 above for an explanation of Swanton's terminology and
translations.

6. Haida Structures of History and Remembering

1 A smaller number of Haida men wear bracelets, and are more apt to do so
on special occasions. Haida men will more often have their crests incorporated into their wedding rings or display them as pendants or tattoos.

2 See for example Raibmon's (2006) account of Tlingit jeweller Rudolph
   Walton.
3 Brown and Bruchac (2006, 209–10, reporting on the work of Michael
   Harkin) note that younger generations of First Nations on the Northwest
   Coast tend to view repatriated artefacts as belonging to the community,
   while older generations tend to see them as belonging to individuals or
   families. For a non-age-graded distinction between community and family
   ownership of repatriated objects, see B. Saunders (1997) and Kramer (2006).
   See also Harkin (1999, 819–20), who argues against Clifford's (1991) separation of Kwakwaka'wakw museums into spaces of political history *or* familial history, insisting instead that both tell political histories: one through the
   use of a particular event hosted by an individual, the other through a focus
   on the traditional wealth of particular families, thus providing them with
   greater legitimacy than the nouveau riche in their community.
4 See also McMaster (2002), Glass (2002, 2011), Jonaitis and Glass (2010),
   Phillips (1998), and Thomas (1997) for an approach to colonialism as
   "interrelated" or "intercultural" histories.
5 Drawing upon Edwards' *Raw Histories* (2001) in which "surface" and
   "deeper" meanings of photographs and acts of photography are inves-
   tigated, Brown et al. also raise the issue of "depth." They caution that
   seemingly superficial observations of photographs, such as the presence
   or absence of braids, can in fact be poignant observations that lead to
   "deeper" historical readings of individuals' and families' experiences of
   historical forces (2006, 148).
6 This interview was conducted on behalf of the Pitt Rivers Museum in
   conjunction with the redisplay of Northwest Coast masks at the museum.
7 See Lehrer (2007, chaps. 3, 4) for a succinct and riveting description of the
   biological reasons taste and smell are powerful memory triggers.
8 In Alaska, Kaigani Haida prepare herring roe on hemlock boughs.
9 And see also Bruner (1986, 11): "We know that participants in a performance do not necessarily share a common experience or meaning; what
   they share is only their common participation."

7. The Place of Repatriation within Collective Memory and Identity

1 Colson hypothesizes that traumatic experiences of dislocation and forced
   evacuation can influence personal strategies and habits in perpetuity, in effect normalizing or constantly reincorporating the (traumatic) memory of
   dislocation (Parkin 1999). See also Nuttall and Coatzee's (1998) conclusion
   that racialized violence in South Africa is becoming normalized through

the quantity and repetition of horrific narratives offered to the Truth and Reconciliation Committee during years of testimony. An outcome of this repetition has been that the categories of "everyday" and "exceptional," "normal" and "traumatic," collapse into each other.

2 See Kramer (2006) for a description of how "theft" has become a central theme in the narratives of another Northwest Coast First Nation, the Nuxalk.

3 *Stolen Spirits of Haida Gwaii* was named Best History Documentary Program and Best Direction in a Documentary Program at Canada's Gemini Awards ceremony in 2005. It also won the Grand Prix Rigoberta Menchu award at the Montreal First People's Festival in 2005, and the Canadian Association of Broadcasters Gold Ribbon Award for Aboriginal Programming in 2006 (Primitive Entertainment n.d.).

4 Among Haidas I spoke with, some were comfortable with Haida objects being in museums because of the history of Haida participation in the tourist art and fine art markets. The sale of family-owned objects to museums garnered more mixed responses, as did unscrupulously collected objects. People I spoke with sought to remedy the absence of historic Haida artefacts within Haida ceremonial and everyday contexts in one of two ways: to repatriate these objects from museums to Haida Gwaii or to renew the skills needed to produce these objects. Relearning the requisite skills, of course, is greatly assisted when makers can get close to objects to study their construction. Speaking of the Kwakwaka'wakw repatriation efforts, Gloria Cranmer Webster (1995) was clear that the community contained all the skills needed to produce the same kinds of artefacts as those held in museum collections; their desire to repatriate artefacts was a specific attempt to correct historic injustices.

5 For Non-Haidas, the pre-1900 period has acted as a cultural benchmark, either as a level of cultural deprivation from which to rescue people or, more recently, as a standard for evaluating the current vivacity of Haida culture through a comparison of the amount, type, and quality of art objects being used and made by Haidas today (see, for example, Gunther 1966, 2).

6 This is reminiscent of work on oral histories that asserts that while particular narratives may be retained in their original form, each new social circumstance allows for the extraction of relevant knowledge, values, and morals. It is the adaptability and multiplicity of meaning within oral histories that encourage their longevity (Cruikshank 1998).

7 Of course, one aspect of this book is its ability to assist in the incorporation of repatriation within Haida collective memory, first, by my own requests

for reminiscences of repatriation, and second, by my inscribing these memories within a document that has been left within Haida villages. Haidas critiquing drafts often interjected comments into the margins that included memories prompted by the text itself, and narrated additional stories to flesh out abbreviated accounts. Their attention to details – individual words, the tone of sentences, the balance between lived life and theory – reinforces the importance of these new narratives and the need for them to be accurate as well as culturally and personally identifiable.

8 There were two series of *Raven and Eagles: Haida Art*, in 2002 and 2003, with one episode introducing the historic collecting of remains and featuring a contemporary reburial in Skidegate, and two episodes telling the stories of the repatriation from the American Museum of Natural History in New York City and early discussions about repatriation with the British Museum in London. The series were produced and directed by Marianne Jones (Haida) and Jeff Bear (Maliseet) of UrbanRez Productions, and included video footage of the repatriation committee's activities shot by Tanya Collinson (Haida).

9 Vince's perspective is explained within the museum exhibition through an excerpt from a *Ravens and Eagles: Haida Art* episode on repatriation.

8. Conclusions and Beginnings

1 For Pitt Rivers Museum staff recollections of this event, see Krmpotich and Peers 2013, chap. 5.

Bibliography

Abu-Lughod, Lila. 1999 [1986]. *Veiled Sentiments: Honor and Poetry in a Bedouin Society*. Berkeley: University of California Press.

Acheson, Steven R. 1998. *In the Wake of the Ya'áats xaatgáay (Iron People): A Study of Changing Settlement Strategies among the Kunghit Haida*. Oxford: Archaeopress.

– 2005. Gwaii Haanas Settlement Archaeology. In *Haida Gwaii: Human History and Environment from the Time of Loon to the Time of the Iron People*, ed. D.W. Fedje and R.W. Mathewes, 303–36. Vancouver: Univerity of British Columbia Press.

Adams, John W. 1981. Recent Ethnology of the Northwest Coast. *Annual Review of Anthropology* 10 (1): 361–92. http://dx.doi.org/10.1146/annurev. an.10.100181.002045.

Alaskan Haida Dictionary (draft). n.d. Juneau: Sealaska Heritage Institute.

Antze, Paul, and Michael Lambek, eds. 1996. *Tense Past: Cultural Essays in Trauma and Memory*. New York: Routledge.

Archibald, Robert R. 1999. *A Place to Remember: Using History to Build Community*. Walnut Creek: AltaMira.

– 2002. A Personal History of Memory. In *Social Memory and History: Anthropological Perspectives*, ed. J. Climo and M. Cattell, 65–80. Oxford: AltaMira.

Atkinson, Henry. 2010. The Meanings and Values of Repatriation. In Turnbull and Pickering, *The Long Way Home*, 15–19.

Augaitis, D., et al. 2006. *Raven Travelling: Two Centuries of Haida Art*. Vancouver: Vancouver Art Gallery/Douglas & McIntyre/University of Washington Press.

Ayau, E.H., and T.K. Tengan. 2002. Ka Huaka'i O Na 'Oiwi: The Journey Home. In Fforde, Hubert, and Turnbull, *The Dead and Their Possessions*, 171–89.

Bailkin, Jordanna. 2004. *The Culture of Property: The Crisis of Liberalism in Modern Britain*. Chicago: University of Chicago Press.

Barbeau, Marius. 1953. *Haida Myths: Illustrated in Argillite Carvings*. Bulletin no. 127, National Museum of Canada. Ottawa: National Museum of Canada.

– 1954. "Totemic Atmosphere" on the North Pacific Coast. *Journal of American Folklore* 67 (264): 103. http://dx.doi.org/10.2307/536218.

– 1957. *Haida Carvers in Argillite*. Bulletin no. 139, National Museum of Canada. Ottawa: National Museum of Canada.

– 1990 [1950]. *Totem Poles*. Foreward by George F. MacDonald. Vols. 1 and 2. Hull: Canadian Museum of Civilization.

Barkan, Elazar, and Ronald Bush. 2002. Introduction. In *Claiming the Stones/ Naming the Bones: Cultural Property and the Negotiation of National and Ethnic Identity*, ed. E. Barkan and R. Bush, 1–15. Los Angeles: Getty Research Institute.

Bashkow, Ira. 1991. The Dynamics of Rapport in a Colonial Situation: David Schnieder's Fieldwork on the Islands of Yap. In *Colonial Situations: Essays on the Contextualization of Ethnographic Knowledge*, ed. George W. Stocking, 170–242. Madison: University of Wisconsin Press.

Bear, Jeff, and Marianne Jones. 2002. *Yahgu Dang Ang* (To Pay Respect) (film). Season 1, episode 13 of *Ravens and Eagles: Haida Art*. Vancouver: Urban Rez Productions.

– 2003a. The New Collectors: Repatriation, Part 1 (film). Season 2, episode 10 of *Ravens and Eagles: Haida Art*. Vancouver: Urban Rez Productions.

– 2003b. The New Collectors: Repatriation, Part 2 (film). Season 2, episode 11 of *Ravens and Eagles: Haida Art*. Vancouver: Urban Rez Productions.

Beider, Robert E. 2000. The Representations of Indian Bodies in Nineteenth-Century American Anthropology. In Mihesuah, *Repatriation Reader*, 19–36.

Bell, Lucille, and Vince Collison. 2006. The Return of Our Ancestors, the Rebirth of Ourselves. In D. Augaitis et al., *Raven Travelling*, 140–5.

Beynon, William. 1941. The Tsimshians of Metlakatla, Alaska. *American Anthropologist N.S.* 43 (1): 83–8. http://dx.doi.org/10.1525/aa.1941.43.1.02a00100.

Binney, Judith, and Gillian Chaplin. 2003. Taking the Photographs Home: The Recovery of a Maori History. In Peers and Brown, *Museums and Source Communities*, 100–10.

Blackman, Margaret B. 1973. Totems to Tombstones: Culture Change as Viewed through the Haida Mortuary Complexes, 1877–1971. *Ethnology* 12 (1): 47–56. http://dx.doi.org/10.2307/3773096.

– 1990. Haida Traditional Culture. In *Handbook of North American Indians*. Vol. 7: *Northwest Coast*, ed. W. Suttles, 240–60. Washington: Smithsonin Institution Press.

– 1992 [1982] . *During My Time: Florence Edenshaw Davidson, A Haida Woman.* Vancouver: Douglas & McIntyre.

– 2011. Charles Edenshaw on the Colonial Frontier. In Glass, *Objects of Exchange*, 49–59.

Bloch, Maurice. 1996. Internal and External Memory: Different Ways of Being in History. In Antze and Lambek, *Tense Past*, 215–34.

Boas, Franz. 1912. *Changes in Bodily Form of Descendants of Immigrants.* Reports of the United States Immigration Commission. New York: Columbia University Press. http://dx.doi.org/10.1525/aa.1912.14.3.02a00080.

– 1921. Ethnology of the Kwakiutl (based on data collected by George Hunt). 2 parts. *Thirty-fifth Annual Report of the Bureau of American Ethnology to the Secretary of the Smithsonian Institution, 1913–1914.* Washington, DC: Government Printing Office.

Boas, Franz, and George Hunt. 1905. *Kwakiutl Texts.* Publications of the Jesup North Pacific Expedition. Vol. 3. New York: GE Stechert/Leiden: EJ Brill.

Boast, Robin. 2011. Neocolonial Collaboration: Museum as Contact Zone Revisited. *Museum Anthropology* 34 (1): 56–70. http://dx.doi.org/10.1111/j.1548-1379.2010.01107.x.

Boelscher, Marianne. 1988. *The Curtain Within: Haida Social and Political Discourse.* Vancouver: University of British Columbia Press.

Bohn, Glenn. 2005a, 5 February. Final Rest for Haida Remains. *Vancouver Sun.* http://www.mail-archive.com/natnews-north@yahoogroups.com/msg00655.html. Accessed 22 April 2005.

– 2005b, 27 June. A Reburial So a New Journey May Begin. *Vancouver Sun,* pp. B2–3.

Bolton, Stephanie. 2005, May 5. The Task Force on Museums and First Peoples, a Decade Later: A Case Study of the McCord Museum of Canadian History. Paper presented at the First Nations – First Thoughts 30th Anniversary Conference, Centre of Canadian Studies, University of Edinburgh.

Bray, Tamara L., and Thomas W. Killion, eds. 1994. *Reckoning with the Dead: The Larsen Bay Repatriation and the Smithsonian Institution.* Washington: Smithsonian Institution Press.

Brody, Hugh. 1994. *The Washing of Tears* (film). Toronto: National Film Board of Canada.

– 2004 [1981]. *Maps and Dreams: Indians and the British Columbia Frontier.* Vancouver: Douglas & McIntyre.

Brown, Alison, Laura Peers, with members of the Kainai Nation. 2006. *"Pictures Bring Us Messages" / Sinaakssiiksi aohtsimaahpihkookiyaawa: Photographs and Histories from the Kainai Nation.* Toronto: University of Toronto Press.

Brown, Deidre, and George Nicholas. 2012. Protecting Indigenous Cultural Property in the Age of Digital Democracy: Institutional and Communal

Responses to Canadian First Nations and Maori Heritage Concerns. *Journal of Material Culture* 17 (3): 307–24. http://dx.doi.org/10.1177/1359183512454065.

Brown, Michael. 1998. Can Culture by Copyrighted? *Current Anthropology* 39 (2): 193–222. http://dx.doi.org/10.1086/204721.

– 2003. *Who Owns Native Culture.* Cambridge, MA: Harvard University Press.

Brown, Michael, and Margaret Bruchac. 2006. NAGPRA from the Middle Distance: Legal Puzzles and Unintended Consequences. In *Imperialism, Art and Restitution,* ed. J.H. Merryman, 193–217. Cambridge: Cambridge University Press.

Bruner, Edward M. 1986. Experience and Its Expressions. In *The Anthropology of Experience,* ed. E.M. Bruner and V.W. Turner, 3–30. Urbana: University of Illinois Press.

Bunn-Marcuse, Kathryn. 2011. Bracelets of Exchange. In Glass, *Objects of Exchange,* 61–9.

Carpenter, Edmund. 1975. Introduction. In *Indian Art of the Northwest Coast: A Dialogue on Craftsmanship and Aesthetics,* ed. B. Holm and B. Reid, 9–27. Seattle: Institute for the Arts, Rice University.

Carsten, Janet. 2000. "Knowing Where You've Come From": Rupture and Continuities of Time and Kinship in Narratives of Adoption Reunions. *Journal of the Royal Anthropological Institute* 6 (4): 687–703. http://dx.doi.org/10.1111/1467-9655.00040.

– 2007. Connections and Disconnections of Memory and Kinship in Narratives of Adoption Reunions in Scotland. In *Ghosts of Memory: Essays on Remembrance and Relatedness,* ed. J. Carsten, 83–103. Oxford: Blackwell. http://dx.doi.org/10.1002/9780470692301.ch4.

Casey, Edward S. 1986. *Remembering: A Phenomenological Study.* Bloomington: Indiana University Press.

Classen, Constance, and David Howes. 2006. The Museum as Sensescape: Western Sensibilities and Indigenous Artifacts. In Edwards, Gosden, and Phillips, *Sensible Objects,* 199–222.

Clifford, James. 1991. Four Northwest Coast Museums: Travel Reflections. In *Exhibiting Cultures: The Poetics and Politics of Museum Display,* ed. I. Karp and S. Levine, 212–54. Washington: Smithsonian Institution Press.

– 1997. *Routes: Travel and Translation in the Late Twentieth Century.* Cambridge, MA: Harvard University Press.

Climo, J., and M. Cattell. 2002. Introduction: Meaning in Social Memory and History: Anthropological Perspectives. In *Social Memory and History: Anthropological Perspectives,* ed. Climo and Cattell, 1–36. Oxford: AltaMira.

Codere, Helen. 1966. *Fighting with Property: A Study of Kwakiutl Potlatching and Warfare, 1792–1930.* Seattle: University of Washington Press.

Cole, Douglas. 1995 [1985]. *Captured Heritage: The Scramble for Northwest Coast Artifacts*. Vancouver: UBC Press.

Cole, Douglas, and Ira Chaikin. 1990. *An Iron Hand upon the People: The Law against the Potlatch on the Northwest Coast*. Vancouver: Douglas & McIntyre/ Seattle: University of Washington Press.

Collison, Nika. 2006. Everything Depends on Everything Else. In D. Augaitis et al., *Raven Travelling*, 56–69.

Collison, W.H. 1981. *In the Wake of the War Canoes*. Ed. Charles Lillard. Victoria: Sono Nis Press.

Conklin, Beth A. 2001. *Consuming Grief: Compassionate Cannibalism in an Amazonian Society*. Austin: University of Texas Press.

Connerton, Paul. 1989. *How Societies Remember*. Cambridge: Cambridge University Press. http://dx.doi.org/10.1017/CBO9780511628061.

Cory-Pearce, Elizabeth. 2007. Creating Ethnography: Differing Notions of Creativity in Anthropological Knowledge Production, a Maori/European Example. In *Creativity and Cultural Improvisation*, ed. E. Hallam and T. Ingold. Oxford: Berg.

Council of the Haida Nation. 2008. History of the Haida Nation. http://www .haidanation.ca/Pages/history/haidanation.html. Accessed 10 February 2008.

– 2009. *Kunst'aa Guu – Kunst'aayah Reconciliation Agreement*. http://www .haidanation.ca/Pages/Agreements/pdfs/Kunstaa%20guu_Kunstaayah_ Agreement.pdf. Accessed 7 November 2013.

Counihan, Carole M. 1999. *The Anthropology of Food and Body: Gender, Meaning, Power*. New York: Routledge.

Crane, Susan A. 1997. Memory, Distortion, and History in the Museum. History and Theory Theme Issue 36: Producing the Past. *Making Histories Inside and Outside the Academy* 36 (4): 44–63.

Crawford, Susan J. 2000. (Re)Constructing Bodies: Semiotic Sovereignty and the Debate over Kennewick Man. In Mihesuah, *Repatriation Reader*, 211–36.

Crosby, Marcia. 2004. Haidas, Human Beings and Other Myths. In Duffek and Townsend-Gault, *Bill Reid and Beyond*, 108–30.

Cruikshank, Julie. 1995. Imperfect Translations: Rethinking Objects of Ethnographic Collections. *Museum Anthropology* 19 (1): 25–38. http://dx.doi .org/10.1525/mua.1995.19.1.25.

– 1998. *The Social Life of Stories: Narrative and Knowledge in Northern Canada*. Vancouver: University of British Columbia Press.

Cubillo, Franchesca. 2010. Repatriating Our Ancestors: Who Will Speak for the Dead? In Turnbull and Pickering, *The Long Way Home*, 20–6.

Culhane, Dara. 1998. *Pleasure of the Crown: Anthropology, Law and First Nations*. Vancouver: Talonbooks.

Curtis, Neil G.W. 2006. "Universal Museums, Museum Objects and Repatriation: The Tangled Stories of Things." *Museum Management and Curatorship* 21 (2): 117–27.

Davidson, Robert. 2006. Reclaiming Haida Culture. In D. Augaitis et al., *Raven Travelling*, 48–55.

Dening, Greg. 1996. *Performances*. Chicago: University of Chicago Press.

Department of Culture, Media and Sport. 2004. *Human Remains Report*. London: Government of United Kingdom.

Downey, Greg. 2010. "Practice without Theory": A Neuroanthropological Perspective on Embodied Learning. *Journal of the Royal Anthropological Institute (N.S.)*, S22–S40.

Drucker, Philip. 1963 [1955]. *Indians of the Northwest Coast. Anthropological Handbook No. 10*. New York: American Museum of Natural History/ McGraw-Hill.

Duff, Wilson. 1964. *The Indian History of British Columbia*. Victoria: British Columbia Provincial Museum.

Duffek, Karen. 2004. On Shifting Ground: Bill Reid at the Museum of Anthropology. In Duffek and Townsend-Gault, *Bill Reid and Beyond*, 71–92.

Duffek, Karen, and C. Townsend-Gault, eds. 2004. *Bill Reid and Beyond: Expanding on Modern Native Art*. Vancouver: Douglas & McIntyre.

Dumont, Clayton W., Jr. 2003. The Politics of Scientific Objections to Repatriation. *Wicazo Sa Review* 18 (1): 109–28. http://dx.doi.org/10.1353/ wic.2003.0003.

Duncan, Kate C. 2000. *1001 Curious Things: Ye Olde Curiousity Shop and Native American Art*. Seattle: University of Washington Press.

Duran, B., and E. Duran. 1995. *Native American Postcolonial Psychology*. Albany: State University of New York Press.

Duran, B., E. Duran, and M. Yellow Horse Brave Heart. 1988. Native Americans and the Trauma of History. In *Studying Native America: Problems and Prospects*, ed. R. Thornton, 60–76. Madison: University of Wisconsin Press.

Durlach, Theresa Mayer. 1928. *The Relationship Systems of the Tlingit, Haida and Tsimshian*. New York: American Ethnological Society/G.E. Stechert and Co.

Edenshaw, Gwaai. 2005. Unpublished interview transcript. Pitt Rivers Museum, University of Oxford.

Edwards, Elizabeth. 2001. *Raw Histories: Photographs, Anthropology and Museums*. Oxford: Berg.

Edwards, Elizabeth, Chris Gosden, and Ruth B. Phillips, eds. 2006. *Sensible Objects: Colonialism, Museums and Material Culture*. Oxford: Berg.

Enrico, John, ed. 1995. *Skidegate Haida Myths and Histories.* Collected by J.R. Swanton. Skidegate, BC: Queen Charlotte Islands Museum Press.

– 2005. *Haida Dictionary: Skidegate, Masset and Alaskan Dialects.* Fairbanks: Alaska Native Language Center, Sealaska Heritage Centre.

Fabian, Johannes. 2002 [1983]. *Time and the Other: How Anthropology Makes Its Object.* New York: Columbia University Press.

Fedje, Daryl, and Rolf Mathewes, eds. 2005. *Haida Gwaii: Human History and Environment from the Time of the Loon to the Time of the Iron People.* Vancouver: University of British Columbia Press.

Feely-Harnik, Gillian. 1991. Finding Memories in Madagascar. In *Images of Memory: On Remembering and Representation,* ed. S. Küchler and W. Melion, 121–40. Washington, DC: Smithsonian Institution Scholarly Press.

Fforde, Cressida. 2002. Collection, Repatriation and Identity. In Fforde, Hubert, and Turnbull, *The Dead and Their Possessions,* 25–46.

Fforde, Cressidar, Jane Hubert, and Paul Turnbull, eds. 2002. *The Dead and Their Possessions: Repatriation in Principle, Policy and Practice.* New York: Routledge. http://dx.doi.org/10.4324/9780203165775.

Fforde, Cressida, Jane Hubert, and Paul Turnbull. 2004. *Collecting the Dead: Archaeology and the Reburial Issue.* London: Duckworth.

Fienup-Riordan, Ann. 1998. Yup'ik Elders in Museums: Fieldwork Turned on its Head. *Arctic Anthropology* 35 (2): 49–58.

Fine-Dare, Kathleen S. 2002. *Grave Injustice: The American Indian Repatriation Movement and NAGPRA.* Lincoln: University of Nebraska.

Fisher, Robert. 1992 [1977]. *Contact and Conflict: Indian-European Relations in British Columbia, 1774–1890.* 2nd ed. Vancouver: University of British Columbia Press.

Fiske, Jo-Anne, and Evelyn George. 2006. *Seeking Alternatives to Bill C-31: From Cultural Trauma to Cultural Revitalization through Customary Law.* Ottawa: Status of Women Canada.

Forest, Marguerite. n.d. Connecting Corridors. *Spruce Roots.* http://www.spruceroots.org/corridors.html. Accessed 10 February 2008.

Fox, Richard G., and Barbara J. King. 2002. Introduction: Beyond Culture Worry. In *Anthropology beyond Culture,* ed. R.G. Fox and B.J. King, 1–19. Oxford: Berg.

Furniss, Elizabeth. 1999. *The Burden of History: Colonialism and the Frontier Myth in a Rural Canadian Community.* Vancouver: University of British Columbia Press.

Geertz, Clifford. 1968. *Islam Observed.* New Haven: Yale University Press.

Gibson, Thomas. 1985. The Sharing of Substance versus the Sharing of Activity among the Buid. *Man N.S.* 20 (3): 391–411.

gii-dahl-guud-sliiaay. 1995. Cultural Perpetuation: Repatriation of First Nations Cultural Heritage. In *Material Culture in Flux: Law and Policy of*

Repatriation of Cultural Property (theme issue), *University of British Columbia Law Review*, 183–202.

Glass, Aaron. 2002. (Cultural) Objects of (Cultural) Value: Commodification and the Development of a Northwest Coast Artworld. In *On Aboriginal Representation in the Gallery*, ed. L. Jessup and S. Bagg, 93–114. Hull: Canadian Museum of Civilization.

– 2004. Return to Sender: On the Politics of Cultural Property and the Proper Address of Art. *Journal of Material Culture* 9 (2): 115–39. http://dx.doi.org/10.1177/1359183504044368.

– 2008. Crests on Cotton: "Souvenir" T-Shirts and the Materiality of Remembrance among the Kwakwa̱ka'wakw of British Columbia." *Museum Anthropology* 31 (1): 1–18. http://dx.doi.org/10.1111/j.1548-1379.2008.00001.x.

– ed. 2011. *Objects of Exchange: Social and Material Transformation on the Late Nineteenth-Century Northwest Coast: Selections from the American Museum of Natural History*. New Haven: Yale University Press.

Godelier, Maurice. 1999. *The Enigma of the Gift*. Trans. Nora Scott. Cambridge: Polity.

Goldstein-Gidoni, Ofra. 1999. Kimono and the Construction of Gendered and Cultural Identities. *Ethnology* 38 (4): 351–70. http://dx.doi.org/10.2307/3773912.

Gosden, Chris and Chantal Knowles. 2001. *Collecting Colonialism: Material Culture and Colonial Change*. Oxford, New York: Berg.

Greenfield, Jeanette. 2007. *The Return of Cultural Treasures*. 3rd ed. Cambridge, MA: Cambridge University Press.

Gulliford, Andrew. 1992. Native Americans and Museums: Curation and Repatriation of Sacred and Tribal Objects. *Public Historian* 14 (3): 23–38. http://dx.doi.org/10.2307/3378225.

Gunther, Erna. 1966. *Art in the Life of the Northwest Coast Indians, with a Catalogue of the Rasmussen Collection of Northwest Indian Art at the Portland Art Museum*. Portland: Portland Art Museum.

Guujaaw. 2006. This Box of Treasures. In D. Augaitis et al., *Raven Travelling*, 2–3.

Gwaganad, Diane Brown. 2004. A Non-Haida Upbringing: Conflicts and Resolutions. In Duffek and Townsend-Gault, *Bill Reid and Beyond*, 64–70.

Haida Gwaii Museum. 2007. Yahgudangang – *To Pay Respect*. Exhibition text.

– 2013, March. *Haida Repatriation & Cultural Committee – Ancestral Remains Report*. Unpublished report.

Haida Laas, Special Issue entitled "*Athlii Gwaii: 25 Years Down the Road*." 2010, November. Council of the Haida Nation. http://www.haidanation.

ca/Pages/Haida_Laas/ PDF/Journals/Athlii_Gwaii.150.pdf. Accessed 29 April 2013.

Halbwachs, Maurice. 1992. *On Collective Memory*. Ed. and trans. Lewis A. Coser. Chicago: University of Chicago Press.

Hallam, Elizabeth, and Jenny Hockey. 2001. *Death, Memory and Material Culture*. Oxford: Berg.

Hamilton, Michelle A. 2010. *Collections and Objections: Aboriginal Material Culture in Southern Ontario*. Montreal/Kingston: McGill-Queen's University Press.

Hare, Jan, and Jean Barman. 2006. *Good Intentions Gone Awry: Emma Crosby and the Methodist Mission on the Northwest Coast*. Vancouver: University of British Columbia Press.

Harkin, Michael. 1988. History, Narrative, and Temporality: Examples from the Northwest Coast. *Ethnohistory* 35 (2): 99–130. http://dx.doi.org/10 .2307/482699.

– 1999. From Totems to Derrida: Postmodernism and Northwest Coast Ethnology. *Ethnohistory* 46 (4): 817–30.

Harris, Cole. 2002. *Making Native Space: Colonialism, Resistance and Reserves in British Columbia*. Vancouver: University of British Columbia Press.

– 1925. *Ancient Warriors of the North Pacific*. London: H.F. & G. Witherby.

Harrison, Charles. 1992. Ritual as Intellectual Property. *Man* 27 (2): 225–44. http://dx.doi.org/10.2307/2804052.

Harrison, Simon. 2012. *Dark Trophies: Hunting and the Enemy Body in Modern War*. Oxford: Berghahn.

Hennessey, Kate, Ryan Wallace, Nicholas Jakobsen, and Charles Arnold. 2012. Virtual Repatriation and the Application Programming Interface: From the Smithsonian Institution's MacFarlane Collection to "Inuvialuit Living History." Museums and the Web 2012 Proceedings. http://www .museumsandtheweb.com/mw2012/papers/virtual_repatriation_and_ the_application_progr. Accessed 8 June 2012.

Henze, Rosemary. 1992. *Informal Teaching and Learning: A Study of Everyday Cognition in a Greek Community*. Hillsdale, NJ: Lawrence Erlbaum Associates.

Herzfeld, Michael. 1995. It Takes One to Know One: Collective Resentment and Mutual Recognition in Local and Global Contexts. In *Counterworks: Managing the Diversity of Knowledge*, ed. R. Farndon, 124–42. London: Routledge. http://dx.doi.org/10.4324/9780203450994_chapter_6.

Hill, Richard W., Sr. 2001. Regenerating Identity: Repatriation and the Indian Frame of Mind. In *The Future of the Past: Archaeologists, Native Americans, and Repatriation*, ed. T. Bray, 127–38. New York: Garland.

Hinsley, Curtis. 2000. Digging for Identity: Reflections on the Cultural Background of Collecting. In Mihesuah, *Repatriation Reader*, 37–55.

Holm, Soren. 2011, 16 March. Removing Bodies from Display is Nonsense. *New Scientist*, no. 2803. http://www.newscientist.com/article/mg20928030 .100-removing-bodies-from-display-is-nonsense.html?full=true. Accessed 15 September 2011.

Hoskins, Janet. 1998. *Biographical Objects: How Things Tell the Stories of People's Lives*. New York: Routledge.

Indian and Northern Affairs Canada. 2003. Terminology. http://www.ainc-inac .gc.ca/pr/info/tln_e.html. Accessed 15 April 2007.

– 2008. *First Nations Profiles*. http://pse5-esd5.ainc-inac.gc.ca/FNP/Main/ Index.aspx?lang=eng. Accessed 10 February 2008.

Ingold, Tim. 2000. *The Perception of the Environment: Essays on Livelihood, Dwelling and Skill*. London: Routledge. http://dx.doi.org/10.4324/9780203466025.

– 2007. *Lines: A Brief History*. Oxford: Routledge.

Isaac, Gwyneira. 2007. Repatriation as a Process of Mediation: Knowledge Networks and the Creation of Cross-cultural Databases. Paper presented at the American Anthropological Association Meetings, Washington, DC, 28 November 2007.

Jaarsma, Sjoerd R., ed. 2002. *Handle with Care: Ownership and Control of Ethnographic Materials*. Pittsburgh: University of Pittsburgh Press.

Jacknis, Ira. 1991. George Hunt: Collector of Indian Specimens. In Jonaitis, *Chiefly Feasts*, 177–224.

– 1996. Repatriation as Social Drama: The Kwakiutl Indians of British Columbia, 1922–1980. *American Indian Quarterly* 20 (2): 274–86. http:// dx.doi.org/10.2307/1185705.

James, Wendy. 2007. *War and Survival in Sudan's Frontierlands*. Oxford: Oxford University Press.

James, Wendy, and Judith Ashton. n.d. *Voices from the Blue Nile*. www .voicesfromthebluenile.org. Accessed 29 November 2012.

Janke, Terri. 2003. *Minding Culture: Case Studies on Intellectual Property and Traditional Cultural Expressions*. Geneva: World Intellectual Property Organization.

Jensen, Doreen, and Polly Sargent. 1986. *Robes of Power: Totem Poles on Cloth*. Museum note no. 17. Vancouver: University of British Columbia Press, with UBC Museum of Anthropology.

Jolles, Carol Zane, with Elinor Mikaghaq Oozeva. 2002. *Faith, Food and Family in a Yupik Whaling Community*. Seattle: University of Washington Press.

Jonaitis, Aldona, ed. 1991. *Chiefly Feasts: The Enduring Kwakiutl Potlatch*. Seattle: University of Washington Press/New York: American Museum of Natural History.

– 2006. Smoked Fish and Fermented Oil: Taste and Smell among the Kwakwaka'wakw. In Edwards, Gosden, and Phillips, *Sensible Objects*, 141–67.

Jonaitis, Aldona, and Aaron Glass. 2010. *The Totem Pole: An Intercultural History*. Seattle: University of Washington Press/Vancouver: Douglas & McIntyre.

Kan, Sergei. 2004. The Nineteenth-Century Tlingit Potlatch: A New Perspective. In *Death, Mourning, and Burial: A Cross-Cultural Reader*, ed. A. Robben, 285–302. Oxford: Blackwell.

Killion, Thomas, ed. 2008. *Opening Archaeology: Repatriation's Impact on Research and Practice*. Santa Fe, NM: School for Advanced Research Press.

King, J.C.H. 1999. *First Peoples, First Contacts: Native Peoples of North America*. London: British Museum Press.

Kirmayer, Laurence. 1996. Landscapes of Memory: Trauma, Narrative, and Dissociation. In Antze and Lambek, *Tense Past*, 173–98.

Koros, Silvia. 2005. Princess Tom and the Alaska Tourist Trade, 1884–1900. *European Review of Native American Studies* 19 (1): 27–30.

Kramer, Jennifer. 2004. Figurative Repatriation: First Nations "Artist-Warriors" Recover, Reclaim, and Return Cultural Property through Self-Definition." *Journal of Material Culture* 9 (2): 161–82. http://dx.doi.org/10.1177/1359183504044370.

– 2006. *Swtichbacks: Art, Ownership, and Nuxalk National Identity*. Vancouver: University of British Columbia Press.

Krmpotich, Cara. 2012. Post-Colonial or Pre-Colonial: Indigenous Values and Repatriation. In *Anthropologists, Indigenous Scholars and the Research Endeavour: Seeking Bridges Towards Mutual Respect*, ed. J. Hendry and L. Fitznor, 162–70. New York: Routledge.

Krmpotich, Cara, Joost Fontein, and John Harries. 2010. The Substance of Bones: The Emotive Materiality and Affective Presence of Human Remains. *Journal of Material Culture* 15 (4): 371–84. http://dx.doi.org/10.1177/1359183510382965.

Krmpotich, Cara, and Laura Peers. 2011. The Scholar-Practitioner Expanded: An Indigenous and Museum Research Network. *Museum Management and Curatorship* 26 (5): 421–40. http://dx.doi.org/10.1080/09647775.2011.621729.

Krmpotich, Cara, Laura Peers, with members of the Haida Repatriation Committee and staff of the British Museum and Pitt Rivers Museum. 2013. *This Is Our Life: Haida Material Heritage and Changing Museum Practice*. Vancouver: University of British Columbia Press.

Lambek, Michael, and Paul Antze. 1996. Introduction. In Antze and Lambek, *Tense Past*, xi–xxxviii.

Lawrence, Erma. 1977. *Haida Dictionary*. Fairbanks: Society for the Preservation of Haida Language and Literature/The Alaska Native Language Centre, University of Alaska.

Leach, James. 2003a. *Creative Land: Place and Procreation on the Rai Coast of Papua New Guinea*. Oxford: Berghahn.

– 2003b. Owning Creativity: Cultural Property and the Efficacy of Custom on the Rai Coast of Papua New Guinea. *Journal of Material Culture* 8 (2): 123–43. http://dx.doi.org/10.1177/13591835030082001.

Lee, Jeff. 2005, 29 July. A New Deal for Natives. *Vancouver Sun,* pp. A1, A12.

Leggett, Jane. 1999. *Restitution and Repatriation: Guidelines for Good Practice.* London: Museums and Galleries Commission.

Lehrer, Jonah. 2007. *Proust Was a Neuroscientist.* Boston: Houghton Mifflin.

Lukovich, Jeff. 2005, 17 September. Place of Wonder. *Vancouver Sun,* pp. H1, H12–13.

Lutz, Catherine. 1988. *Unnatural Emotions: Everyday Sentiments on a Micronesian Atoll and Their Challenge to Western Theory.* Chicago: University of Chicago Press.

MacDonald, George F. 1983. *Haida Monumental Art.* Vancouver: University of British Columbia Press.

MacFarlane, Nathalie. 1993, 21 September. *The Recovery of Haida Artifacts and Human Remains from Culver City, California to the Queen Charlotte Islands Museum in Skidegate, Haida Gwaii.* Unpublished report.

Marchand, Trevor H.J. 2001. *Minaret Building and Apprenticeship in Yemen.* Richmond, UK: Curzon.

– 2009. *The Masons of Djenné.* Bloomington: Indiana University Press.

– ed. 2010. *Making Knowledge: Explorations of the Indissoluble Relation between Mind, Body and Environment.* Oxford: Wiley-Blackwell. http://dx.doi.org/10.1111/j.1467-9655.2010.01607.x.

Mauss, Marcel. 1990 [1954]. *The Gift: The Form and Reason for Exchange in Archaic Societies.* Trans. D.H. Walls. London: Routledge.

May, Sally K., Donald Gumurdul, Jacob Manakgu, Gabriel Maralngurra, and Wilfred Nawirridj. 2005. "You Write It Down and Bring It Back ... That's What We Want" – Revisiting the 1948 Removal of Human Remains from Kunbarlanja (Oenpelli), Australia. In *Indigenous Archaeologies: Decolonizing Theory and Practice,* ed. C. Smith and H.M. Wobst, 110–30. London: Routledge.

McKeown, C. Timothy. 2002. Implementing a "True Compromise": The Native American Graves Protection and Repatriation Act after Ten Years. In Fforde, Hubert, and Turnbull, *The Dead and Their Possessions,* 108–32.

McKinley, Judy. 2008. Land Use Agreement Marks Beginning of a New Relationship. *QCI Observer,* 18 January 2008. http://www.qciobserver.com/Article. aspx? Id=3071&Archive=1. Accessed 25 March 2008.

McMahon, Kevin. 2004. *Stolen Spirits of Haida Gwaii.* Film. Toronto: Primitive Entertainment.

McMaster, Gerald. 2002. Our (Inter) Related History. In *On Aboriginal Representation in the Gallery,* ed. L. Jessup with S. Bagg, 3–8. Hull: Canadian Museum of Civilization.

Meighan, Clement. 1992. Some Scholars' Views on Reburial. *American Antiquity* 57 (4): 704–10.

Merrill, William L., Edmund J. Ladd, and T.J. Ferguson. 1993. The Return of the Ahayu: da: Lessons for Repatriation from Zuni Pueblo and the Smithsonian Institution. *Current Anthropology* 34 (5): 523–67. http://dx.doi.org/10.1086/204205.

Merryman, John Henry ed. 2006. *Imperialism, Art and Restitution*. Cambridge: Cambridge University Press.

Meuli, Jonathan. 2001. *Shadow House: Interpretations of Northwest Coast Art*. Amsterdam: Harwood.

Mihesuah, Devon A., ed. 2000. *Repatriation Reader: Who Owns American Indian Remains?* Lincoln: University of Nebraska Press.

Miller, Bruce G. 1995. Folk Law and Contemporary Coast Salish Tribal Code. *American Indian Culture and Research Journal* 19 (3): 141–64.

– 1997. The Individual, the Collective and the Tribal Code. *American Indian Culture and Research Journal* 21 (2): 183–205.

– 2003. *Invisible Indigenes: The Politics of Non-Recognition*. Lincoln: University of Nebraska Press.

Miller, Bruce G., and Michael Kew. 1999. Locating Aboriginal Governments in the Political Landscape. In *Seeking Sustainability in the Lower Fraser Basin: Issues and Choices*, ed. M. Healey, 47–63. Vancouver: Institute for Resources and the Environment, Westwater Research, University of British Columbia.

Milloy, John. 1999. *A National Crime: The Canadian Government and the Residential School System, 1879–1986*. Manitoba Studies in Native History no. 11. Winnipeg: University of Manitoba Press.

Modest, Wayne. 2012. Material Bridges: Objects, Museums and New Indigeneity in the Caribbean. In *Anthropologists, Indigenous Scholars and the Research Endeavour: Seeking Bridges towards Mutual Respect*, ed. J. Hendry and L. Fitznor, 185–95. New York: Routledge.

Morphy, Howard. 1994. The Interpretation of Ritual: Reflections from Film on Anthropological Practice. *Man N.S.* 29 (1): 117–46.

Murdock, George P. 1936. *Rank and Potlatch among the Haidas*. Yale University Publications in Anthropology no. 13. New Haven: Yale University Press.

Nadasdy, Paul. 2003. *Hunters and Bureaucrats: Power, Knowledge, and Aboriginal-State Relations in the Southwest Yukon*. Vancouver: University of British Columbia Press.

Neylan, Susan. 2003. *The Heavens Are Changing: Nineteenth-Century Protestant Missions and Tsimshian Christianity*. Montreal/Kingston: McGill-Queen's University Press.

Nicholas, George P., and Kelly P. Bannister. 2004. Copyrighting the Past? Emerging Intellectual Property Rights Issues in Archaeology. *Current Anthropology* 45 (3): 327–50. http://dx.doi.org/10.1086/382251.

Nicks, Trudy. 1995. Task Force on Museums and First Peoples. *Material Culture in Flux: Law and Policy of Repatriation of Cultural Property* (theme issue), *University of British Columbia Law Review*, 143–147.

– 2003. Introduction: Museums and Contact Work. In Peers and Brown, *Museums and Source Communities*, 19–27.

Nicks, Trudy, and Tom Hill, eds. 1992. *Turning the Page: Forging New Partnerships between Museums and First Nations*. Ottawa: Assembly of First Nations and Canadian Museums Association.

Nisga'a Final Agreement. 1999. http://www.ainc-inac.gc.ca/pr/agr/nsga/nisdex_e.html. Accessed 25 March 2008.

Noble, Brian. 2002. *Niitooii* – "The Same That Is Real": Parallel Practice, Museums, and the Repatriation of Piikani Customary Authority. *Anthropologica* 44 (1): 113–30. http://dx.doi.org/10.2307/25606064.

Nora, Pierre. 1989. Between Memory and History: Les Lieux de Mémoires. *Representations* 26 (Special Issue on Memory and Counter-Memory), 7–24.

Nuttall, Sarah, and Carli Coatzee, eds. 1998. *Negotiating the Past: The Making of Memory in South Africa*. Oxford: Oxford University Press.

O'Hanlon, Michael, and Robert L. Welsch, eds. 2002. *Hunting the Gatherers: Ethnographic Collection, Agents and Agency in Melanesia, 1870s–1930s*. Oxford: Berghahn.

Old Massett Village Council Heritage Resources Department. 2006. *Haida Memories*. http://www.virtualmuseum.ca/CommunityMemories/AEAW/000a/Exhibits/E nglish/index.html, Virtual Museum of Canada. Accessed 30 November 2007.

Oliver, Lindsay. 1993, May. *Found Human Remains, Queen Charlotte Island Museum, Skidegate, Q.C.I. from the "Gessler Collection."* Report prepared for Archaeology Branch, Ministry Responsible for Culture, Victoria, British Columbia.

Pannell, Sandra. 1994. Mabo and Museums: The Indigenous (Re)Appropriation of Indigenous Things. *Oceania* 65 (1): 18–39.

Parkin, David. 1999. Mementoes as Transitional Objects in Human Displacement. *Journal of Material Culture* 4 (3): 303–20.

Peers, Laura. 2004. Repatriation – A Gain for Science? *Anthropology Today* 20 (6): 3–4. http://dx.doi.org/10.1111/j.0268-540X.2004.00309.x.

Peers, Laura, and Alison K. Brown. 2003. Introduction. In Peers and Brown, *Museums and Source Communities*, 1–16.

– eds. 2003. *Museums and Source Communities: A Routledge Reader,*. New York: Routledge.

Phillips, Ruth B. 1998. *Trading Identities: The Souvenir in Native American Art from the Northeast, 1700–1900.* Montreal/Kingston: McGill-Queen's University Press.

– 2003. Introduction: Community Collaboration in Exhibitions: Towards a Dialogic Paradigm. In Peers and Brown, *Museums and Source Communities,* 19–27.

– 2011. *Museum Pieces: Toward the Indigenization of Canadian Museums.* Montreal/Kingston: McGill-Queen's University Press.

Pine, Frances. 2007. Memories of Movement and the Stillness of Place: Kinship Memory in the Polish Highlands. In *Ghosts of Memory: Essays on Remembrance and Relatedness,* ed. J. Carsten, 104-125. Oxford: Blackwell Publishing.

Poignant, Rosalyn, with Alex Poignant. 1996. *Encounter at Nagalarramba.* Canberra: National Library of Australia.

Posey, Darrell A. 2004. *Indigenous Knowledge and Ethics: A Darrell Posey Reader.* Ed. Kristina Plenderleith. New York: Routledge.

Pratt, Mary Louise. 1992. *Imperial Eyes: Travel Writing and Transculturation.* London: Routledge.

Primitive Entertainment. n.d. Awards, Nominations and Festival Screenings. http://www.primitive.net/awards.html. Accessed 1 April 2008.

Pullar, Gordon L. 1994. The Qikertarmiut and the Scientist: Fifty Years of Clashing World Views. In *Reckoning with the Dead: The Larsen Bay Repatriation and the Smithsonian Institution,* ed. T. Bray and T. Killion, 15–25. Washington: Smithsonian Institution Press.

Pynn, Larry. 2010, 18 November. *Lyell Island: 25 Years Later.* First Nations Fisheries Council website. Available at http://fnfisheriescouncil.ca/index.php/fish-in-the-news-/1125-lyell-island-25-years-later-nov-1810. Accessed 10 October 2012.

Raibmon, Paige. 2006. *Authentic Indians: Episodes of Encounter from the Late-Nineteenth-Century Northwest Coast.* Durham: Duke University Press.

Ramsay, Heather and Kwiaahwah Jones, eds. 2010. *Gina 'Waadlux̲an Tluu – The Everything Canoe.* Skidegate: Haida Gwaii Museum Press.

Riding In, James. 2000. Repatriation: A Pawnee's Perspective. In Mihesuah, *Repatriation Reader,* 106–120.

Robertson, A.F. 2007. Memory and the Regeneration of a Catalan Community. Paper presented at Department Seminar Series, Institute of Social and Cultural Anthropology, Oxford, UK, 19 October 2007.

Rosaldo, Renato. 1984. Introduction: Grief and a Headhunter's Rage: On the Cultural Force of Emotions. In *Text, Play, and Story: The Construction*

and Reconstruction of Self and Society, ed. S. Plattner and E. Bruner, 178–95.
Washington: American Ethnological Society.

– 1986. Ilongot Hunting as Story and Experience. In *The Anthropology of Experience,* ed. E. Bruner and V. Turner, 97–138. Urbana: University of Illinois Press.

Rosenblum, Amalia. 1996. Prisoners of Conscience: Public Policy and Contemporary Repatriation Discourse. *Museum Anthropology* 20 (3): 58–71. http://dx.doi.org/10.1525/mua.1996.20.3.58.

Rowlands, Michael. 2002. Heritage and Cultural Property. In *The Material Culture Reader,* ed. V. Buchli, 105–14. Oxford: Berg.

Royal Commission on Aboriginal Peoples. 1996. *Report of the Royal Commission on Aboriginal Peoples.* Vols. 1–5. Ottawa: Canada Communication Group.

Saunders, Barbara A.C. 1997. Contested *Ethnie* in Two Kwakwaka'wakw Museums. In *Contesting Art: Art, Identity and Politics,* ed. J. MacClancy, 85–130. Oxford: Berg.

Saunders, Nicholas. 2004. Material Culture and Conflict: The Great War, 1914–2003. In *Matters of Conflict: Material Culture, Memory and the First World War,* ed. N. Saunders, 5–25. London: Routledge.

Scheper-Hughes, Nancy. 2001. Ishi's Brain, Ishi's Ashes: Anthropology and Genocide. *Anthropology Today* 17 (1): 12–8. http://dx.doi.org/10.1111/1467-8322.00041.

Schildkrout, Enid, and Curtis A. Keim, eds. 1998. *The Scramble for Art in Central Africa.* Cambridge: Cambridge University Press.

Schneider, David M. 1980. *American Kinship: A Cultural Account.* 2nd ed. Chicago: University of Chicago Press.

– 1984. *A Critique of the Study of Kinship.* Ann Arbor: University of Michigan.

Sealaska Heritage Institute. 2007. *Xaat Kil.* http://www.haidalanguage.org/ways-of-writing.html.

Seguin, Margaret. 1985. *Interpretive Contexts for Traditional and Current Coast Tsmishian Feasts.* Ottawa: National Museums of Canada.

Seremetakis, Nadia C. 1994. The Memory of the Senses, Part 1: Marks of the Transitory. In *The Senses Still: Perception and Memory as Material Culture in Modernity,* ed. C. Seremetakis, 1–18. Chicago: University of Chicago Press.

Simpson, Moira G. 1996. *Making Representations: Museums in the Post-Colonial Era.* London: Routledge.

Skidegate Repatriation and Cultural Committee. 2006. www.repatriation.ca. Accessed 30 November 2007.

Sledge, Michael. 2005. *Soldier Dead: How We Recover, Identify, Bury and Honor Our Military Fallen.* New York: Columbia University Press.

Spencer, Frank. 1992. Some Notes on the Attempt to Apply Photography to Anthropometry during the Second Half of the Nineteenth Century.

In *Anthropology and Photography 1860–1920,* ed. E. Edwards, 99–107. New Haven: Yale University Press/London: Royal Anthropological Institute.

Stearns, Mary Lee. 1990. Haida since 1960. In *Handbook of North American Indians,* vol. 7: *Northwest Coast,* ed. Wayne Suttles, 261–6. Washington: Smithsonian Institution Press.

Steltzer, Ulli. 1984. *A Haida Potlatch.* Seattle: University of Washington Press.

Stewart, Hilary. 1984. *Cedar: Tree of Life to the Northwest Coast Indians.* Vancouver: Douglas & McIntyre/Seattle: University of Washington Press.

– 1993. *Looking at Totem Poles.* Vancouver: Douglas & McIntyre.

Stocking, George W. 1968. *Race, Culture, and Evolution: Essays in the History of Anthropology.* New York: Free Press.

– ed. 1989 [1974]. *A Franz Boas Reader: The Shaping of American Anthropology, 1883–1911.* Chicago: University of Chicago Press.

Stoler, Ann Laura. 2008. Imperial Debris: Reflections on Ruins and Ruination. *Cultural Anthropology* 23 (2): 191–219. http://dx.doi.org/10.1111/j.1548-1360 .2008.00007.x.

Stoller, Paul. 1989. *The Taste of Ethnographic Things: The Senses in Anthropology.* Philadelphia: University of Pennsylvania Press.

Strathern, Marilyn. 1999a. *Property, Substance and Effect: Anthropological Essays on Persons and Things.* London: Athlone.

– 1999b. What Is Intellectual Property After? In *Actor Network Theory and After,* ed. J. Law and J. Hassard, 156–80. Oxford: Blackwell.

– 2004. Losing (Out on) Intellectual Resources. In *Law, Anthropology, and the Constitution of the Social: Making Persons and Things,* ed. A. Pottage and M. Mundy, 201–33. Cambridge: Cambridge University Press. http://dx.doi .org/10.1017/CBO9780511493751.007.

– 2005. *Kinship, Law and the Unexpected: Relatives Are Always a Surprise.* Cambridge: Cambridge University Press. http://dx.doi.org/10.1017/CBO9780511614514.

Stuart, George E. 1999. Conclusion: Working Together to Preserve Our Past. In *The Ethics of Collecting Cultural Property,* 2nd ed., ed. P.M. Messenger, 243–52. Albuquerque: University of New Mexico Press.

Suttles, Wayne. 1958. Private Knowledge, Morality and Social Classes among the Coast Salish. *American Anthropologist* 60 (3): 497–507. http://dx.doi .org/10.1525/aa.1958.60.3.02a00080.

Sutton, David E. 2001. *Remembrance of Repasts: An Anthropology of Food and Memory.* Oxford: Berg.

– 2006. Cooking Skill, the Senses, and Memory: The Fate of Practical Knowledge. In Edwards, Gosden, and Phillips, *Sensible Objects,* 87–118.

Swanton, John R. 1905a. *Contributions to the Ethnology of the Haida.* The Jesup North Pacific Expedition. Memoir of the American Museum of Natural History, New York, vol. 5, pt. 1. Leiden: E.J. Brill/New York: G.E. Stechert.

– 1905b. *Haida Texts and Myths: Skidegate Dialect*. Smithsonian Institutions Bulletin no. 29. Washington, DC: Government Printing Office.

– 1908. *Haida Texts, Masset Dialect*. The Jesup North Pacific Expedition. Memoir of the American Museum of Natural History, New York, vol. 10, pt. 2. Leiden: E.J. Brill/New York: G.E. Stechert.

Tapsell, Paul. 2000. *Pukaki: A Comet Returns*. Auckland: Reed.

Thom, Brian. 2000. Precarious Rapport: Harlan I. Smith and the Jesup North Pacific Expedition. *European Review of Native American Studies* 14 (2): 3–10.

Thomas, Nicholas. 1992. Inversion of Tradition. *American Ethnologist* 19 (2): 213–32. http://dx.doi.org/10.1525/ae.1992.19.2.02a00020.

– 1997. *Oceania: Visions, Artifacts, Histories*. Durham/London: Duke University Press.

Thornton, Russell. 2002. Repatriation as Healing the Wounds of the Trauma of History: Cases of Native Americans in the United States of America. In Fforde, Hubert, and Turnbull, *The Dead and Their Possessions*, 17–24. http://dx.doi.org/10.4324/9780203165775_chapter_1.

Tourtellot, Jonathan B. 2005. Destinations Scorecard: National Parks. http://www.nationalgeographic.com/traveler/features/nprated0507/nprated.ht ml#magazinetext. Accessed 12 November 2007.

Townsend-Gault, Charlotte. 1994. Northwest Coast Art: The Culture of the Land Claims. *American Indian Quarterly* 18 (4): 445–67. http://dx.doi.org/10.2307/1185391.

– 2004. Circulating Aboriginality. *Journal of Material Culture* 9 (2): 183–202. http://dx.doi.org/10.1177/1359183504044372.

Trope, Jack F., and Walter R. Echo-Hawk. 2000. The Native American Graves Protection and Repatriation Act Background and Legislative History. In Mihesuah, *Repatriation Reader*, 123–68.

Turnbull, Paul. 2010. The Vermillion Accord and the Significance of the History of the Scientific Procurement and Use of Indigenous Australian Bodily Remains. In Turnbull and Pickering, *The Long Way Home*, 117–34.

Turnbull, P., and M. Pickering. 2010. *The Long Way Home: The Meaning and Values of Repatriation*. New York: Berghahn.

Turner, Nancy J. 2004. *Plants of Haida Gwaii*. Winlaw, BC: Sono Nis Press.

Union of BC Indian Chiefs. 2005. Background on Indian Reserves in British Columbia. In *Our Homes Are Bleeding* (digital collection). http://wwwubcic.bc.ca/Resources/ ourhomesare/teachers/index.html. Accessed 20 May 2008.

Vaillant, John. 2005. *The Golden Spruce*. Toronto: Vintage Canada.

Verdery, Katherine. 1999. *The Political Lives of Dead Bodies: Reburial and Postsocialist Change*. New York: Columbia University Press.

Vilaça, Aparecida. 2005. Chronically Unstable Bodies: Reflections on Amazonian Corporalities. *Journal of the Royal Anthropological Institute* 11 (3): 445–64. http://dx.doi.org/10.1111/j.1467-9655.2005.00245.x.

Virtual Museum Canada. 1998. *Haida Spirits of the Sea.* http://www .virtualmuseum. ca/Exhibitions/Haida/nojava/english/home/index. html. Accessed 20 April 2005.

Ward, Doug. 2005, 5 July. Remote B.C. Park Tops Poll as Best in North America. *Vancouver Sun,* pp. B1, B4.

Webster, Gloria Cranmer. 1991. The Contemporary Potlatch. In Jonaitis, *Chiefly Feasts,* 227–48.

– 1995. Potlatch Collection Repatriation. In *Material Culture in Flux: Law and Policy of Repatriation of Cultural Property* (theme issue), *University of British Columbia Law Review,* 137–41.

Weiner, Annette. 1985. Inalienable Wealth. *American Ethnologist* 12 (2): 210–27. http://dx.doi.org/10.1525/ae.1985.12.2.02a00020.

– 1992. *Inalienable Possessions: The Paradox of Keeping-while-Giving.* Berkeley: University of California Press. http://dx.doi.org/10.1525/california/ 9780520076037.001.0001.

Weston, Kath. 1997. *Families We Choose: Lesbians, Gays, Kinship.* New York: Columbia University Press.

Wilk, Richard R. 1999. "Real Belizean Food": Building Local Identity in the Transnational Caribbean. *American Anthropologist N.S.* 101 (2): 244–55. http://dx.doi.org/10.1525/aa.1999.101.2.244.

Wright, Robin. 2001. *Northern Haida Master Carvers.* Seattle: University of Washington Press.

Yates, Francis. 1966. *The Art of Memory.* London: Routledge & Kegan Paul.

Yellowman, Connie Hart. 1996. "Naevahoo'ohtseme" – We Are Going Back Home: The Cheyenne Repatriation of Human Remains – A Woman's Perspective. *St. Thomas Law Review* 9:103–16.

Zimmerman, Larry. 1987. The Impact of the Concept of Time on the Concept of Archaeology. *Archaeological Review from Cambridge* 6 (1): 42–50.

– 1989. The Present Past: An Examination of Archaeological and Native American Thinking about Law and Time. In *Thinking across Cultures,* ed. D. Topping, 32–42. Hillsdale, NJ: Lawrence E. Erlbaum.

Index